# Books by George Riemer

## and a play for reading:

# The
# New
# Jesuits

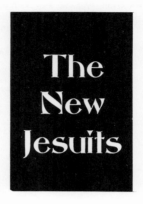

# The New Jesuits

## George Riemer

*Little, Brown and Company*
*Boston—Toronto*

LIBRARY OF CONGRESS CATALOG CARD NO. 79–135433

01238   W0751   T02/71

FIRST EDITION

*Published simultaneously in Canada*
*by Little, Brown & Company (Canada) Limited*

PRINTED IN THE UNITED STATES OF AMERICA

To Jack Teeling, S.J., whose letters
and laughs kept me in the Society
twenty-five years after I had left it

*A lot depends on whether we lose our nerve, whether we keep thinking it's something worth fighting for. Jesuit survival is not going to depend just on Jesuits. We're going to have to keep looking outward to see how we can work with and help people outside. If we don't do that, we'll die.*

*— Paul J. Weber, S.J.*

# Contents

*xii*

# Jesuit Facts

Jes'u·it (jĕz'û·ĭt; jĕzh'–), n. [N.L. *Jesuita*, fr. *Jesus.*] 1. A member of the clerks regular of the Company (or Society) of Jesus, a religious order founded by Ignatius Loyola in 1534 and approved by Paul III in 1540. . . . The order was suppressed from 1773 to 1814. Jesuits were among the first missionaries and explorers in the territory that now forms the United States, and were established as an order in the United States in 1807. The title *Jesuit* originated in religious polemics but is generally accepted as an unofficial designation of the order. Abbr. S.J.

> — *Webster's New International Dictionary of the English Language,* 2nd ed.

2. (usually l.c.) *Offensive.* A crafty, intriguing, or equivocating person: so called in allusion to the methods ascribed to the order by its opponents.

> — *Random House Dictionary of the English Language*

In 1969 there were about 35,000 Jesuits, 7,775 of them in the United States. About 2,400 of the U.S. Jesuits were "scholastics" in various stages of training for the priesthood, and 1,200 were "brothers," that is, those who live as Jesuits but do not intend to become priests.

In the United States Jesuits run twenty-eight colleges and universities and fifty-four high schools. Most Jesuits here either teach or are getting ready to be teachers, but some are retreat masters, chaplains, and administrators for the order itself. In *Hyphenated Priests*, William H. Cleary argues that priests today must have a second profession in order to relate to society and presents the Jesuit-lawyer, -engineer, -psychiatrist, -sociologist, -journalist, -poet, -musician, -economist, -builder, and -theologian.

---

Shall we not have regular swarms of them here, in as many disguises as only a king of the gypsies can assume, dressed as printers, publishers, writers and schoolmasters? If ever there was a body of men who merited eternal damnation on earth and in hell, it is this Society of Loyola's. Nevertheless, we are compelled by our system of religious toleration to offer them asylum.

— Former President John Adams
in a letter to President Thomas
Jefferson, 1816

---

By 1650, only a hundred and ten years after their founding, the Jesuits controlled over five hundred colleges in Europe and were directing them according to their own master plan for education, the *Ratio Studiorum*. As part of their educational design, they operated a chain of some three hundred and fifty theaters. In these, they developed a drama form that bridged medieval morality plays and grand opera. Between 1650 and 1700 Jesuits wrote one hundred thousand plays. Few of these were printed but about three hundred still survive. Documents credit Jesuits with choreographing well over ten thousand ballets, and a Jesuit invented the *magica lanterna*, a forerunner of the motion picture camera. They were the experts and consultants of that day and their strongest specialty was communication.

Jesuits developed an enormous power and prestige, so, inevitably, they made fast friends and fast, fierce enemies. The most traumatic event in Jesuit history was their legal annihilation, forced by Portugal, Spain, France, and the two Sicilies in 1773. This event, called the Suppression, figures strongly in the talk of radical Jesuits who believe the Society's finest moments are struck when it is being persecuted.

Pope Clement XIV enacted the Suppression on July 21 by a famous brief, *Dominus ac Redemptor*. The brief opens by citing a long series of precedents for the suppression of religious orders by the Holy See, then briefly sketches the objectives and history of the Society. It tells how Jesuits defied their own Constitutions, which forbade them to meddle in politics; it speaks of the great ruin to souls caused by their quarrels with local bishops and the other religious orders, their practice of stooping to adopt heathen customs and usages in the Orient, and the disturbances resulting in persecutions of the Church which they had stirred up even in Catholic countries. In consideration of these facts, and for reasons, Clement said, that had been "suggested to Us by the principles of prudence and which We retain concealed in Our Breast," the Society of Jesus with all its houses, colleges, schools and hospitals was "suppressed, extinguished, abolished and abrogated forever."

The Suppression struck 22,589 Jesuits — 11,295 of whom were priests; it stripped the general and other superiors of all their authority and transferred it to local authorities; it stopped the order from recruiting new candidates and forced it to dismiss men in training. Jesuit priests could join other orders or serve as secular priests under bishops. Those Jesuits who were engaged in education were permitted to continue on condition that they abstain from "lax and questionable doctrines" apt to cause strife and trouble. They were no longer allowed to read heretical books.

The pope appointed a congregation of cardinals to take possession of all properties possessed by the Society. He threw Lorenzo Ricci into prison where the general died in 1775.

Jesuits fought the Suppression at first, then withdrew into

territories of the free-thinking sovereigns of Russia and Prussia, Frederick II and Catherine II, who protected them.

Pius VII revoked Clement's Act of Suppression in 1814 and restored the Society to corporate legal existence.

## TRAINING: THEN AND NOW

Ten years ago, a man entering the Society of Jesus was prepared to undergo a training period lasting fifteen years.

*Novitiate:* the place and time for the first stage of training. After two years, the novice took perpetual vows of poverty, chastity and obedience.

*Juniorate:* the house for the two-year schooling period reserved for studies in the classics of Greek and Latin antiquity. As a novice, the Jesuit was called "Brother." As a junior, he began to be called "Mr." He was now a "scholastic." The junior worked toward a Bachelor of Arts degree.

*Philosophate:* the house for the three-year course of philosophy. It was taught in Latin, ended in an oral examination and gained the licentiate, or Ph.L., somewhat like the Master of Arts degree.

*Regency:* a three-year period of work in a foreign or Indian mission or of teaching in a Jesuit high school.

*Theologate:* the house for a four-year program of theological studies. At the end of the third year, the scholastic was ordained a priest. Theology was taught in Latin.

*Tertianship:* the final year of training; a course of study, prayer and self-examination before beginning the active ministry.

The following description of Jesuit training appeared in 1970 in *Jesuit Directions*, a brochure published by the Jesuit

Vocation Bureau. One great difference not shown is that philosophy and theology are now taught in English.

Preparation for Jesuit life is serious and extensive. An entering candidate for two years meditates, practices Ignation living and studies. Through the *Spiritual Exercises* of St. Ignatius he learns the mystical character of the Order.

Next, he completes his undergraduate work. A Master's Degree is mandatory for men planning ordination [to the priesthood].

The following three years can be invested in a variety of human experiences. Depending on the individual and the responsibilities of his province, he may be given the opportunity to teach in a high school or university. He may travel to an emerging nation to assist other Jesuits working there, or to other ministries of action within his province. Given the talent to pursue further graduate study, almost any university from Stanford to Fribourg to Harvard is a possibility.

A Jesuit studies Scripture, liturgy and dogma thoroughly. He learns how to link sacramental rites to men's lives. He plunges into deeper meanings hidden in the revealed word of God. After ordination, briefly in seclusion, he intensifies his contact with God and strengthens his ideals.

With these long years of training in asceticism and learning completed, a Jesuit enters his apostolate as a "contemplative in action." Altogether, preparation may occupy the first four to six years of Jesuit life, eight to ten years for those choosing to be ordained.

*Novice Master:* spiritual guide and director of training in the novitiate.

*Rector:* superior of a house or community. The "house" may be a big building or an apartment in the ghetto.

*Minister:* superior in charge of practical matters such as supplies, travel, expenses, house maintenance. There is a father minister in each major house.

*Provincial:* superior of a province. The United States *assistancy* is divided into ten provinces: Maryland, New England, New York, Missouri, Wisconsin, California, Oregon, New Orleans, Chicago, and Detroit.

*General:* superior of the entire Society of Jesus, with headquarters in Rome.

# The
# New
# Jesuits

# Will Jesuits Be
# the New Protestants?

I am an ex-Jesuit. I entered the Society of Jesus at Florissant, Missouri, in September 1940, at the age of twenty and
left seven years later. I'm back now at Florissant walking
over old grounds and I'm wondering what those years did to
me, and could I have done better with my life without them,
and what had I wanted here in the first place? Just a year
earlier a Jesuit friend had written to me from Florissant and
had promised me nostalgia if I once came back to these
grounds:

> . . . *the years and miles between have disappeared
> and I'm back in the times during the war when we
> were here. . . . The repainting job in the chapel
> which seemed so harsh and modern when it went in
> has faded and become quaint like the art work in the*
> Saturday Evening Post *of the '20's. The vineyard
> and the front land with its two tall rows of trees are
> gone, but they seem more than ever present in their
> very absence. . . . Meals are served buffet style now
> but remember how those carts used to roll from the
> kitchen, steam trailing after, loaded with whole roast
> chickens or brown betty or Brother Huseman's hand-
> churned ice cream? I haven't seen a single cart. . . .
> The huge Mo Province baroque pulpit still stands in
> the refectory but now it's wheeled out only for special
> talks. Microphones make voice exercises in the base-
> ment unnecessary. There is bottled beer now but it*

*seems to have no special attraction. Guitars and folk
songs have replaced the silence of the chapel and no
scholastic has ever heard "We hail Thee, Francis
Xavier" let alone knows the words . . .*

I drove into St. Stanislaus at 11:30 one night in August
1969. As I turned into the driveway, my lights swept across
three young men waiting for me at the start of the walk that
led to all the buildings. They approached, not seeing me, but
smiling into the headlights. They wore no cassocks; I guessed
they were novices. "You're up late," I said.

"We've just been into the city. We saw *Midnight Cowboy.*"

I had never once been in the city during my four years at
Florissant and in that time never saw a film. My first film
had been in St. Louis the year I started philosophy. I saw
*Going My Way.*

The novices led me to the juniorate building where a room
had been prepared for me on the second floor. When they
had gone I put out my lights and stood at the window facing
west, looking toward Howdershell Road, the cow barns beyond it, and beyond them the three- or four-mile dirt road
leading to the Jesuit rest and recreation villa above the Missouri River. Good times there, singing and talking, every
Thursday. *"Everybody out, rain, snow, or cold. At steep
grades, those nearest the food wagon help the horses by
pushing."*

On your way to villa, you had to pass a shaggy, overfed
oak that wore a shrine on its chest, a storm veteran whose
back was braced with lightning rod. It stood rooted near a
weary, old lichen pond that could have been its wife, the two
grown ancient together. Two or three miles farther up the
road was a column of plumelike maples I'd never forgotten.
About thirty of these trees curved upward toward Charbon-
niere on the Missouri bluffs, in all seasons different. In all
weathers, in all lights of day, they used to make me ache
from wanting to possess them, they were that beautiful. Now,

4

at the window, I wondered whether any of them were still standing.

*Come to Stanislaus*
*On Howdershell Road*
*That's where the Jebbies*
*Have their abode*

*We came to Stanislaus*
*Look how we grew*
*We owe it all*
*To corn bread and stew*
— OLD VILLA "HYMN"

I left my room and walked out in the corridor. The junior-ate could house about a hundred men. My class, the first to occupy it, had filled about forty rooms. But in 1969 only eight men took vows at Florissant. I passed room after room that was empty: bare mattresses and uncased pillows, chairs upside down on bare desks. I walked back and forth along the corridor from end to end trying to remember my room as a junior, but I couldn't remember it. I thought my body must have some kinesthetic memory of it and tried to sense what it was but without success. There was no room that I could be certain had been mine. I couldn't remember where anyone else had lived either, but this was understandable because an important house rule prohibited visiting.

I left the juniorate on its eastward side and walked out on the grounds. Back in New York I would never dare to walk in Central Park this late. It felt wonderful to walk on grass and under trees and around shrubs in the dark without fears of being mugged. But this feeling of security was interrupted suddenly when I remembered that a gruesome double murder had been committed a few hundred yards from the seminary grounds nearby on Howdershell Road while I was a first-year junior.

Once I had been able to tell blindfolded where I was on

*5*

these grounds. Father Dent had taught me that. Dent had worked in Patna, India, and when I knew him he was living in the infirmary. His health was broken, but I don't know how. He spent much of his day on the lawns rooting out dandelions, his eyes almost closed and his right hand pressed hard against his temple. He said the light hurt his head. He wanted me to learn Sanskrit and used to tell me the Indo-European roots of words. He showed me how to identify grasses and trees by their smells and the sounds that breezes made rushing through them.

They were intensely sensed, my Florissant years, because they were years of silence and waiting.

The highest ground at St. Stanislaus is at the southeast corner pointing down toward Lambert Field and St. Louis. When I was a novice, in lonely, rebellious moments I sometimes stood at that corner and wished I were in the city. I could look over miles of dark, brooding lands and see no house lights at all, but far off a low, flat mushroom of light squatting on the horizon was St. Louis. That was "the world" out there, that was the CITY. I used to strain all my senses trying to feel and smell its body heat.

I had loved the city. I remember my first night in the St. Louis philosophate: I sat tight against the window, too exhilarated by the sounds and the air to sleep. There was a soft rain. I couldn't see the traffic signal but I saw its wavery red, green and gold lights spilled across the wet road. What I loved best was the warm, rubbery throb and *slcc* of car tires. That was life. Cicadas and crickets make interesting sounds but nature doesn't answer when you ask it for love. I really did prefer those tire sounds. They were human. They carried people — lovers or travelers, people going to work or coming home.

I cut across the grass heading toward that city corner now, passing the greenhouse, the white marble angel and the little stone chapel. I expected to be entertained by nostalgia. I thought waves of old language, prayers, complaints, popular songs I had once shouted into the wind stream up there would come rolling back to overwhelm me.

When I reached the land peak, I was shocked to see St. Louis had moved and was standing hard up against the grounds. Florissant Valley, jammed with houses and slashed by superhighways, looked like an Italian street festival. There was a wedding celebration a few houses away sounding so close the accordion could have been in the little chapel behind me and the Polish whoops come from the angel.

I didn't like people so close to the grounds. I wanted to have that great dark space moat back again with St. Louis out there off in the distance tempting me.

Usually, when I'm near a Jesuit house, I stop at the switchboard and look over the names to see if anybody I know is living there. At Stanislaus the next morning I walked through the cemetery. When I had been a novice, the cemetery meant nothing to me. You have to have experience to appreciate a graveyard.

I saw a stone marked FRANCISCUS PREUSS. Tall, elegant, Cambridge-toned classicist; wearing a blue cap, blue knit sweater: hauling logs, digging, laying in road beds, putting in culverts to save our villa road from eroding into the Missouri River. His class on Aristotle's *Poetics* was among the most important classes I can remember attending.

I saw GULIELMUS WADE. Bill Wade — I name him now by way of dropping a flower in memory of a great teacher. Wade is engraved more deeply in me than in his stone and I challenge the stone to contradict this. He used to write everything you said on the blackboard as you said it. I can see him writing down the words of my tribute now, isolating "great" with a chalk circle, then shooting arrows into it, or laying a platform of heavy underlines below and bombing it. Wade treated every question with respect, everybody's question. "It has to be important," he once said, "because it comes from your mind." I remember one of his three-hour psychology exams: Wade said the prayer before class, wrote the Greek word for mind (*nous*) on the board, then walked out. The exam was to figure out what he wanted.

I stood at a stone block that told me Harlan Edwards was dead. When I entered the Society, Edwards was one of the five *secundianni* — second-year novices — assigned to introduce me and the other new men to community living. He had blond hair and blue eyes, and spoke with what I learned later was a St. Louis accent. I remember listening to him trying to correct it down in the basement, practicing "Martha, Martha, the Lord is here," which St. Louisans liked to say as, "Mortha, Mortha, the Lard is here."

Edwards explained the daily order and some house regulations: we would get up at five and go to bed at ten; there was to be no talking "except during the appointed times." If it was necessary to speak, we were required to use Latin. The "appointed times" for speaking English were the thirty- to forty-five-minute recreation periods after lunch and supper, villa days and Sunday afternoons. The last fifteen minutes of both after-meal "rec" periods were to be spent in Latin conversation with assigned partners. We were to try to know everyone and not seek to have particular friendships. On walk days we were to leave the grounds in threes: walk partners were assigned and their names posted on the bulletin board. I still remember how some of us grinned when Edwards told us the rule of *tactus:* meaning we weren't to touch anyone, not even as a joke; therefore no horseplay, no backslapping, no contact sports. We thought this was funny because one of Edwards's front teeth had been chipped down on the soccer field.

I really didn't know Latin before I came to Florissant, though four years of it had somehow passed over me in high school. Now I had to learn it or choke from frustration. All food was passed at the table so no one would starve from ignorance, but I'm surprised today that our ravenous hungers were not so exploited. If I had been told, "No Latin, no food," I might have become a classicist. I believe the quality of our Latin may have been good because a feeling of disdain prevailed against *culina* Latin — "kitchen" Latin, or slang. Fractured Latin puns had some currency but in general were discouraged: *sub ubis* (under + where) for "underwear" and *quercus* (oak) for "o.k." are the only two puns I can remember at this sitting. Once, while dusting statues in the chapel, a novice cracked off Jesus' finger. He carried it to Brother Vasquez, the sacristan, and whispered: "*Digitus Dei est hic*" (the finger of God is here) — the phrase Pope Paul III was supposed to have said to Ignatius in approving the Society.

It took me time and work to learn that silence was something more than not talking. I came little by little to realize there were all kinds of ways I was breaking silence: by my gestures and facial expressions, by noticeable exhalations or inhalations, by false struggles to suppress a smile, by eye directions, by the way I walked or sat or wore my cassock or hitched my cincture.

If you live in a community of silent men, the man who keeps clicking his ball-point pen button may drive you up the cloister wall. You start imagining his intentions. You accuse him — in your mind, of course — of being thick and insensitive. A lot of silence is hard on paranoiacs.

One day an announcement went up saying there would be an *exercitium modestiae* at eleven in the morning. No one asked, "*Quid est exercitium modestiae?*" though the *primianni* stood reading the sign longer than usual. The *secundianni* wouldn't have answered anyway. At a signal given by the manuductor, *secundianni* and *primianni* walked to the walls of the *ascetary*, our meeting room, and formed a horseshoe-shaped line. The novice master entered and sat at a table facing the mouth of the horseshoe. He explained that the exercise was intended to help each of us become aware of faults, personality traits, and rule violations that annoyed the community. He asked each man to report his observations

*9*

as objectively as possible without rancor and warned all not to interpret motives or intentions.

After this introduction, the first *secundianni* in alphabetical order walked to the center of the horseshoe and knelt on the floor. The first man in line to his left along the wall said: "Brother has a shattering, loud kind of laugh. He comes too close to your face when he talks." When the admonitor had finished, he yielded to the next man in line, who added his criticisms. The criticisms unrolled until the novice master stopped them. The exercitant might collect as many as twenty or thirty distinct criticisms. He would write these down later, then bring them to the novice master for discussion.

Some of the novices dreaded this exercise, some were shocked by it. I liked it, though I admit it was more interesting to be the critic than the criticized. The *exercitium modestiae* served several purposes but one of its chief effects was to discharge grievances and tensions backed up or suppressed by silence. It gave us the chance to become aware of ourselves as others sensed us. The feedback was honest and was given in friendship. We knew our critics were not conspirators since each had made his own observations in his own silence.

During my first months in the Society, I resented the fact that my recreation and walk companions were assigned. I never tried to figure out the selection system but I remember we were kept mixed so that I never got the same two men a second time. At least one *secundianni* was appointed to each trio; he set the walk destination and was supposed to keep the conversation on some "spiritual" level. "Spiritual conversation," I suppose, was to keep us from wasting our precious talk time comparing old girl friends or discussing corn bread and stew and brown betty. But we were too immature to discuss spirituality with any sophistication. God, how awful some of those conversations were! People would ask quite bluntly, "Did you have any special lights in this morning's

*10*

meditation we can discuss?" I began to see that human talk was not always better than total silence. There were some people you liked being with: what they laughed at and how their faces reacted to you told you who they were. If you could join them without manipulating the rule, you were happy. Yet I have to say that some of the Jesuits who later became my very good friends were men I would have avoided during the novitiate if I'd been given my free choice of friends.

Some novitiate rules, those against room visits, *tactus*, and particular friendships, worked together to prevent homosexual relationships, cliques, exclusive groupings, and conspiracies to overthrow the house. Were they effective? Yes, they were. During my four years at Florissant no one overthrew the house. I remember no exclusive cliques, and to my knowledge there were no overt and consummated homosexual relationships.

I do remember of myself that during my second year as a junior I developed an intense and exciting fondness for one of the men in my year. I never told him or anyone else about my feeling, but I believe he was aware of it. I wanted to touch him and put my arm around him, and I sensed he would have let me, but I could never bring myself to do it. One Sunday I asked him to go on a walk with me. I helped him put on his sweater, though he certainly didn't need help and though I'd never helped anyone else with a sweater. I led the way making sure our destination took us climbing up a rocky ravine and over some bridge pilings just so I could help him and get his help, thus being able to clasp his hand or arm. We rested on the high ground of a sloping meadow, sat in the hot dry air of the field with its sweet grass and the roaring buzzy sounds of bees and flies. We just sat there and did a lot of not talking, and then we went home. Yet I felt guilty about it. My passion from start to finish lasted about a month and it died as unexpectedly as it had started. It was humiliating and embarrassing while I had it, for though it gave a specific

*11*

pleasure, it was a pleasure I generally didn't want. It was humiliating because it had led me into some undignified little games. Even now, I'm ashamed more of the petty phoniness than of the homosexuality. Did *tactus* "save" me? I don't think so. It was a rule I could easily ignore in the press of strong feelings. If anything stopped me, it was fear of the mystery of homosexuality and disgust at my cowardice in not being more open.

Harlan Edwards had helped me carry my trunk to the trunk room where I was to store my winter clothes and some schoolbooks I had brought along thinking they might be useful. I gave him $7.40 — all the money in my pockets, and he put it in a brown envelope with my name on it for storage in the house safe. Some men came to Florissant with enough money for their return trip home. I came expecting to stay. I felt my first hurtful pangs of loneliness and separation when Edwards took me to Brother Diaz, the house tailor. Diaz had already received my cassock measurements by mail a month earlier and now needed me for one last fitting before Cassock Day, the day the new men met all of the *secundianni* and were admitted into the full Florissant community. The cassock is a sensible, simple, lightweight, loose-fitting garment and ought to be revived as an academic fashion. Ours were well made of good fabric and I was proud to get mine. What made me feel bad was the pair of black cotton trousers Brother Diaz gave me to wear under it. There was no going back to the outside world again, I saw at once; not in those pants. I felt they were strictly for under-cassock wear and not to be publicized. When I look back I can't really think of anything wrong with them. They had light gray stripes and looked like morning trousers. Maybe what bothered me about them was that Edwards and Diaz wore them too. Everyone wore them, in fact. They were community pants. We were expected to be more concerned with our Roman-collared neck image than our pants image.

September being the month school starts, I've had a lot of bad Septembers, but I can't remember any September that was as bad as that first one at Florissant.

Humid, hot weather made the banisters and woodwork feel sticky, gave us prickly heat, salted the armpits of our cassocks, and made us stink of vinegarish sweat, yet house rules required us to wear long sleeves even during tennis or handball down at field. Showers were strictly limited to one a week because of the annual water shortage. The community used rain water collected in cisterns as it ran off the various roofs, and the cisterns could never take in enough to last through a dry, hot summer. We had to take basin baths in our cubicles. Our showers were down in a whitewashed, dungeonlike basement that needed just a dash of water to charge the air with acrid fumes and casein smells. You could almost hear the fungus start creeping: white furry cultures on the walls, great green splotches of mildew over the shower curtains, mysterious brilliant orange growths reaching up out of the floor drains. As a "special treat" one hot September afternoon we were allowed to swim in a concrete box filled with muddy water backed up behind a cofferdam at the pump house. We had "monk's knees" — callous pads like those you see on surfboard riders, and we compared knees to see who had been kneeling most.

Daily order with the full novice community turned out to be a seventeen-hour race through a maze of brief activities controlled by bells. It left very little time for self-pity, low moods, or sexual frustration. Meditation started at 5:30 in the morning and lasted an hour. It was followed by Mass and then (at last!) we had breakfast. I forget what happened at eight but we were always in a frenzy to shave (cold water), make our beds, clean out our cubicles, brush our cassocks, and polish our shoes before eight. The shortest activity lasted exactly a minute and the longest, I believe, about two hours. There were no formal studies during the novitiate, but we had one class each of Latin and Greek. *Gymnicum*, or calis-

13

thenics, took five minutes each day. *Manualia* — physical work in the kitchen or laundry or about the house and grounds — lasted about an hour. We had a lot of required reading in Jesuit traditions. There were conferences and lectures every day. There were two examinations of conscience each fifteen minutes long. We had voice exercises in the basement, rehearsals for Latin talks and for the "Mariennum," the pulpit speech every novice had to give to the house. The rosary and litanies were recited by all novices together in Latin and in march time out on the paths or in the cloistered walks.

At about nine at night I used to start thinking, "It'll all be over soon." I had never before been so glad to stretch out in bed, let my muscles go, and stop thinking. But then, just when the after-hum of the bells had stopped and all the bones in my face, my back, my arms and legs had one by one slipped clicking back into their sockets, just about three minutes after I'd dropped into a serious, beyond-recall sleep, the 5 A.M. tower bell would slam in my head and I'd be up fumbling for my shoes and plunging into my cassock for another seventeen-hour race.

I studied Harlan Edwards and other *secundianni* frequently during that first September trying to observe them when they were off guard. They looked healthy and normal enough. I mean they didn't have abnormally shaped heads. They were intelligent and quick; some were athletic. They weren't effeminate. They seemed sincere. Because of his chipped front tooth, when Edwards was conscious of being watched he covered his mouth while he laughed. Yet I noticed he laughed easily and frequently *without* covering and this assured me he wasn't faking some kind of religious joy for our benefit. Edwards, I decided eventually, could have made it outside. He was in the Society by desire and choice, not because he had no other options. Why did I feel it was important that he be able to succeed "out in the world"? I guess I needed to convince myself that I hadn't put in with odd or inept people who were using the mysteries of religion to disguise their personal failures. I was making up my mind whether to accept the Society's training or to rebel or to get out.

On September 29, 1940, all first-year novices began the long retreat, a period of intensive meditation and self-scrutiny. It lasted to the end of October, relieved by three break days, but otherwise conducted in total silence with none of the usual recreation periods. On the eve of this retreat, each of us received a clothbound book holding exactly 125 four-by-seven pages. I still have my copy. Its binding is cracked and a glue flake falls into my hand as I open it. I leaf through it now for the first time in many years and I'm again surprised at how barren it seems. *The Joy of Cooking* is more vividly written. Yet this book has influenced me more than any other book in my life. It is the *Spiritual Exercises* of St. Ignatius, the series of meditations and self-examinations composed by Ignatius between 1521 and 1548. It is the heart and soul of the live and moving Jesuit. I suppose I could have endured that first quarter year at Florissant — with its silence and Latin, the grotesque monk's knees, the forced integration, and the loneliness, I could have taken all this without the long retreat but it wouldn't have made sense to do so. The retreat's first and immediate effect on me, therefore, was to make the novitiate intelligible, even reasonable, and its discomforts tolerable. It confirmed the religious life as an adventurous search for radical truths and feelings.

The *Exercises* cannot merely be read or be read about, but must be personally experienced. They intend to bring you before the barest, most basic image of yourself it is possible to have, before a self stripped of cosmetic effects, deceptions, masks, false fronts, false bottoms, false supports and securities, false goals and false pasts. Once you have had this vision of your naked self and accepted yourself as you are, then you are ready to consider the meaning of Jesus. The meditations and prayers try to crack through the hardened language shells covering the story of Jesus' life, his dialogue with people he knew, his activism and commitment to revolution, his love of people, his special relatedness to children and women, his rejection and murder, his resurrection and his plea that we live out his love and express his values in our own world today, each of us in our own way according to our own insights. The *Exercises* intend to create a crisis of insights and feelings that challenge you to serve love, growth and life. If you now arrange your time and begin to work for this cause, the *Exercises* have helped to Christianize you. If you commit all your time to such work under Jesuit leadership, you are a Jesuit. The *Exercises* leave their mark far back in those inner caves of the self where decisions are born and a person so marked is never the same again.

Altogether I spent four years at Florissant: two in the novitiate and two studying Latin, Greek and English classics in the juniorate. When I left Florissant my career ahead was clearly marked for me. I would spend three years in the philosophate followed by three years as a regent in one of the Jesuit high schools. After the regency period, I would go to the theologate for four years where in my third year I would be ordained a priest. After a fourth year of theology, I would spend a year in the tertianship, a year set apart for spiritual renewal.

I expected the three years immediately ahead of me to be successful ones. I looked forward to probing the great human questions in philosophy and I was eager to do some creative writing in my advanced English courses.

But as things worked out the three years were failures. I was bad at managing my own time and didn't prepare for classes. I got a bad start in English by failing the graduate school entrance exam. The department head told me I could repeat the exam and let me take graduate courses anyway. But during the year I discovered that my concept of English did not match the department's. The department was interested in writers of the past, not in developing new writers; while it talked history and criticism, I was listening for ideas that would help me write. When I took the entrance exam over at the end of the year I proved the first test had been right by failing again. Philosophy was a disappointment too. Aside from superb classes taught by Bill Wade and by Robert Henle, philosophy revealed itself as something for Latin technicians and professional scholars. It was a dialogue between the masters and a ring of bright students blinking back and forth brilliantly, delighting each other. All who were not part of this ring were asked to be convinced that philosophy was hands-off except for super-intellects. Only a few had the talent to be professional philosophers; the many who did not have this talent were warned to shut up. As with English I searched out my own course. One of the questions that excited me was the concept of freedom. I chased down every word I could find on it and took it to my room for meditation.

I found myself more and more in conflict with my rules or my superiors. I fell in love with two or three girls in the university and the thought that I would spend a long womanless life as a Jesuit priest sometimes troubled me. I seemed to be always feeling either anxious or worried or guilty. I relieved some of my tensions by becoming a frenzied practical joker: I just now remember going into Andy Maginnis's room just before noon one day and hiding on top of his huge old eight-foot-high armoire. Andy came in and knelt at his prie dieu for the angelus. At the words "the angel of the Lord appeared unto Mary" I jumped from the armoire crashing to the floor in front of Andy and then galloped out of the room. (Andy later repaid me for this shock by carpeting the floor of my room wall to wall with trash dumped from all the hallway barrels.)

During my last year in the philosophate, I was called down to the provincial's residence and told I would not be given minor orders with the rest of the men in my class — a warning that my eventual ordination to the priesthood was

*17*

being questioned. Another superior suggested that if I didn't develop a sense of prudence I might never be allowed to write or publish, and that far from working with people I might be assigned to the basement library in St. Mary's, Kansas.

One night I was pacing some of my problems around the university's tarred quad, a sooted St. Louis drizzle stinging my eyes, when an answer burst in my mind. It was clean, simple and direct. It was both exciting and frightening. To that moment it had been unthinkable. The next day I went to my education director and told him I thought I should leave the Society. I expected him to be surprised, but he nodded and shook my hand. He said, "I've been waiting for you to discover that by yourself."

I left the order because of a conflict of interests: I wanted to be a writer and I wanted to be a Jesuit. In those days you couldn't be both without getting into trouble. Back then no good Jesuit would have dreamed of picketing a bishop or of demonstrating against a Jesuit university. He would never have talked to the press about contraception or abortion or trial marriage without first getting his ideas cleared through his provincial.

I felt that to be a writer I had to meet and know all kinds of people and experiences and then write what I honestly thought and felt. I was assured I would never be free to do this. With S.J. after my name I could never write and publish just for myself. As a member of a historic international organization I had to respect the organization's image and help protect it. As I was told again and again by my superiors, I had to be "prudent."

I've never blamed anyone but myself for leaving the Society — that is, I've always thought it was my own misfit behavior that made me out of place in the order. I've never accused the Society of being inhuman or unfair to me, and while I've objected that parts of the training were wrong or irrelevant so far as I was concerned, it never occurred to me that the training itself might have been wrong or irrelevant. But in recent years a surprising number of Jesuit priests and scholastics have left the order: from 1965 to 1970, almost three thousand; five hundred of them Americans. Jesuit recruitment has fallen off severely. The Society admitted four hundred new men in the year 1960, but only 149 in 1967. This exodus of men and also the changes that the Society has made in its training program makes me now look more critically at my own training. Instead of asking, "Where did I go wrong?" let me ask this time, "Where did the Society go wrong?"

Some of the Jesuits that I've talked with during the past two years seem to wish they could rewrite history and cut out the fact that Ignatius Loyola was a soldier and expected a soldier's obedience from his men. I think their discomfort with Ignatius's metaphor comes from the fact that they see it only from the soldier's point of view. But if Ignatius wanted Jesuits to obey their superiors and if he also wanted them to confront the world in a radical Christian style, wasn't he assuming that the superiors would themselves be radical? When Ignatius said his Jesuits should entrust themselves to their superiors as dead bodies being carried, surely he intended that the superiors be alive. If Ignatius Loyola's image of swift military obedience isn't relevant today, it's because Jesuit superiors in the United States are too prudent, safe and sedentary. The provincial's *visit* is less the tense, electric Paul Revere kind of contact, and more the small town watchman's making sure the lights are all out.

If Ignatius wanted his men to be poor, it was so they would be free to move fast, drop everything, and go. He didn't want a man to get hung up on a job or on a climate or on a woman or a language or get too settled or too involved with his family; any of these conditions could drag down the man in motion. This is the meaning of the vows: poverty, chastity and obedience are supposed to give freedom of action. The Jesuits that I've talked with aren't afraid of motion — at least they weren't when they first entered the Society. It's their superiors who have settled down, who have gotten themselves all involved with the care and feeding of buildings. The only orders that I've seen requiring military speed and detachment have come from superiors who suddenly wanted to get rid of a problem Jesuit — like Heithaus sent to Milwaukee, or Dunne sent to Los Angeles, or Berrigan to South America.

Militant Jesuits say that only innovative, time- and life-consuming work, radical and risky activism can justify their being poor, chaste, and obedient men. A young Jesuit priest told me: "I'm not going to give up having a son just in order to prefect a study hall. Any married teacher can do that. If the superior doesn't have anything better in mind for me, and if he just sits on his ass and convinces me that this is his Society, I'm getting out. It's not the game I signed up for."

Since the novice master is responsible for preparing the young Jesuit to cope with his future, the Society's image of its own future must be found in the mind of the novice master and the minds of his advisors. What was the image of the future that guided my own novice master back in the past? Did he anticipate Vatican II? The Peace Corps? A U.S. President and a senator and a Nobel prize-winning Negro assassinated? Did he think ahead to a world in which a Jesuit would be on the staff of *The Atlantic*, and one would be a fugitive from justice, and another would run for a congressional seat, when novices would learn to dance and would drink cocktails on a feast day, and when the Society would ease its way out of Latin? Speaking for my own novice master, no.

The Jesuit ideal projected for me in my day was one of personal sanctity, an introspective vigilance over the minute conflicts that could shake up my peace of mind. I would achieve inner holiness by control over my bodily impulses, my sexual impulses, my eating and drinking desires. I controlled communication by controlling my body, my gestures, my facial expressions. I taught my skin to be at rest, my hair to stay down, my eyes not to rove, my teeth not to grind. I was expected to be prudent, to be orderly, to manage my time well. I was supposed to look past ad hoc disturbances and not rock the status quo.

I wonder whether today's superiors might not be in agony because they were picked by superiors of a generation earlier who knew them to fit patterns they themselves had been trained on. World War II unexpectedly put the United States in a dominant world position. It wasn't ready. Its new ambassadors couldn't speak the languages of the countries they were assigned to, didn't understand their problems, didn't like their food or their music, and didn't relate to their customs. Isn't this also somehow the Society's problem? Since Vatican II the Society has been expected by many of its own men to be a kind of this-world power, a power that can read a fast-changing world and communicate with it. But hadn't their superiors been picked because they were "other-worldly" and inner-holy people born during years of spiritual isolationism?

A German actor in Munich who had acted in a Bertolt Brecht play under Brecht's direction told me that during the first week of rehearsal everyone in the cast had to read his part in strict monotone. No one was allowed to inflect or emphasize a syllable, word or phrase. There were to be no gestures or facial expressions. The voice had to be held neutral and as barren of interpretation as humanly possible. If the cast couldn't work this way, Brecht would walk out and come back only after the cast was able to comply. Then, when Brecht was satisfied that his actors had emptied themselves of their prejudices and biases regarding his play, he would begin to guide their inflections and stresses. He thus made sure his actors worked together to project his play and not theirs.

This certainly isn't the only way to direct a play, and I don't suggest it's always the best way. I use Brecht here as a brutal and perhaps clumsy metaphor to describe how I understand Jesuit basic training as it was when I was there. Brecht demanded that his actors empty themselves and come to work clean; only then could they understand and act out his play properly. This is virtually what my novice master and provincial asked me to do. They gave me three tests: the first was to pull myself away from entangling distractions in the secular world; the second was to make myself *alone*, to withdraw not only from the world outside but, in effect, from my own fellow novices; the third was obedience — I was to submit myself to God's will and hold back no will of my own. God's direction would be made evident to me in commands and suggestions communicated by my Jesuit superiors.

I met my first test easily by cutting myself off from home and friends, giving up photographs, rings and pins as souvenirs of a former identity. I put away the clothes I'd come with and put on the black cassock. From September of 1940 until V–E Day in 1945 I didn't see a newspaper or hear a radio. I saw none of my former friends and I saw my parents three times when they came to visit me. I didn't make any telephone calls during this time and didn't receive any. I wrote only to members of my immediate family and their letters were the only ones I received.

I still agree with the logic of this first demand. I came into the order an uncouth adolescent, encrusted with my own peculiar Milwaukee habits, language patterns, and prejudices affecting everything I heard and saw. Some of these accretions had to be stripped back, not necessarily because they were bad but because they might interfere with my new growth. I had to clear away the debris of old self-images so that an entirely fresh image might emerge.

The second test was much harder to pass than the first. I was helped to cut away from past connections by my geography: we were buried out in the country; no cabs, buses or trains, and one telephone in the rector's hallway. But geography worked against me in this second test. It was hard to withdraw from the other men. We had all voluntarily marooned ourselves together on this isolated ground, yet a variety of rules now restrained us from communicating with each other. The novitiate's second demand expected me to be my own individual monastery (*monos*=one, alone) and regard even my own brothers in Christ as aliens. The fact that we tried to speak Ciceronian Latin to each other helped remind us that we were foreigners. The need to look up a word in the dictionary frequently made us question whether it was necessary to use the word at all. Room visits and particular friendships were forbidden. Silence, meditation and prayer, *tactus*, "modesty (that is, control) of the eyes," and the various interior businesses connected with self-watching all helped to establish the fiction of interpersonal distance.

Ignatius Loyola founded his Society on the principle of absolute, immediate and heartfelt obedience: "Each one should convince himself that they who live under obedience must allow themselves to be carried and ruled by God's Providence through their superiors as though they were a dead body which allows itself to be carried in any direction and to be treated in any manner whatsoever." The third novitiate test, therefore, was obedience. A house rule said there was absolutely no eating between meals. In obedience to this rule we picked huge golden peaches, Winesaps and Tompkins Kings, sweet Boscs, and bushels of plump purple grapes as if we were handling inedible waxes, unless the manuductor called *"Dentalia!"* — the signal permitting us to eat. Each of the hundred or so activities that raddled our various daily orders began by bell and ended by bell. We tried to become experts at cheerful promptness, learning to stop whatever we were doing and move on to the next activity at the bell's first stroke. The bell signaling the end of recreation, for example, could cut a word down in midsyllable and a guffaw abruptly at guff—.

An essential part of these three tests or demands was silence. Silence was profoundly vital for mental prayer. It was equally important for obedience, for if Jesuits were going to let themselves be ruled by "God's Providence through their superiors," they would have to listen to the superiors. Wordlessness was necessary for hearing the Word. Silence was the binder that held all other rules in place and made it easier for them to work. It prevented conspiracies, grumbling, back talk and open revolt. Silence wrapped each man, separating him from his neighbor. It encircled the *secundianni* and separated them from the *primianni*. It separated all novices from juniors, since the two divisions never talked except on a "fusion" day, one of the rare holidays when the silence and Latin rule was lifted for a few hours and the whole house talked. *Secundianni* silence was more experienced and firm than *primianni* silence. *Primianni* were instructed to live each day as it came and not to ask what lay ahead. Consequently, each new activity or feast day or variation of regular order came as a surprise: for example, the first villa day, the first Christmas season, the long retreat, the marching May litanies. These were surprises controlled by the *secundianni*. While the *primianni* were learning the silence of not asking, the *secundianni* were learning the silence of not telling. It was important to learn both kinds of silence because both were operating all through the Society in the obedience relationship.

Silence sometimes worked with immaturity in the novitiate to create ridiculous situations, since almost anyone with any kind of authority became the transmitter of God's will into your life. You felt you had better not disobey anybody or your power connections would be cut off. At field you might find yourself wondering if the man serving the ball at tennis was acting in God's place toward you.

In an environment of silence all communications become more vivid. Loneliness is more poignant and fear more disturbing. Secrets are better kept and executive action can be more decisive and clean-cut. When my provincial notified me that my request for dismissal from the Society had been granted and that the necessary letters from Rome were on their way, he ended his letter: "In the meantime, go quietly

*24*

about your work, and please do not discuss your departure with your fellow philosophers." That was the custom, disappear suddenly in night and fog. It was a brutal way to leave friends. They would come to the study room one day and see your desk emptied out and your chair upside down on top of it.

The Society never diagrammed its organizational structure for me but I used to imagine a chart that had an eye inside a triangle at its top center: that was for God. A ray from this triangle shot in a straight line downward to a tiara: the pope. From there the line angled over and down to a black biretta with "General S.J." printed on it: our Father General. The line then passed from Father General to a biretta marked "Mo. Prov. Prov.": the Father Provincial of the Missouri Province. Next it shot down to the novice master in the novitiate or to the rector and minister in other houses. Once inside the house the line branched downward becoming rootlets that passed through the spiritual father, the infirmarian, the teaching faculty, the choir director, the refectorian, and the beadle. God's medium was most frequently the bulletin board. He often used your mail bin and in emergencies your napkin box.

While the Society didn't use a box and line organization chart, such charts and progress graphs were so much a part of American thinking in the early forties that the mind supplied one for you. Since an organization chart is a metaphor, we could have used the image of a well-oiled machine with all of the parts contributing to the machine's function. But liberal arts people don't like to see themselves as cogs in any machine, no matter how important the cog or how beautiful and productive the machine. The favorite organization chart for religious orders is the human body. It's practical — you don't have to memorize the diagram. It's not demeaning: all parts of the body have their proper dignity and get their share of attention, concern and love. It points up the values of teamwork, of everyone going to his place and doing his

25

job: "Does the foot try to be the head?" Most people will accept as logical that the health of any body is best served when all its parts are integrated and coordinated with the head. These values are not only important for the organization's efficiency but essential for its very survival. But there is a danger of getting carried away by this metaphor. If you are the head, your danger is arrogance. The head has to be incorruptible, reasonable, fair, good, believable, and fully informed. The head may not assume it is all these things merely by reason of being the head. If you are not the head, your danger is apathy and overcompartmentalization. You say it is not your responsibility to think or feel. You say too easily: "That's not my job."

In an environment of silence, you can actually hear and feel the power lines of an organization chart hum. You must not let the chart hypnotize you. You must learn how to escape its automatic locking mechanisms by pretending fatigue, by indulging your sense of humor, and most important, by acting vigorously from conscience. I believe silence was violated less by those of us who broke it by talking than by the superiors who used our silence to prevent the organization chart from being questioned.

In 1943 all schools in Missouri were racially segregated. John Markoe, a Jesuit parish priest in St. Louis, started action to integrate St. Louis University. The president of the university, Father Patrick Holloran, S.J., agreed to put the issue of integration before his regents and deans, but afraid that an alumni backlash reaction could cost the university thousands of dollars in withheld or canceled support funds, he first sent the alumni a form letter presenting the pros and cons of integration. He also sent along a blank ballot asking for a yes or no vote. Markoe smuggled a copy of the letter and a ballot to the *St. Louis Post-Dispatch*, and despite protests from Holloran, the paper published both. When the university regents and deans finally met, only two of fifteen faculty members voted for integration. Thirteen voted no: "It will lower the standards of the university." "All the white students will leave." "It can't be done."

Claude Heithaus, a Jesuit anthropologist at St. Louis University, was incensed at this decision. He had never given thought to the racial problem before but now he made up his mind to fight for the university's integration. He was scheduled to preach a sermon to the university student body and decided he would confront the students. He told them:

> Some people say that if the Society of Jesus gives Negroes the Catholic education the Church wishes them to have, our white students will walk out on us. Is this true? I deny it! I say it is a lie and a libel. I challenge the whole world to prove that even one of our Catholic students will desert us when we apply the principles from which Jesus Christ suffered and died.

> I will go further and prove the opposite. I will prove it here and now. Catholic students to whose welfare I have dedicated my life and all that I have, listen to me. St. Louis University admits Protestants and Jews, Mormons and Mohammedans, Buddhists and Brahmins, pagans and atheists, without even looking at their complexions. Do you want us to slam our doors in the faces of Catholics, because their complexion happens to be brown or black?

> It is a lie. I see that you repudiate it with indignation. You scorn it all the more because you know that some of the very people who disseminate this lie have themselves sent their sons to Harvard and Yale, where they were glad to sit in the same classrooms with Negroes. These people bow in reverence before Oxford and Cambridge, the University of London and Sorbonne, but if they ever attended these great universities as I have, they would soon learn that in the world of scholarship there is neither white nor black, brown nor yellow.

I've quoted only three paragraphs of Heithaus's talk here, but the *St. Louis Post-Dispatch* printed all of it, the whole thing. It reported that at the end of Heithaus's sermon the students rose to their feet in a show of support for integration. President Holloran ordered Heithaus to be silent on the topic of integration and gave the *Post-Dispatch* a statement denouncing the anthropologist for his action. The entire city got involved, telephoning, writing letters, some promising prayers and vigils if the university would open its doors to Negroes, others threatening to close the school and lynch Heithaus if Negroes came in. Holloran gave way to pressures for integration and the university admitted its first Negro student a few months later.

I came into St. Louis University in September of 1944 totally ignorant of this struggle. I first heard there were racial troubles when Holloran announced that fall that the university was welcoming Negroes to academic equality, but that "in the wider and less well-defined field of social relationships, contacts and activities we do not approve, nor shall we attempt to enforce, identity between white and colored students." At noon recreation a few days later I heard that Claude Heithaus had astounded the students at Mass that morning by denouncing Holloran's policy as un-Christian.

Holloran locked Heithaus out of the pulpit. Heithaus came back by writing an editorial for *The University News* on integration. It took almost the entire issue and was picked up in its entirety by the *Post-Dispatch*. Holloran now banned Heithaus from *The University News*.

One night at the start of dinner in the refectory I heard Claude Heithaus called by name and saw him get up from his seat. Heithaus, a tall, lean man, looked like Gary Cooper and his movements were like Cooper's; the likeness shattered when you compared the way they communicated. Usually there was a lot of plate and bowl clattering as the community, about four hundred men, started passing food and getting ready to eat, but now there was silence. Back behind us at the rear of the refectory the lector up in his pulpit announced in Latin that Father Heithaus was being restricted to his room for three days of isolation and prayer. Everyone listened with their heads bowed and their eyes downward, ashamed, I guess, either of Heithaus for getting the penance or of Holloran for imposing it. Heithaus got up and walked back to his chair at the table. Then I saw a remarkable thing. All the men at Heithaus's table took off their birettas in a salute to him. They smiled and I saw that others around the hall-like refectory were also smiling at Heithaus and taking off their birettas. And up at the administration table there was Holloran, university president but also rector of the house, and he was grinning at Heithaus too and taking off his biretta. I still don't know what it all meant. I know that at the time I felt proud being in the room while it was all going on. I felt less proud shortly after when Heithaus was assigned to Marquette University in Milwaukee. George Dunne and John White, who had publicly supported Heithaus, were also sent away, Dunne to Los Angeles and White to British Honduras. Today I ask: where was I? What did I do to help Heithaus? The answer is easy: I prayed. The answer is easy: nothing.

On my most recent visit to Florissant as I walked around the Stanislaus grounds I realized that I was remembering sounds more than seen events. Here is a place where we had *gymnicum* and I hear Brother Haller barking from the side of his tough jaw: "Chop wood! One. Teeeoo. Three. Foe. One. Teeoo. Three. Foe." I find sounds bunched up at every gateway because the gates were cutoff lines for talk on field or walk days. Here are the benches where as a novice on Sunday mornings I used to eavesdrop on music played in the juniorate. And now on this dark-gray, moonless night I stand near the greenhouse and look down valley over sections of land that were once posted for grapevines. I think I hear the shrill rustling of autumn grape leaves. Shrill because the leaves' edges were hard and dry and the wind whistled across them and across the naked stretches of wire on which vines hung dying. Suddenly I turn and look behind me. I feel uneasy. I'm afraid. Is that a face there inside the greenhouse? Is somebody in there watching me?

While I was a *secundianni* in the novitiate, one of the first-year novices, a tall, broad-shouldered St. Louisan, used to fascinate me with explanations of Plato's philosophy. Whenever possible at villa or at field during a handball game or during bits of the recreation period, he explained the Platonic idealities of goodness, truth and beauty. I had never known anyone who had studied philosophy and talked it as part of conversation, so these were heady discussions for me. I was sorry to have them stop when I became a junior and we were separated by the rule that said novices and juniors were not to break division by talking.

It was during the grape harvest in my first year as a junior that the rector of the house called us together for the gruesome news that the parents of one of our second-year novices had been axed to death on Howdershell Road near the seminary. I almost feel again the extraordinary dry chill I felt — as if a long cold steel chisel had parted me inside — when I learned that the victims were the father and mother of my own Plato tutor and that the killer had been his brother.

Now let me confess an astounding fact: it was only during my recent visit to Florissant that I realized I had never told this young Jesuit, this brother, this man how sorry I was for his loss and his suffering. Granted that words might have been useless, I never stepped through the rules of silence, *tactus* and division that separated us. I could have gripped his hand to remind him I was his friend, that I cared and wanted in any way he'd let me to help him carry the burden of his excruciating tragedy. He would have understood. He would have felt my feelings. It is possible that silence was a relief for him; he didn't have to explain things to anybody and didn't have to endure awkward condolences. I am positive that the novices, the novice master, the rector, the provincial and all the faculty gave him comfort and help. He himself surely didn't expect any of us to come through to him. I knew he was away from the house much of the time, perhaps with relatives. I know all these mitigating, extenuating, justifying conditions. Yes, they're all possibly true but they don't take away the fact that by letting the institution operate for me I had dehumanized myself. If obeying those rules was being Christ-like, wouldn't the world be more human without Christians? How close, how loud must the bell toll to toll for a Christian?

Some Jesuits say that the glory years of the Society were those that brought on their suppression and banishment. Will the Society of Jesus die of deflation this time rather than suppression? Will it be abandoned rather than banished?

The Society of Jesus is supposed to serve where there is need. Is there any greater need in this time than the need for credibility? Doesn't the world need a model for love and dialogue?

The Roman Catholic Church today is confronted by its second massive protest-ant revolution, a bloodless one this time since the Pope has no army. The Society of Jesus succeeded in turning back and containing the Protestant revolution four hundred years ago. Will today's Jesuits be the new protestants?

The eleven men interviewed in this book are not typical Jesuits, because it's hard to type Jesuits. If one thing draws these talks together, it's that the Jesuits here all show a strong concern for man, for the human. The human black. The human poor. The suffering, war-hurt human. The urban, polluted, violent human. The searching and learning human. The unborn human. The insensitive human. The communicating human. The young and future human. The fact that I present eleven Jesuits does not mean that they are symbolic — one man for each good apostle. It just happened to work out that way.

PHOTO BY GEORGE RIEM

*Let's say NO
if it needs saying.*

# Daniel Berrigan, S.J.

*There is a yellow plastic sign fixed to Dan Berrigan's apartment door in Ithaca, New York. It was taken from some fence surrounding demolition and construction work and it tells the truth. It says: HARD HATS MUST BE WORN ON THIS JOB.*

*Berrigan's job has two parts: the first is to help young people grow an honest conscience. The second is to make room for that growth by opposing what is death-oriented, false, corrupt, irrelevant and antihuman in the establishment.*

*Berrigan's demolition-construction work consists of writing books and plays, recording poetry, teaching, counseling, opposing the war and the draft, demonstrating, bothering bishops, suffering arrest and search and disciplinary exile.*

*Two posters stuck to his office wall, one by Sister Corita, speak for his style of life: "Damn Everything But the Circus," and "Look, Love is Here to Stay and That's Enough."*

*The interview with Berrigan started about two in the afternoon and stretched toward eleven at night. The very last part was recorded in my motel room, with Berrigan beginning to tire, sitting cross-legged on a bed, his eyes half-closed, his neck bent. He addressed the recording microphone in his hands as if it were a chalice and he were speaking into it the consecration of his life.*

*Berrigan was ordered by the federal court to begin a three-year prison sentence on April 9, 1970, for destroying draft files. Instead of surrendering himself on that date, he went into hiding until August 12, 1970, when he was arrested in Rhode Island by the F.B.I. Berrigan is now a federal prisoner in the penitentiary in Danbury, Connecticut. The following interview was concluded in early April.*

---

*What do you feel other Jesuits think about you right now?*

You'll get as many answers to that as Jesuits, especially depending on their age. I don't want to go into interpreting their minds. Put that question to them.

*Have you been criticized by Jesuits who are embarrassed by your "escapades"?*

Oh, sure. There's always a tremendous undercurrent of that. The opposition and suspicion of the older Jesuits and the superiors is probably the hardest thing I have. But my mixing with Jesuits is quite rare these days except for Jesuits I encounter who are in the movement. A number of younger Jesuits have come through. They spend a few days going over some things connected with their lives. But I don't have to justify myself before large numbers of Jesuits in a Jesuit house. That would be very upsetting. I don't have to live with the kind of mix of Jesuits who would make their unhappiness with me apparent.

I'm just about tolerated. There have been several moves to get rid of me, but they can't quite get away with it. There is too much public sentiment against this war and the Church is awakening to it. So the Society couldn't take the heat of throwing a man out because of his peace activities. I have sympathy and support from younger people in the order, but I have no illusions of getting any real moral support from the level of authorities.

*What does your family think of your behavior as a Jesuit?*

Well, we have a very mixed family scene. There are six boys. Phil and myself are the youngest. I think it's a good, even exciting family. We have everything from war hawks to prisoner. And the criminals of peace are the priests, Phil and I. The really interesting people are our parents. My father died last November at ninety and my mother is eighty-six. They have faced bitter times, and faced it in their old age and with bad health, yet they've never wavered in their support of us. They'd say, "Since it's your conscience and since you are willing to go this far, we see it better and we go with you." They would never have seen it if it hadn't been their own sons.

*What precisely did you do that is sending you to a federal prison?*

Nine of us went into a draft board office in Catonsville, Maryland, in May of '67. It was a small board carrying only three hundred eighty I-A files. We took all these files to a parking lot and put them into trash baskets there. We burned the files with homemade napalm, then waited around for the police.

The Catonsville demonstration was the first in which a Jesuit was involved. Since then Jesuits have been involved in draft file destruction in Chicago and Washington, Boston and Philadelphia. Catonsville won attention because there were a large number of very diverse people and there were several of us who were quite prominent. Let's see, there were three priests involved.

*What made you zero in on Catonsville?*

It's near Baltimore. My brother and his associates lived and worked down there. They had cased the draft office there and knew it was wide open and easy to get to. I came in with only two days to go. They had done all the ground work over a period of two to three weeks. We all made the napalm together and we did this deliberately so we'd be unmistakenly involved. We made it from a formula in a Special Forces Handbook published by the School for Special Warfare at Fort Bragg. We made a crude form consisting of two parts gasoline and one part soap flakes, we left it in liquid form so it would pour.

The papers were calling us "the Catonsville 9." We're only eight now. Dave Darst was killed in an auto accident in Nebraska on his way to visit prisoners of conscience. He burned to death. Dave was a Christian Brother. His order didn't deserve him, and that was a fact. But the fact was not something David was anxious to make much of. His order had produced him, that was the real point. He was celibate, bright as quicksilver. In his very brightness was all the joy and pain of being a man today; but a *young* man! A face at its best when surrounded by others.

He could have lived in that middle ground of partying, study, female fluttering, sacred and secular bread, and circuses that make up the lives of so many clerics today. No great loss, no great gain. But something else happened to him. He could not live with death. He had no bargaining skills.

*You're forty-eight years old and you've been a Jesuit thirty years. Are you disappointed in your order?*

Well, let me put it this way, I'm not at all sure it's going to make it. This is probably the last generation in which the Society will be recognizable in its present structure. I think that's a good thing, if we could pace the speed up and start pointing to alternatives by way of a lot of experimentations. But I sense in the Society, beginning with the general himself, with whom I talked at some length — I sense a great resistance to any real change beyond Band-Aids and fooling around within the structure. My own experience proves people won't accept real change.

*Were you quite satisfied with your early Jesuit training?*

Oh, I was a very young boy. Given those times it wasn't that bad. That's thirty years ago.

*You entered in 1939 before the Second War and heard nothing about it. Right?*

A little bit. Nothing by way of any critique. It was never submitted as a moral question. That was the tragedy. In theology ten years later, there was one man to whom I'm eternally grateful who was just beginning to raise the question of, not of nuclear weaponry, but of saturation bombing. Father John Ford. For various reasons that I regret very much, he got sidetracked and never really went into modern war. He did begin at least to ask whether or not one could move as we did into Tokyo and Dresden with our massive bombings of their civilian populations. But we were so terribly retarded that it was years before any of us caught up. Most of us never did.

I would have to go very slow, as I have the last years, encouraging young people to come into the Jesuits. I agree with Thomas Merton, who once said to me that he never thought that he himself should be anything but a monk, but that if he were a young person he would never become a monk. That's about where I am too.

*You sense a great resistance to change in the Society and you fear her immobility to make serious changes dooms her. Is the Society so property-heavy she can't move?*

Oh, I think that's very true. Especially in the States here. We're just too thoroughly American to be deeply Christian.

We can't really grab the sources of change and move with them.

The Jesuits are a Western expression of a Westernized Church. We're just part of a kind of Promethean drive toward technological domination of the universe and control of the people of the world. We are one instance of this, a very powerful and a kind of shameful instance of this.

Once you get down beyond all the rhetoric about "God's will," "obedience" and "authority," you come to this clutching and protection of property. This is even true of some very good men. This is a sign of the de-Christianization of what we like to call "the religious life." We cannot really answer the summons of God because we have real estate. Those who place that in jeopardy by their moral activity get it in the neck. Witness me.

*Jesuit decisions become a defense of territory.*

Oh, yes. Yeh. Property gives us a very strong clutch to whatever kind of identity we have. Most Jesuits come from middle-class families into a very powerful middle-class ethos in the order. Most have never known anything else and really haven't had to search out their own meaning beyond where they were born. The Society never offered anything — I don't think — radically beyond that. It offered a very powerful justification for that middle-class ethos, a kind of spiritual interpretation of it, and in many cases a very admirable kind of field of action. I love the Society very much, but I've had to look at it in a very real way since all this broke over me. I think that we're going to die rather than change. I would put it that simply. We've kept all the rhetoric about poverty, humility and detachment while the substance has just drifted away.

Under the umbrella of "God's will," we were treated to a justification for the endless acquisition of property, and an endless kind of immunity from taxation. There was the obvious supposition that we would be free from the draft, but at the same time serve the war machine through chaplaincies, the ROTC, and even military academies, and through the indoctrination of young people in the military ethos. All this was part of the unexamined package called "the will of God" that was purveyed by the hierarchic Church through our superiors. That box has now been opened.

*Jesuits are moving into secular professions such as medicine. I see them as word men moving into the land of numbers, humanizing technology and research.*

I can understand and maybe rejoice in this up to a point. This has always been part of the Jesuit genius, this full kind of human entrance into the intellectual and cultural scene. But I have reservations. The question of professional training ought to be quite secondary to our tradition. We all come out of long years of ascetical and Biblical meditations and prayer and discipline. It seems to me that these should tend to sharpen a man's conscience and awareness of life and death around him. I have the greatest respect for the adaptability of the Society. But acculturation has horrifying aspects because you can't survive as a kind of a relic.

Recently the *National Guardian* pointed to me as the most notorious example of new forces operating among American Jesuits. I was used as a kind of a springboard for interviews with various Jesuits around the country, mostly younger men. One of them said something so disappointing, I remember not being able to sleep that night — you know when you're angry how you compose letters? — this was a young theologian, just ordained a few years. He said, "Well, Berrigan is an obvious proof that the Jesuits will not only survive but will flourish more than ever." The interviewer asked, "What do you mean?" The young theologian said, "Consider whether General Motors or the *New York Times* would allow someone like Berrigan around."

Now there's a theologian whose operating metaphors had nothing to do with the Bible or the life of Christ or the tradition of the Society. He was appealing to the most atrocious kind of corporate life as a point of comparison with the American Jesuits. That was theology to him — that the American Jesuits were much more liberal and ongoing because they would allow me to hang around rather than throw me out, which General Motors would have done. I was appalled. He totally ignored the issues, as though I were on some absurd campaign advocating vegetarianism.

Jesuits are not called just to humanize professional life, but also to judge it, to exercise a Biblical judgment upon it. To say no to its killing aspects. To root out all its duplicity, its hatred of life, its hatred of the poor and the powerless, and its racism.

I see our guys entering with great skill and great resources into the cultural scene, for example, medicine. But I wonder if their presence doesn't help justify the scene. By being there they enhance the good name of the Society but at the cost of reinforcing the worst aspects of the culture. They have no resources to offer in most of these scenes beyond the resources of the scene itself.

That's not what I'm about. I'm out of the Bible. I'm out of Christianity. That's why I'm not getting along too well at Cornell, and that, I might add, with a whisp of odium, is why I've never gotten along in the Church.

*When you say "out of," you mean "begot by"?*

Yes. That's my *tradition*. That's *why I was born.*

*Specifically, whom do you honor? Who's your root in the Bible?*

Jesus.

*I was wondering which specific prophets you honored in the Bible.*

Well, the prophets are very important obviously, but did I make my point? Jesuits have honored every profession all over the world and have a great reputation for that. But we do not have a great reputation for telling the world that it is the enemy of man. We don't do that.

*Do Jesuits in secular institutions get too caught up in the secular apparatus?*

I don't like to set up abstract kinds of norms for people because everything is so flexible now. But let me say this. The graduate students in this big scene here at Cornell hang around their own field and avoid areas of conflict. On the issues of the war, the graduate students weren't really heard from until their immunity was threatened a year ago. Now the Jesuits who come here disappear into that scene. I'm not blaming them. I'm just trying to report. Their reputation is very good. They always do well. But as far as exercising the kind of judgment on this scene that the SDS is trying to exercise or that the blacks are trying to exercise, or that a few of us in the clergy are trying to exercise, no.

*But haven't the clergy and even teachers always been timid about political involvement?*

Sure. Right. But you know our Jesuit rhetoric about ourselves is very different. The *Exercises* aren't timid. The rhetoric of our retreats isn't timid. Our liturgy isn't timid.

Our rhetoric asks for a profound radical disassociation from the ways of exercising power that are proper to the world. The *Exercises* tell me that a Jesuit's reputation and honor are second to the good repute and honor of Christ.

*45*

*The "Kingdom of Christ" as Ignatius describes it in the Exercises, the Christian Camelot, is a very stirring vision.*

The whole Kingdom idea is not timid — that we should be ready at a minute's notice to lose our lives for the honor of Christ and for human life in the world. We've been nurtured on this kind of language. But substantially we don't bring the concept to a cultural scene where we could exercise great leverage.

*Do you have any Jesuit leaders that you respect?*

There are many people in the Society I respect but none of them are leaders. Though by no means are any of them followers. If you see what I mean.

A couple of years ago, a superior said to me with considerable heat: "If only you would wait, until we have the difficulties in the order settled, before bringing on these crises from outside!" Could it be that the God of our Scriptures (and presumably of our lives) might be urging a different timetable on us? Like, how can you live in a house dedicated to better housekeeping with children dying on the front lawn? What sort of picture can you bear at the picture window?

This is the kind of mortician mentality and dread of living experience that operates at official levels, and says to me by implication, silence and exclusion, and by shunting me to the edge: "You just don't count, because we don't trust experience, therefore we don't trust you. What we really trust is the past and the hierarchy, and the letters of the generals, and our investments."

*"And the success that's come from this combination."*

Yes. This thing worked, so who are you to criticize? Or, as a black power kid might put it, "What else is new, nigger?"

46

That's the word I get. Well, I don't want to dwell on my personal case. I don't want to be in trouble with anyone. I don't particularly relish it.

*You don't and yet you do. You'd be bored if there were nothing to bitch against.*

I would be unhappy if things seemed okay but were really false or cruel. I just long for the kind of Church in which I could be in full communion. I haven't had that for a long time.

Why should I despair of having an authority who can be interested in the welfare of the powerless, the prevenient power of life over death, the contempt of all those forms of death that Jesus also refused to submit to?

I would like the authorities to stand where I stand because I think that that's what authority should be in the Church. In other words, I don't see that *I* ought to be at any edge of things. I don't see why the Jesuit provincial shouldn't be as angry at the Vietnam war as I am. Or why he shouldn't be as determined to follow Gandhi and Christ into jail. I'd love to have him where I am. I think he should be.

In four or five years of the most atrocious, genocidal, uncivilized warfare we do not yet have a single bishop who will stand with us. I don't mean by burning draft files, I'm not being immodest. I mean stand with us by saying in public: these men have a case. Or by visiting young Catholics in prison. They visit the troops every God-damned Christmas. Spellman did it, now Cooke is doing it. They go down and rub noses in the White House and give lousy sermons to Nixon and they betray the Church.

But that kind of Church doesn't stand up very well when human life is in breach and when civilians are being bombed and when Jews are being incinerated. There's no real change in sight. As far as I can see. Maybe you can see it.

*No. I can't see any big changes.*

And yet it does seem a very small change.

*No. It's a big change to expect.*

It's a big change from the kind of the Caesaro-papist union we've gotten used to, but it's a very small change if you pick up the New Testament and read Matthew 5, The Sermon on the Mount.

*Peacemakers, poverty of spirit — to live these ideals and act them out would be no small change.*

It does seem fairly simple. That's part of my difficulty. I guess I'm primarily a kind of very intolerant fundamentalist.

*But you're still in the Society. Some intolerant people simply walk out. Your intolerance takes a different form.*

Right. I have some leverage for dialogue.

*But you do see yourself in a dialogue then?*

There are a hell of a lot of ways of carrying on a dialogue. I'm in print continually and I say what I want to say. When they come and say, "We have serious reservations because you're not telling the truth," then I'll say, "Please tell me where? In what?" But every time I've had very tough troubles with censors, it's been because I was trying to say something that special interests did not want said. So I go ahead and say what I should.

*Has the traditional close relationship between the Society and the pope kept Jesuits from attempting radical change?*

Yes. Even recently Paul the Sixth invoked that image of running to horse when the pope speaks. He made a very explicit thing of it when he released the encyclical on birth control. *Humanae Vitae* was a loyalty test that the Jesuits above all others were required to pass. Well, it's the most horrendous kind of Machiavellianism, whether he realizes it or not.

*But the Jesuit in training was never taught to confront his superiors. He was taught to obey.*

You're speaking of something extraordinarily rare and very difficult. Nothing of a serious radical nature happened in my life as a Jesuit much before the age of, well, forty. Yet now I see it happening to men in their thirties and late twenties. Everything inevitably is pushing down younger all the time. The most radical people now on campus are freshmen. Young Jesuits are now asking questions we never did in our early years. The whole thing is a keg of dynamite. My kind of thing is proliferating to a new generation.

This is a tough period. And of course, I have to have almost bottomless sympathy for the perplexity of trying to be an authority in the Church these days. But it does seem to me that the Spirit is breathing in very unusual places and it's not helpful to put the lid on it.

*You say you didn't make a radical change in your life until you were forty?*

The occasion for laying my life on the line hadn't arisen. I'm not saying it shouldn't have arisen, because the '50's were marked with some terrible bloodletting in the civil rights movement. When I made an attempt to get with that, I was very harshly reproved by my superiors. At that time I thought one should obey.

*At least once a year women's magazines run an article called something like "Middle-Age Rebel." A forty-year-old man who married at twenty looks in the mirror and asks: "What's happened to my life? I'm working like a dog, going mad in a rat race for kids who don't care. Who am I? What am I getting out of this?" Some of these men divorce or acquire a mistress; some quit their jobs or professions. Do you think your "marriage" to the Society is running through such middle-life turbulence?*

That's probably a good way of putting it. But I regret so few of my own generation have gone through this change. Somewhere along the line they had their veins cut open and they lost most of their blood before they got to forty. It's quite tragic to me. What's happened to them is probably only slightly less ruinous than what's happening to people in the outside culture. The majority of them disappear into these various machines and are ground into hamburg by the time they're forty. They never really become achieving persons in the spiritual sense. My hope for the Church is a very slim one, but the Church does slightly less harmful things to people than the culture does.

*Would you agree that the Jesuit order's survival index might be found in the health of Jesuit community life?*

I guess every question brings up every other one. Yours is very, very complex. It seems to me *health* is the key word. Can a community of Jesuits deeply institutionalized by its very geography be considered healthy? Or is the real health going to be found in numbers of Jesuits who cut loose from the institutions, without cutting loose from the Society, keeping some spiritual bonds but living at its edges?

The best things I find happening in the Society are the small communities of Jesuits who have totally disestablished and are living in the middle of the real world. This is being tolerated by the Society as an experiment.

*You feel that mere toleration is a rather stingy form of support?*

Well, I've gotten used to it without ever ceasing to mourn that it has to be that way.

It's been a source of great unease to my superiors that I've been here living in an apartment alone for about two years and my community is Cornell. After all, I'm a university employee, the first priest ever hired here.

I'm officially connected with LeMoyne College in Syracuse, but my links are loose and I think they've been happy to leave it that way. Nobody is really inclined to push issues up against the wall. The public supports those who are resisting the war in a thoughtful way. Though superiors are not enlightened, they are aware.

Speaking of a community, I was urging a year ago that we seek positions at Cornell for Jesuits. They showed some interest, but it never seemed to get off the drawing board. Anything innovative is very rare these days.

*You say Cornell is uneasy about your presence here. How welcome do you think a band of radical Jesuits would be?*

The question doesn't arise. There isn't such a band — and even if there were it would probably be a mistake to come here. Too isolated and watchful and self-centered to be useful for us.

*Should Jesuits dump their properties and work on secular campuses as you do?*

I guess there are no black and white answers here. It would be foolish to set up a rigid norm right now. We're too much in a state of flux and perplexity.

I do want to make my own position clear, because I do have one here, even though I don't believe in a rigid expression of it. It seems to me that as men of faith, we have no right to take positions of power which will compromise our possibilities of speaking for human rights. That to me makes it unimportant where a Jesuit is, whether it's in one of our own institutions or Cornell University. That's why for a Jesuit to get tenure or become dean at a secular school induces more questions. The really radical kids are saying that professors should not be tenured, that deans of men are bought out.

I'm taking a rather large salary from Cornell. I don't like the sources of that money, but at least I'm here in a way which is making Cornell uneasy. I'm asking questions. It appeals to me as some sort of Biblical stance, that you're not silenced by your geography, or by the form of authority that you take on. If you remain at the edge of it, you remain a critic of it.

*When you say geography, do you mean real estate?*

No. Geography in an analogous sense. I mean one's place. One's position, job, status, all of those things.

The temptation of someone invited to a place like this is to be mesmerized by its superficial aspects: the affluence, all the enormous resources and the beautiful scene. To try to sense the underlying currents of the antihumanistic, death-ridden, exploitative racist power operating here, and then to be a critic in a way that will be significant to it, and to reject its corrupt securities: I think that's the only reason for being here.

As far as the rhetoric about this place is concerned, it's just about as truthful as the New York archdiocese. Perhaps worse, because it's bigger.

*If you put yourself in a posture of criticism towards any environment that you're in, you must live an uncomfortable life. What does the gadfly do for fun? Chew betel nuts?*

I'll have to try that. No, that's pretty true. This kind of life is absurd without faith — though a life of faith has absurd elements too. But this kind of life is not only absurd without faith, it's also lethal. It could kill a man. It could unbalance him, as it does to many of these seculars wandering around in despair. They go to drugs. They go into various forms of suicide.

*Or they decompartmentalize themselves. They think and feel one way, and behave another way.*

Yes, and this strikes deeply at good, young radical people too. The question being do they have the resources to continue in the long haul required for real change? Those resources have to be deep. But, as you find in the SDS here and in many parts of the radical movement, such resources aren't available. Gadflies do go mad. But those in power go mad too — don't let me neglect to say that. They go mad in other ways.

*When you say "the long haul," you refer to an objective. You can't really define whether a long or short haul is called for unless you have some kind of goal and a series of standards to mark progress.*

Nobody is going to reach his mark in his own lifetime. That is beside the point. One wants to be a sign of some human future, of some human community, and, in a time of great violence, of some nonviolent resources, and ride with that. Ride with that.

I don't have any five-year plan. I've always avoided those. When I came here, President Perkins asked me what my goals were. He was very unsettled. He had found out who I was only after getting a lot of flak from benefactors and alumni who read reports that I was coming here. But he had already signed my contract.

I said to him very simply, I said, "Mr. Perkins, I don't have any purpose in coming here." I said, "I think that's the language of engineering schools and I refuse to be engineered or to be engineering others." I said, "I don't have any purpose beyond living for others and with others. I come here to mix with people and to be available and to encourage and to perhaps show that man's life is a little more important than his machinery, his toys, his bank account." I said, "I am quite willing to let happen what happens, including leaving here." Of course, that was very unsettling language for him. His language was quite barren and quite mechanized. It was unsettling that a man would be that free and not have *his* language.

*When you say you are here to involve yourself in change but have no prescribed goals or objectives determining the pattern of change, you are echoing Marcuse. Do you intend that?*

I hadn't thought of it. He certainly isn't very important to me. I consider him a frightening man, I would just as soon go with Perkins as go with him.

*If the Vietnam thing suddenly stops, what will you do? Keep beating the country for having been in it? Find another war?*

Oh, no. I think the country will take care of that for me. *I* won't have to find another war. *It* will. When you've got a military as big as ours, you've got to keep it in shape or it gets rusty. Oh — there will be other wars. That's why we've been insisting now for five years that Vietnam is only a symptom of a very profound illness in the whole body.

*You said the country would provide you with a new cause. What do you mean?*

54

It isn't as if the Christian has to go around like a dog looking for shit, you know, for an issue. He just has to know how Caesar acts in the world and what Christ says to that. He's supposed to know a little bit about both. He can read the *New York Times* and he can read the Bible.

Do you see what I'm getting at? I'm trying to say this: that as long as the powers and dominations spoken of by Paul, and the inhabiting devils spoken of by Jesus, continue to presume to rule history, then the Christian has some task. He doesn't have to concoct one because to secular powers "death" will always have dominion and "life" will always be cheap. The Christian will say, "No! Human life is infinitely precious. Human death is not to be preferred to the life of a man."

Vietnam is the merest edge of the iceberg of power. After Vietnam, you start with things we should have been at years ago. For example, what are we doing for the majority of man, as Pope John would say, "the third world"? What's happening to those who were cursed from conception to live and die in misery? We're pounding the resources of the world down the rathole of military hardware. What are we doing to the resources of the world through our ecological destruction?

*Do you think the radicals against Vietnam have been ruthlessly silent about some other very inhuman things going on in this country?*

I do. I do. I've been appalled at times by the young radical movement. The '69 SDS convention, the Hiroshima Day parade in New York, the Weatherman violence in Chicago — it's insane.

The SDS kids come in here to talk all the time. I must say that up to spring '69, Cornell had one of the better national chapters. They were doing outstanding work in very important areas of need.

The underground press conducted the first real analysis in anybody's memory of the sources of power and money, and therefore the sources of our moral impasse at Cornell.

None of the departments here dared to ask where the trustees got their money. No one in the sciences had asked where their foundation money was coming from. No one asked where government grants were leading the university.

Suddenly these kids come along. They're bright, independent, in trouble with the courts on the draft, many of them are awaiting jail. They were able to turn a searchlight on Cornell which no one else had the guts, the enterprise to do for fifty years. They bared the bones, the skeletal articulation of this whole thing: where is it moving? What is it like once you get beyond all this fatty tissue?

I can't spend a lot of time criticizing young people without also making it understood how they've been forced into this. The longer the war goes on, the longer insanity is in the air, the closer these kids get up against the wall. The pressures they're under are just enormous — from the draft, from the war, from racism, from the cities, from the university, the pressures from their own families to conform, all this, and then the silence of the churches.

I balance my disappointment with the SDS and young people with a reminder that we're much more deeply at fault.

*Doesn't resistance and the understanding of what to resist require some maturity and some depth and balance?*

The kids are growing up fast. It's hard to generalize about them because some mature so quickly and understand so much so well. But when young people are in despair with all that energy and all that moral passion, they strike out in a way which is murderous and undefined — it's like a scythe in the hands of a madman. You can't tell your enemies from your friends when you reach that stage. You even refuse to distinguish. But let's match that kind of saturation with the kind of saturation killing of people introduced by our technology.

*Let me get your feeling about drugs on the campus.*

Well, what's the relative damage in the middle class wrought by alcohol? Alcoholism continues and is accepted. Yet we have this terrible kind of overkill attitude toward the drug scene. Our treatment of the young is lethal, because we're afraid of change. It proceeds from the same fear that makes us kill blacks or Vietnamese.

I submit that the laws are the last resort of the desperate. If everything else fails in human communication, enact the law and lock the bastards up. Whether they are war resisters or Vietnamese or blacks or priests. Lock them up.

*You're describing law as a form of force.*

Form of *violence*. I want to be clear on that. A form of violence against human change — human change which is not meant to be contained, but welcomed and listened to and rendered human by human community and dialogue. Law, as we presently conceive of it, stops that.

The judge said to us: "I can respect you as human beings and understand what you have tried to do, but the law is the law." He could not be a human being, as he confessed, and be a judge.

*The judge as a human being must interpret the law and modify it to suit circumstances — is that what you mean?*

The judge as a human being is invited to be a human being. Being a judge is merely putting a black nightgown over your suit.

*Will the students question advertisers, for example, on the morality of cigarette advertising?*

Young imaginations have the power of attacking certain objects or conditions as the symbols of everything else. If they aren't directly attacking cigarettes, it's because they're attacking napalm. Anybody who can read can draw the implications.

*Why haven't the students been active about Biafra?*

Only because you have to pick and choose, and the Americans are not directly involved in the deaths in Biafra, and they're Americans.

*We don't gain peace easily and not by slogans. It takes sacrifice and hurts. I just can't believe that love for peace comes at an early age.*

Our expectations lead us to believe that as a person got older and wiser and got more authority, his conscience got more acute. But the exact opposite happens!

*I was referring to young persons who are so articulate about Vietnam. Why couldn't they be equally articulate for the lost and the hurt in other areas? They don't seem to give a damn.*

They do give a damn. But they only have one life and so many hours. They say no to the whole damn bag.

*Right, well, we are limited in our time. Each of us only has one life and so many hours. Are you free to criticize where the young go wrong? Aren't you perhaps, in danger of getting some "real estate" yourself that will inhibit you?*

Well, there certainly is a danger. I would admit that. I disassociated from institutional aspects of the SDS. I'm friends to individuals but I don't generally attend their meetings and I had a lot of fights with their leadership. Luckily, most of those leaders are gone now, which might be better again for us actually.

There were three hundred fifty Cornell students who came to our trial in Baltimore and turned the streets into a very beautiful, nonviolent, thoughtful scene. For a week. That was two years ago this October. But then last year they wrote us off.

Some very profound differences arose between my style and theirs. They turned much more toward the rhetoric of Maoism and radical Leninism and the cult of violence stemming out of Guevara and the Latin American scene. They knew quite clearly what I buy and what I don't buy, and they knew also that the destruction of draft files is still about the only form of nonviolent protest that I'm interested in right now. They didn't offer any good alternatives beyond their rhetoric. So we had an argument.

Many of them even forget the war as an issue. In fact, the resistance movement here seems to have died out. We don't have people handing in draft cards in any great numbers any more. All that has gone. It may revive again.

*As I see it, credibility is the key to communication. Since the kids are communicating with you, they must trust you. How do you get their trust?*

If you live in a way which is trustworthy, you will be trusted. The way to be trustworthy is to live for others and damn the torpedoes.

*Even if you live for others, they have to trust that your life is for others.*

It's a very delicate balance to keep between aligning yourself with the young and selling out to everything that's coming along. Right now there's an enormous amount of disassociation and sickness and alienation and madness in the young. My contribution is also to declare that they can take me or leave me. They can find me credible or not — I don't give a damn. Because I'm proceeding out of a certain tradition and going in a certain direction. They may link with me or ricochet off. I will never cease talking with them, but I also will not sell out to them any more than I would sell out to anyone. Now that's easy to say but it's a very tough thing to live and it's fraught with all sorts of dangers.

*Do you think you might have to leave the Society to prove to the young people that you are committed to their service?*

No. They bring up this question, but it's not particularly interesting. I could as well challenge them about leaving the University or the SDS or their families, or the Church. Every institution is up for the cruelest kind of critique and every one is ambiguous. To stay with one or to leave one is a secondary question.

Modern man is simply inconceivable without institutions. That's not a defense of old institutions. It's just an encouragement to get new things going that will be more serviceable and flexible and celebrational, that will welcome such resources as joy, and hope and patience, and above all human differences rather than human stereotypes.

Many people are converging from the edge of the old, rather than the center of the old. I think it's absurd to think that one can be without institutional life. One, perhaps, had best be at the edge of institutional life though, so that he can meet other people coming and going at that edge.

*Looking at the new films and new theater and new politics as part of a grand mosaic, what do they tell you?*

I think we're dealing with aspects of whatever future society may be like — its celebration of leisure, of the life of the

60

senses, of a healthy, outward-looking sexuality, of personal affection as a basis for politics, of compassion as a basis for social service.

My generation can only hope to be learners at one end of this spectrum. We can encourage and enable these things to happen, rather than initiate them ourselves, though I don't want to turn that possibility off entirely.

The areas of danger are always the areas of power and these are the areas held by my generation. The new generations have to work up through powerlessness to new forms of power. I think our job is to say no to existing forms of power so that the young may move further. I think also our work — listening and being teachable and humble — is to bury the already dead elements of human life — those that have been used up, and to have the courage to say no to them in order that new things may be born.

Of course, that's very cruel on us because we came up through another shape of things and it's difficult for us to welcome or even to concede the fact that certain things die.

*You seem to have learned your role toward change and the young from your parents.*

Okay. Right. Yes. It is really, really remarkable. They kept very cool. They stayed with our stages as we moved along.

Getting back to theater, I was most intrigued with the Living Theater and all I had read about it. I had never seen it. I wanted to invite Beck to put on some real street theater in Baltimore, so I phoned Yale about two weeks before our trial. The message for various reasons never got to him. At any rate his group didn't come.

They came here to Cornell in the early spring, and I met both Becks. They were very warm and appreciative of what we had done at the trial. They are peace people from way back. Judith Melina was in jail in the forties — in the forties, imagine! — for refusing to take shelter during one of those horrible bomb practice things in New York.

When I met them Julian Beck said, "Tonight we'll do our play for you and the Catonsville 9, and we'll do it the best that we can." So I went. It was one of those ironies because I walked out after about two hours. I had had all I could take. I thought the whole thing was terrible. It had to do with a very simplistic kind of incantatory politics, and with mob scenes and with the awakening of the worst kind of instincts in young people. It just wasn't where I was. I had been through all this already at the Pentagon, and I'd had it. I struggled through it again with friends later, and we concluded that there were very mixed reactions and I was just one reaction.

*What do you mean you had been through this at the Pentagon?*

I was subjected to mob scenes that could have been very degrading if you didn't have a lot going for you. It was very hard. But I didn't want to get into that same thing and call it theater.

The nudity was quite natural. For one thing they were rather elderly people. About my age and about as attractive nude. Ha-ha-ha! There was no danger of any sexual outbreak. (I was even hoping for something better!)

They moved among the people in various stages of undress. In fact Julian Beck himself made an epiphany in the balcony by hotting up the scene with an elderly lady. We thought it was a put-on. But she was just an old, little woman, sixty or seventy years old, who had bought her ticket like everyone else. He began to rage at her, to scream at her, to undress in front of her, and do degrading and threatening things. It could have been very damaging to her but the Becks themselves were damaged in the eyes of many of us. We're going to have to have a different theater than that, I think.

Let me say this: Several times when I've gone to jail, I've been stripped to the buff. And I've been told to bend down and had my ass reached up — looking for drugs. And I don't particularly go for that. I put up with that because that's where I am and that's what I have to live with these days.

When I came home from Hanoi, we were roped off: two of us at Customs. Luckily we were prestigious items; newsmen all around and these things get recorded. But they held us there for a half hour going through every stitch of our clothing and seizing everything we had brought. I had taken notes everywhere in Hanoi. I had taken notes by cigarette lighter in a bomb shelter while being bombed. I had them in an American paperback on ten or twelve yellow pages.

You can submit to a lot of indignities because your dignity is beyond the reach of those who would like to destroy it. But some things you're not going to give up. You'll die first. I was not going to give those notes up. I said to myself, "God damn it. If they want to take these notes, they're going to have to kill me first. I'm going to keep these notes." That was the point at which I said NO. They must have sensed this, I think, and they handed the book back before they let us go. The notes were the basis for my book *Night Flight to Hanoi*.

What am I saying all this for? . . .

I just don't want invasions of human life and human dignity perpetrated in the name of art. If we have to go through them in the name of Caesar, I'll put up with that because I'm speaking for powerless people. But I won't pay for it and grin under it as though it were art. Well, there's my hang-up.

Some of the SDS and some of the young incendiaries now say, "Let's put up with anything because blacks do it." It's very unpopular right now to say that blacks shouldn't do certain things. I say, "Let's say NO if it needs saying." That applies to everyone, the Becks and to the black power people and to the SDS and the Catholic Church. Let's get a minimum denominator of how a human being operates and say, "No further. No further."

From the *Cornell Alumni News*, May, 1969:

Editor: The following is a copy of a letter I have sent to President Perkins:

*I wish to include my name with those alumni who are gratified that Father Berrigan is a member of the Cornell staff. I say this despite the fact that I am not in accord with all of the opinions or remedies for social ills which have been attributed to Berrigan. It is easy to respect his courage and the calibre of his intellect and eloquence. What seems to me more unique and most important about this man, however, is the balance he strikes between his imaginative and active involvement at the frontiers of social change and his explicitly emphatic refusal to countenance or condone impulsive, unnecessary violence for the sake of mere rebellion.*

*As a school psychologist working with young people, I feel that such a man can appeal to and constructively channel the enormous passion for change which so stimulates today's youth. He is an idealist who possesses control and responsibility.*

*I believe many thoughtful adults recognize the delicate razor edge of balance which must be maintained in our existing social ferment. We must preserve what is of value and relevance in our institutions and traditions while we seek to change what is anachronistic or evil. But our society is in great danger. Our young enthusiasts will not be turned aside or repressed but many of them lack the tempered perspective that only maturity can provide.*

*It seems to me that Father Berrigan is aware of this danger and, at the same time, his courageous witness serves as an appealing and positive model for our young people.*

*Marjory Buchen Seymour '42*
*Allendale, N.J.*

64

*"Special service" never means the Pope
is above and beyond comment.*

# John Padberg, S.J.

*Someone at St. Louis University told me that John Pad-berg had received the E. Harris Harbison Award for Distinguished Teaching. Before my appointment hour with Padberg, I went to the University's publicity office to pick up a news release describing this award. The receptionist had trouble locating it. Suddenly, she said, "Here it is! Somebody's filed it under 'Harris, E.'" I told Padberg. He said "That's just what I need: the* heresy *award."*

*John Padberg was born in St. Louis in 1926. He is the fortieth Padberg since 1886 to attend the University. His Doctor of Philosophy degree is in intellectual history from Harvard. He is now Academic vice-president.*

*My interview was to last from 10 to 11:15* A.M. *with the next available date eleven days away. Padberg packed a sheaf of papers into his desk drawer when I came in. "It's a bad time of year," he said, his forehead deeply ridged. "I've been working on the budget and need about three million."*

*With the budget put away, his desk was totally clear of papers. A red-wrapped book lay shining on his desk next to a golden quart of Old Jeb bourbon. The book spine read:* Padberg/Colleges In Controversy/Harvard.

*Padberg listens well. You know from his eyes and hands that he's listening. He must be aware of the telephone and of that red three million in his desk drawer, but you don't feel you're being pushed. His words have time for warmth. He chooses them carefully, uses the most necessary, and uses these with feeling. You seem to have a weekend rather than a slot between the accountant and a press conference.*

*About a week before giving up this book to my publisher, I got a telephone call from St. Louis. Padberg: "Did you send it in — the interview?"*

*"Not yet. Next week."*

*"We stopped short. I had to go. Remember you said something about the Mafia and I said it was like the Jesuits?"*

*"That's right," I said. "That's how we ended."*

*"Listen, could you just add a few words? Just that I . . . I want to make this clear — that I love this Society. I want no doubt about that."*

---

The biggest decisions this country will have to face in the next five years will deal with quality of life: what kind of a life do we want for our people and what kind do they themselves want?

If we don't first have a complete explosion here, there'll be reasonable racial integration — and by reasonable, I mean total. Then, as our affluence increases, and if we don't have a nuclear war, people are probably going to have a shorter work week, more money, and more opportunity for vacations. What will we want to do with our new leisure? Are we going to be purposeless, or are we going to have more people wondering "Well, what's it all about"?

The changes facing the United States are the same as those now confronting our universities. But the government will look increasingly to the universities for ways to handle these changes. The government is going to have to give more than bread and circuses, TV and popcorn. How? What? I'm not certain.

The overriding decision in international situations deals with peace. How much do we trust other people and other nations? And how much of ourselves personally and of our money are we going to put into the development of other nations?

Then there's the question of genetic manipulation. What implications will this have for the family and for social life? How will it affect the way young people are brought up? Now, no university alone is going to be able to give all the answers to this problem, but it will probably provide some of the material out of which government entities, social foundations or individual persons will create their answers.

A twelve-year study of professional education conducted by the School of Engineering and Applied Science at UCLA recommends that since doctors, lawyers, clergymen and all other professionals operate through decision making, all professional schools ought to require the same basic courses in decision making.

Perhaps even more important than decision making would be the problem of recognizing how you train or sensitize people to recognize problems. Decisions can be pretty askew if they're not decisions on the real problems and questions that the profession ought to be concerned with. For example, look at our planned interstate highway system. Did the engineers recognize the problems they would inevitably bring along with their highway system? Engineers don't ask whether they should work or not. They get a contract and act.

*Their decision making follows the contract. You're saying they should ask some questions before the contract.*

Yes, like what will a big highway do to the neighborhood? Will it split it in half? Will it kill small businesses? Highways push up the price of land and push out marginal business operators to make room for filling stations and shopping centers. All you have to do is drive down any American highway and you'll see the commercial slums we've built.

71

*If we're going to be having more leisure, what are the schools doing to prepare people for it?*

Not very much, I'm afraid. By leisure, I don't simply mean a passive enjoyment of anything, whether it's baseball or Beethoven. I mean what kind of active use are you going to make of leisure? Are you going to go out, let's say, and tutor in the inner city? I want to see our graduates become activists.

*Speaking of activists, are you ready for the day when a radical nun occupies your office and drinks your Old Jeb in a demonstration for women's rights?*

I can foresee a radical nun doing just about anything!

*A group of women faculty members at Columbia University issued a report showing that about twenty-five percent of the doctoral degrees went to women but that women accounted for only two percent of the tenured graduate-school faculty. The women said they were puzzled by the graduate school's commitment to train women but not hire them.*

They have a right to be more than puzzled. Most Jesuit colleges and universities are no better off than other U.S. educational institutions in not knowing how to educate women for their future roles in society. A tenured graduate-school post demands a lot of time and work. I think this interferes with our normal idea of a woman's role in the family. Now whether that normal idea is the one that ought to prevail, that's another question.

*How would you react if blacks were to confront the Society with a claim for reparation, saying that Jesuits in the past have owned slaves?*

*72*

I'd say they were historically silly! I really would. Because to whom and for whom is the reparation going to be paid, and for what? The term "priest slave" once meant an easy life. I don't justify slavery! But to talk about reparations I think is meaningless here. That the Society has an obligation as it always had, to do something about the poverty in the world, about racism — yes. By all means. But this reparation thing I have real problems with. Real problems. You see I'm really too much of a historian not to feel that this is meaningless. Reparation means I pay back, or I repair an injury done to someone by doing something in response. I'm afraid this reparation claim is reverse racism. If we are really going to be serious, I have to urge reparation for the Indians of the United States, and on a much greater scale, a far, far vaster scale. If the black communities are going to be serious about it, though God knows the whites have practiced enough injustice, the people from whom they ought first to claim reparation are their own fellow blacks in kingdoms in Africa who sold them into slavery.

*Was capitalism founded on slavery?*

Capitalism I don't think was founded on slavery. I think it was founded on exploitation, but all exploitation is not slavery. All capitalism? There was capitalism a long time before slavery. I think Lenin was right when he called colonialism the last stage of capitalism. He was trying to justify the non-fulfillment of Marx's inevitable dialectic, you know, in the industrial nations the rich get richer and the poor get poorer, and they are going to do that. What happened was that in the industrial nations the rich *did* get richer, but the poor *did not* get poorer. In Britain, in Belgium, in Germany, and France in the nineteenth and early twentieth century. Well, then Lenin says, "Ah! The reason they haven't become poorer is that they, the petit bourgeois and the workers have made an alliance with the capitalists so that the real people who are being exploited are no longer the workers on the continent. They are the people in the colonies." Lenin was right on that. By all means he was right on the exploitation of colonies.

*Is religion an essential element in education, do you think?*

Yes. I really do think so. The openness to mystery, an awareness that there are problems, possibilities, depths that go beyond simply the things we can see and touch and taste, feel and measure and weigh.

*Then accepting that State and Church should be separate, should the State be involved in education?*

You mean in religious education? Or in all education?

*In education. Since public school teachers are saying they can't mention religion —*

Oh, that's not true! That they can't . . . Well, they're just crazy! Let's just take it from the basis of an academic discipline. For a man to be really educated and not to know that most of mankind, throughout most of its history, has been involved in a religious dimension, is to pauperize the education of that man. It's simply to deny a whole portion of reality. Suppose that somebody in power in a particular country denied the germ theory of disease: "It doesn't exist; our education, therefore, will ignore this theory." Well, he can do it if he wants to, but he is hardly dealing with reality.

*I wrote a textbook recently that applied Martin Buber's concepts of dialogue to communication during the dating period. The book was originally intended for Catholic schools. Then it was thought the public schools might use it for sex education classes. I had one section explaining that the "Thou" in "I–Thou" was God in Martin Buber's original thinking. I*

74

*was asked to take this out because some of the public school board members would object to it.*

Oh, I'm sure it would annoy and confuse a lot of them. What that all points out is the utter vacuity of intelligence that exists on a lot of education levels in the United States. There are plenty of countries in the world that are equally free, equally democratic, equally devoted to liberty for their people, who manage with intelligence and goodwill to have religious education or religion as a factor in education. Go to our north border, Canada. They manage to conduct religious schools which are supported by the State along with public schools which are also supported by the State. Now why Canada can do it and we can't is beyond me. Our failure can be explained only by a whole series of historical accidents and reasons, the blame for which has to be shared equally by Protestants and Catholics. I think some of the early bishops of the United States, some of these specially in the East, frankly the New York Irishmen, were much at fault. They made a big mistake in consistently denigrating the public schools, which were indeed effectively Protestant schools, and often openly inimical. The age of dialogue has not yet begun.

*Are you satisfied that Jesuit schools are doing enough to prepare their students as future decision makers, to meet all the changes before them?*

They are not doing enough. But of course, no institution is doing enough. I think we're getting into such things. For example, here at St. Louis University, we're just starting the Institute for Organizational Psychology. The Institute for Molecular Virology is also new. It's pretty high-powered, very highly funded by the federal government and foundations. It will study population, but from the research basis of the ultimate material constituents of life, both molecules and viruses within the biological sciences. Now, is that going to reach an awful lot of people directly? I don't know. It is the kind of research we hope will make some difference ultimately. The Divinity School has finally moved onto a university campus where it can interact with all of the other disciplines and call upon the specialized expertise of those disciplines to begin asking questions about the nature and quality of life for the future. In some way the questions you ask are more important than the answers you give.

Now what do we do with the ordinary undergraduate students in arts and sciences? Well, I hope they get an awareness that there is no one discipline and no one study that gives answers to all questions. The curriculum in arts and sciences now is no longer a major-minor thing, but rather it has an area of concentration where, for example, if I'm specializing in nineteenth-century English literature, I am sort of under the control of the English department but I can take courses in nineteenth-century political history, sociology of the nineteenth century, nineteenth-century art. Perhaps for reasons of organization in the past we've cut off knowledge into discrete and separate sections. It ain't that way. It just never works for man. Maybe we'll begin, maybe, having people see the complicatedness of life and of knowledge that really follows life.

*What are the changes and decisions facing Jesuits about their own organization, the Society of Jesus?*

Well, it's a cliché, but let me use it anyway: Shall the Society of Jesus be relevant? Everybody says, "Yes, obviously." But how? How is the Society going to live with a world that's much more complicated, much more open to all kinds of experiences and ideas? How will it serve the Church? I think our best service will be to push it forward, to be loyal gadflies. That's difficult to do. It's not too hard to say I'm in the service of someone when I passively obey or react to an order or a wish. There are times when that's appropriate, but I think our greater service is to be a thorn in its side. Perhaps we ought to provide a place of controversy within a tradition. We would be its prophets and critics.

*The Jesuits would dialogue with the Church.*

Yes. And dialogue doesn't mean passing vapid generalities back and forth. It would have to be a vigorous questioning. What do we really think is the truth. There are various ways of presenting the truth. You can do it with a rude harshness that will win nobody because the presentation itself is not particularly good. Confrontation is not always the best tool. I want to convince someone not only that this is true but that it is *good*, and that therefore one ought to do it and put his energy into his decision.

*Is confrontation sometimes the best tool?*

It might be, yes. I'm not the kind of person, myself, who thinks you get very far by banging on desks. Maybe it's just my temperament.

*I suppose one really can't live in an organization or a community and keep fighting it without let-up.*

Well, let me put it one step farther back. One can't live without living in an organization or a community of some kind.

*But you can't live there and be a thorn all the time.*

Oh, no. I don't see how you can either. The common bond you have with a community can't simply be one of constant complaint. Like those who say, "The one thing that we all have in common is that we're against them" — whoever "them" happens to be. I don't see that at all.

Neither do I see that I can be happy or psychologically balanced as a member of any organization that tells me what to do and doesn't ask me to make any decisions.

*Dan Berrigan at Cornell says that too many Jesuits accepted into a secular school or community go along with it and never raise questions about its own behavior or being.*

I agree. I agree that's not only a temptation but an actuality. I have no quarrel with that statement at all.

*Why are Jesuits swallowed up like this? Are they afraid to protest?*

Oh, I don't think it's so much fear as it is . . . well, most of us seldom see the deeper implications of our actions. We're too much caught up with the daily affairs, you know, of signing papers and sending out memos, preparing or teaching classes, or whatever else it is, to see the underlying root problems and difficulties of the society or organization that we live in. It takes a certain amount of emotional energy just to accomplish one's ordinary work. Secondly, it takes a certain amount of emotional and intellectual investment to make oneself part of a group, whether the group is St. Louis University or the American Historical Society. Your self-investment alone takes a lot out of you. Often there's not enough, let's say, free capital around to put into something else. And the something else may be the standing back from the group and saying: Oh . . . maybe yes, and maybe no.

*What are the threats challenging the Society's future?*

I think first of all, is the Society going to be up in the front questioning a lot of things that most other people are comfortable with? I think it has to make a decision whether it wants to be there, certainly as it was in its very best days.

78

There are two temptations, either of which the Society could succumb to. The first is the *Supportive Back Brace Temptation:* The Society finds the future so threatening that it turns to its past and tries to structure a set of rules designed to keep the people inside of it comfortable and firm. The designers might model their set of structures from the old Society, take certain rules and say this is Jesuit life and this is how the Jesuit must live, ought to live. In other words, go back to the monastic life. Despite the rigidity and the difficulties of some of the rules, some people would find it comfortable to know this is right, this is wrong, this accepted, this forbidden, this you can do now, this you can't do now.

The second is the *Gentlemen's Club Temptation.* It comes from the possibility that a certain number of people entering the Society and wanting to stay in it could make it simply an organization of very high-minded people who are little more than just secular humanists.

The only motive that gives this whole Jesuit venture sense is the imitation of Jesus Christ. I don't mean by that, you know, that I'll go around barefooted and wear a beard and a bed sheet wrapped around me. I think the Society is going to move increasingly toward the life-style of a secular institute. It will *not be* a secular institute, but will have surely, resemblances to one. Now I say "toward" because I don't think it will ever fully get there. The Society has got to find the kind of balance and tension between a situation in which each of its members very much does his own thing, yet does it as part of a community apostolate. This will include a community decision to determine our priorities.

*Is that community you foresee one of residence or one of interinvolvement? Will the community members merely share gas, electricity and rent, or will they also be committed to each other and the community?*

I don't think either alone. In other words, is the Society I foresee made up of people who live together because they have a project to do in common, or is it made up of people who live together, who support and sustain each other, and only incidentally go out and do something? I don't think it is either one of those.

For Jesuits, the service of man is not a consequence of loving God, but the very form of loving God. That's not easy because you can get lost in the service of man. In some ways it's easier to be purely secular or totally Trappist.

*Does the Society's Constitution encourage comradeship rather than friendship for its members?*

I don't think the genuine, original spirit of the Society was against friendship. You have to read the letters of Ignatius. He'd write to Xavier and end the letter, "Yours forever," or "Yours in a way that I cannot express." Just read their lives and see that these people really meant something to each other.

*I feel this is quite important for the survival of the Society.*

Sure. So do I. If it's just comradeship, it won't work. But if it's friendship in the very best sense of the word, it will.

*Is the growing number of ex-Jesuits a vote of no confidence in the order's ability or willingness to confront and cope with the changes facing it?*

That depends on why they are ex-Jesuits, and also on how they regard the Society once they've left.

For some, leaving may well be a vote of no confidence. If it is, for God's sake we had better take it very seriously. But others had personal reasons for leaving the Society. They weren't in disagreement with its work or how it was doing it, but they felt that they personally were not fit for that. I think it's more, in a way, a vote of confidence in the Society and in the Church, that even from within the Society they feel free to look at themselves and the Society honestly. There used to be a lot of pressure from one's family and the outside community that kept men in the priesthood even when they personally felt they didn't belong. It took a lot more guts in the past to leave than it takes now. That doesn't mean that the people today are any less courageous. That isn't so. I just say that the whole general community around us is so changed that people can leave much more freely. I'm glad they can, if they really decide they ought to.

If a person decides that this is not the kind of life that he, in his circumstances, given his background, and his temperament, can find conducive to his being what he ought to be as a Christian, I say fine. He ought to leave.

*The Salvation Army has a unique way of solving celibate loneliness. If an officer — that is, minister, wants to marry, he or she must marry another officer.*

I'd hate to see that kind of thing happening to the Society. I'd hate to see Jesuits marrying Jesu-ettes!

*Do you foresee a Society of Jesus made up of married Jesuits and celibate Jesuits?*

I don't foresee it, but I have no personal difficulties with it. I mean I wouldn't think that it would violate the essential nature of the Society, but I think that the whole view of the religious life in the Church would probably have to be changed. You'd have to deal with two conditions before you could make any changes: a misogynist tradition in the Society and a misogynist tradition in the Roman Catholic Church. There've been mixed communities in the Church but they were celibate, not married groups. There was one famous community of several hundred men and women at Fontevrault — it's the place in France where Richard the Lion-

Hearted, Eleanor of Aquitaine, and Henry the Second are buried. It consisted of a monastery for men and one for women, a penitential monastery, a monastery for pilgrims, and a refuge for the sick, I believe.

*Did they have a monastery of chaperones who supervised them?*

I don't know about that. The two most interesting things about it were that their superior general was supposedly always a woman, and that all of the other women took vows of perpetual silence. I'm not sure, but probably the men decided that.

*But it didn't last?*

Only seven hundred and some years which is pretty good. The only reason it didn't last after that was that the French Revolution pitched them all out. Napoleon made it a prison. It's a magnificent place, a really great place to see. I've been told the British government regularly makes discreet inquiries as to why their two kings and queen should not be brought back. The French response has been that if these English has enough sense to wish to be buried in France, why should they be disturbed?

*You said before that the Jesuits have a misogynist tradition. How did Ignatius feel about women?*

Ignatius had quite a bit of correspondence with women, especially with several Spanish women who were immensely generous during his pilgrim years after he had left military life and before he founded the Society. Ignatius had very warm relationships, very generous, and, in some senses of the word, affectionate relationships, but also very troubled relations with women. They wanted to join the Jesuits and, I think, al-

82

most decide how the thing was going to be run. His difficult experiences led him to be pretty definitive that there weren't going to be any female Jesuits.

Ignatius's letters show the problems he had with some of the women, but they also show, I think, the real respect he had for them. A famous book, *Ignatius Loyola's Letters to Women*, was published in 1956 on the occasion of the four hundredth anniversary of Ignatius's death. It was edited by, not Karl, but by Hugo Rahner. The general of the Society is supposed to have asked: "Father Rahner, of all the things you could have done for the anniversary, why did you choose to edit his letters to women?" Rahner's reply was said to have been: "Father, it's just like the other side of the moon. We never get a chance to see it."

*I think that the bad image of marriage, when a kid of eighteen or nineteen has it, cuts out marriage as an option for what he's going to do with his life.*

Well, it would be foolish to deny that that's a possibility. But I suppose what you have to do is ask a fair number of Jesuits, "What was your image of your parents' marriage?" Then, of course, when they say it was a very happy image, you can say, "Ah, but you didn't know the Freudian implications or the psychosexual implications there. Maybe really deep down in your subconscious it was an unhappy image." So, of course, you can't win with those kind of rules for the interpretive game. Personally, all I can say is, my own mother and father with six kids — I always had a very happy image of marriage.

*In the* Spiritual Exercises, *Ignatius recommends an ability to "discern spirits." Does this quaint phrase have meaning today?*

I don't like the term, "discernment of spirits." It's an awkward and strange kind of term for modern ears. But Ignatius is talking about our being able to discern, to understand, to get at the bottom of our changeabilities. He wants us to recognize what's involved in the changeability, and what we might do about it.

We aren't going to be somebody like Complete Control Yokum in *Li'l Abner*, you know, where the thing that is really important is that one never wavers and never changes and never has different views. If you want that, for heaven's sake, get an IBM machine and program it completely.

*I do like the way as a historian you probe back at the original meanings of words. The fact that you go to the Constitutions rather than the institute demonstrates that in a bigger way.*

Well, see, the institute is the compilation of prescriptions, ordinations of the General Congregations of the Society, the decisions of the generals and other material of that type. They were written for particular circumstances, particular times. I have no quarrel with that at all; obviously such decisions are necessary. They are historically conditioned. But to canonize them and to say that's where we go to really understand what the Society is, instead of going back to the Constitutions misses one point. In going back to the Constitutions, I'm certainly doing what the Vatican II says: "Go back to the original spirit of the founder." Now notice it said not necessarily the original *work* of the founder. We don't have too many problems with the Society in that regard, but what do you do if you happen to belong to the Order of Our Lady of Mercy for the Ransom of Captives from the Muslims? You know? How are you really going to carry out the work?

*What does the March of Dimes do after polio has been . . . ?*

Yes. That's the spirit of the thing. It seems to me that such an order couldn't do a better thing in accord with the spirit of its founder than work in the inner city.

*84*

*So what are they doing?*

I don't know. But several of the religious orders have real hang-ups on this, I know of one: The Slaves — and I mean slaves is the word used — of the Virgin Mary. Well, what does it mean?

*The false language of piety, the way it encumbers you and hangs on you, literally it's a drag. It makes the users either dishonest or stupid.*

Yes. Read some of the Acts of Consecration to the Sacred Heart, for example. To say that one really feels the things that are set down there, except rarely in one's life, and to proclaim it here, right here and now — you know: "My heart overflows with the feeling of absolute confidence, as from wellsprings of pure joy, I prostrate myself here before you . . ." This just creates a false conscience, it seems to me. It's also the application of Gresham's monetary law to words: bad words drive out good ones.

*I was at Florissant recently when the men took their vows. Here were guitars, songs created and sung by scholastics, banners and vestments made by scholastics. With so much free, individual expression I expected each man would vow his commitment his own way, but they read a formula. It began with something like, "I, in profound humility, recognizing my own worthlessness . . ." I concede that one man at some particular moment might experience such a profound feeling, but for eight men or thirty men each in turn expressing such a feeling is not only incredible but ridiculous. The vow formula repeated like this invites inattention and disrespect. If a man recognizes his worthlessness so profoundly, why is he up there vowing his life? Another thing: the vows were made "in the presence of Mary and all the angels." What about us? Were we supposed to be eavesdropping?*

85

*The vows are a public declaration meant for human ears. That's why they were put into English.*

I felt a jarring note in the formula itself, too. It's a far better translation than others I had seen before, but I expect men will soon be stating their vows in their own words.

*Are the traditional religious vows of poverty, chastity and obedience obsolete? What do they mean today?*

The ways we live them have to be different for us today. The external circumstances for poverty, obedience and chastity have changed since the sixteenth century. One good example is the life of St. Aloysius. We used to be told his self-control and modesty were evident in the fact that he always wore black and never looked others directly in the face. Hogwash! It may be true that he did this, but the ordinary fashionable clothes for a sixteenth-century noble, if you look at the paintings of the time, is often dark or black. For instance, look at Bronzino's famous "Portrait of a Young Man." It was a mark of the highest impoliteness to look in the face of another man speaking to him, unless you were his superior.

*So generations upon generations of Jesuits have been lowering their eyes because —*

Yes, because of circumstances which were perfectly understandable in their own times, but don't necessarily exist today. And take poverty. You can talk all you want about Jesuits being poor men, but you have to put all kinds of qualifications on that. Even if we say they are living in the most Spartan temporal conditions in their rooms, poor men don't get the education Jesuits have. Jesuits, though they never own books, certainly read more than poor men. Poor men aren't encouraged to develop their talents, their emotions, their attitudes, their abilities, the way Jesuits are. No poor man could get the Harvard education that I got. Nor have traveled as broadly. He doesn't have the kind of job I have. A Jesuit may wear the same clothes and eat exactly the same food as a poor man, but never with the same thoughts and associations about them.

I would prefer, I think to substitute the word *simplicity* for the word poverty, but I can't get very far selling this substitution to my friends. They say, "Here you are a historian and you're throwing overboard hundreds of years of history." But I think I'm keeping two thousand years of Christianity. People then say, "Ah, but that means you don't denude yourself of all temporal things." I agree. Practically, I do not denude myself of all temporal things.

What we live isn't poverty in the contemporary meaning of the word. It isn't. But calling it poverty may give people a false conscience or it may give them a superficial idea of what poverty is. If they think, "What we're doing *is* poverty," they'll never get really passionately concerned with what *real* ghetto poverty is like. "We're living as poor people." The devil we are. The whole program of a government and of modern society should be the elimination of poverty. So what do we mean, then, when we come along and say that we're vowing it? We sound anomalous, to say the least.

*I was instructed to think that asking for permission — say to buy a suit or take a trip — was symbolic poverty.*

It may be symbolic, but symbolic of what? The need to get permission doesn't make for poverty. At least it doesn't seem to me that it does. It's not the same as begging. It's not being on welfare. A Jesuit will always get what he needs when he asks for it. A poor man doesn't.

*An ex-Trappist told me his order was having some doubts about its own poverty. When it was founded, it gave up meat and ate cheese, the food of the poor. Over the years it devel-*

*oped many of the great cheeses — Port du Salut, for exam-*
*ple, that are now regarded as gourmet foods. The poor can't*
*afford them. So the Trappists may start eating hamburgers.*

That's interesting. Since we don't eat as poor men, I really
think calling our food simple rather than poor is more
honest.

To equate poverty simply with mere objects and external
circumstances, like clothes or money, shows gross ignorance
of the life of the poor. This is wrong. I argue, many times,
that it's a misleading term to talk about a vow of poverty.
We know today that poverty also includes a whole mind set,
a set of attitudes that you almost can't help having if you
have to struggle day by day for existence.

*Your insight into the vow of poverty as a middle-class façade*
*shocks me. I see I've had a superficial understanding of the*
*vow. Now I wonder what you see in the other two vows.*

In a way, the three vows might be better expressed as a
radical faith, hope and charity. We start with the radical assumption that the world is good, that the world's enterprises
are good, man's hopes and aspirations, man's desires, man's
creations, man's production, are good things. In themselves
they're good. Not just because they refer to a higher image,
but, because they are such in themselves.

Now, here are my vows. First, I say that despite the fact
that all material things are good, I never put my complete
trust, never my complete confidence in them. I always say
that there is someone, something totally beyond any material
thing, to whom I give myself: God. Well, I don't see him as
I see the material goods about me. That's *faith.*

And secondly, we talk about chastity. I think probably
what we say is something like . . . how would you put it?
. . . something like this: Not only do I believe there is someone, something beyond all the material things: I want to pos-

88

sess that someone, that person, eventually. And I have confidence that I shall do so. When we talk about possessing God in Scripture, the closest analogy we have for it is married love. And, we say, I bear witness to the fact that however deep and intimate and fulfilling the total possession of one human person by another may be, the mutual possession of God and self is deeper and more intimate yet. But I only know this in a radical *hope*, in confidence in that God.

The third, obedience. I think what we are saying is that I can't give myself even here, now, to another in free surrender except in the context of some kind of a love relationship with all that this implies of surrender of yourself and yet retention of your selfhood.

Now, I want to do an awful lot more working out of these thoughts. Basically, it seems to me that the three vows, away from the juridical context in which they are written and in which we talk, go to those three fundamental virtues of the Christian. And by pronouncing the vows of poverty, chastity and obedience we commit ourselves to be radical witnesses to faith, hope and charity.

*Let me add this: belief and trust support any friendship, whether sexual or nonsexual, married or nonmarried. Trust or credibility or faith is what makes communication possible between persons; hope makes communication exciting and persevering.*

*Why do we have three vows or virtues? Aren't these only distinctions of logic rather than reality?*

If you look at Scripture, and you look at the words used for faith, hope and charity, there is a root congruity between the three of them. They aren't the neat, nice separate things that we made them in dogmatic theology, by any means. All three of them go together. Faith makes no sense without hope, hope makes no sense without faith, and neither of them make any sense unless I feel a love relationship.

*You say love of God is traditionally compared with "married love." In the same way that we've learned more about poverty haven't we learned much more about "married love" than we knew at the time this analogy was first made? Therefore, does this traditional analogy make clear sense to us today?*

The analogy makes deeper sense today because we have learned more of married love. We understand more about the communion of personalities in marriage.

*When I was in the Society, the mark that characterized the Jesuit was instant obedience to his superior. Superiors obeyed higher superiors and the chain of command ran right to the pope. Is obedience still regarded this way?*

I really don't know how obedience is going to be changed. But I think it's going to be. I know it has been within the Society in recent years. For example, the old notion that an obedient person was one who when asked, "What do you think about this?" said, "Well, you make up your mind. You're the superior." This was a sort of a caricature, but one that was sometimes presented to us as an ideal of obedience. This certainly isn't true any more.

To my mind, if I have this vow of obedience in and to the Society, I have an obligation, not just the right but the obligation, to present my views on a particular subject or particular thing I'm asked to do. Not just right but obligation.

Now this would not have been said before. There are many changes going on in the Society and other religious orders too, for which the theoretical justification will only come later. With that I'm perfectly happy. I think we have had far too much theory to which practice then sort of had to be *krrwachkpp* [sound of something being squashed to fit] — fitted. Maybe this is just the pragmatic strategy of Americans coming through.

*Before an individual Jesuit speaks on contemporary or controversial matters, ought he get permission from his superiors?*

That depends on him. Whether he thinks he ought to. That's changed. Oh yes. Certainly it's changed. Father Berrigan is one of the very best examples of that. But there are plenty of others who feel the same way.

*I asked Father George Shoup this with regard to abortion and population control. He thought and then he said, "I wouldn't know whom to ask."*

Yes. Whom should I ask? I might ask, "Shall I speak?" But I certainly can't ask someone who doesn't know something about the history of the Society in the nineteenth century. There is nobody that I know of in this country who knows as much about the European Jesuit schools in the nineteenth century as I do. Whom am I going to ask about what I say on this matter?

I think it's also true that I'm an absolute fool if I don't recognize that so speaking, though I may not wish to commit the Society, I'm certainly speaking partly as a representative of the Society, I'm getting a certain amount of notoriety on that account. I think when I speak I ought to take into account "What is this going to do for and to the Society." Also, I am not just speaking as a private individual. I wish I could. There are many times I would love to write to newspapers, but haven't because rightly or wrongly, people would think I was talking as a voice of the Jesuits, or *a* Jesuit instead of as John Padberg.

*Or as St. Louis University.*

Yes. That's even more of a problem.

*What about the pope? Would the Society's tradition of special servicę inhibit Jesuits from criticizing the pope?*

I hope that we don't lose the tradition of special service, but I also hope that special service never means that we feel the pope is above and beyond comment, above and beyond the Church, as the Church itself is not above and beyond comment.

*Then do you suppose the Society's superiors will muzzle individual Jesuits who condemn Vatican errors?*

I don't think so. It depends an awful lot on what you say, how you say it, circumstances in which you say it, what your intentions are — Now, who's going to determine intentions? You criticize or you comment, not only by your words but also by your actions. And sooner or later the American Church is going to have to recognize that we often say things in ways other than by mere words. Much of the Church in this country has been hung up on the verbal interpretation of the Code of Canon Law. We have got to get used to — recognize that there are ways other than words of saying, "I think this is good or bad or better or worse."

At the time of Ignatius a religious order had to have all of its members regularly singing choir. Ignatius fought this. Until the Holy See imposed choir on the Society, he insisted that choir was *not* an essential of the religious life. The Society didn't have to go around putting placards up on the wall, "Choir Not Essential." All it had to do was live, and insist that it was living a religious life without choir; to say in one way, comment upon, and indeed to criticize, what was probably the more general notion at that time, that you had to have choir in order to be a religious.

*You don't believe that the comments ought to be made to the public at large? Through media such as television and so on?*

Sometimes they ought to be. Yes. There is hardly anything that is private in the Church any more. There is no private kind of teaching of the Church which we are going to keep hidden behind doors any more.

*Can you foresee a Society that accepts temporary vows of its members? Will a man be able to be a priest for a promised number of years rather than a lifetime?*

I can see it, yes. I think it presents an awful lot of problems. Most of which I have not had the time to think about. But I do not see this as intrinsically impossible.

*In the light of many studies affirming the prime importance of early childhood and the person's intellectual and emotional development, how is it that Jesuits continue to ignore preschool and elementary school education as an area for their involvement?*

You can't do everything. That's about all that we can really say. Partly it's because we have not the tradition of doing this kind of thing and tradition bulks very large. I would like to see Jesuits in, let us say, educational psychology, working on the kind of things that Piaget did.

*Right. That's what I mean . . .*

But the tradition has just been so much against it. The unwritten tradition. Where would a man like that fit? In the United States schools, he'd have a hard time. Throughout his training in the Society, before special studies, he'd be out of phase. Now, I'm not saying you shouldn't have such people, but — most of us have a very difficult time doing something that hasn't been done before.

Let me just cite my own case here. Intellectual history is hardly the most radical thing in the whole wide world, but, for me to go into this was an unusual thing. I did it, not, originally, because of what people in the Society said, but simply because I heard about it from someone else. I was encouraged to do so by people later on, but there was not the same kind of day-by-day encouragement that I would have had if I had gone, say, into straight political history. And history, you know, is a relatively common discipline for Jebs to go into.

*But isn't childhood development one of the great areas of change in education?*

Okay. And what you would really need there to get Jesuits involved is someone who recognizes these areas of change and has a dominant kind of personality. For example, Jesuit involvement in geophysics in this country is due very much to one man. Really. That was Macelwane. Some of the involvement of the University of California at Berkeley in geophysics is due to Macelwane. He helped set up the department out there. If you get some aggressive person who is interested, one who attracts others to follow, you'll have Jebbies going into preschool research.

We unfortunately — or maybe fortunately — don't have the kind of master plan that people think we do. Or let me put it this way: If we were one-tenth as efficient and intelligent, as farsighted, and as ordered as people say we are, we would be ten times more efficient, ordered, intelligent and farsighted than we really are.

*We usually attribute to the Mafia a greater efficiency and ability to be evil than it really has. Valachi showed us the Mafia is often bumbling and clumsy.*

That sounds like Jesuits, too! We blunder a lot . . . But I couldn't imagine being with better men.

*By suppressing the creative side of our men,
we've turned out a lot of cold fish.*

# John J. Walsh, S.J.

John Walsh was a protégé of Mme. Maria Ouspenskaya, a famous exponent of Stanislavski's "Method" acting. He is a doctoral graduate of the Yale Drama School, and has studied drama in Japan, Italy, Austria and France. Between 1951 and 1964, Walsh directed the Marquette University Players in Milwaukee. His players were invited five times to represent the United States at the Delphiade Festival in Europe. The Delphiade invites only one school from each country. Former players now working in New York say Walsh gave them the equal of professional experience. During Walsh's tenure at Marquette, he presented over sixty plays: "We did things like Chelderode's Christopher Columbus, which nobody understood. From the audience's point of view that was a big bust. We did Ionesco's The Bald Soprano, which ended up by my having to go out and give a lecture before performance, simply because there was so much dismay and griping about it . . . Life is much too serious these days for Under the Yum-Yum Tree over and over and over. The important playwrights are returning to the major, basic, human relationships. Important theater has to deal with man's relationships, either to God or to himself or his fellow man."

Since 1964 Walsh has been teaching Jesuit scholastics at St. Stanislaus Seminary and St. Louis University. It was in St. Louis and at Florissant that I interviewed him. A silence of word and gesture and expression stands about Walsh. It's

99

*a live, creative silence: it asks you to speak, to be. There is no rejection or criticism in his face. You feel welcome to be yourself. His blue eyes look frail. He doesn't interrupt you. He's not listening for a break so that he can jump in. He's not competing.*

*Finally you think: well, it's his turn now. He should talk. He talks unhurriedly, not expecting you to interrupt him. You do, however, and you're sorry, but you interrupt again. Each time you interrupt, he falls back, listening. There is no anger on his forehead, no annoyance. But his silence says: "I'm here. There's no need to shout." Your voice gets quieter. Pauses begin to give your words more room. You're open to listening.*

*During the early minutes of my first meeting, my eyes would dart to the tape machine needle to make sure the recorder was working properly. Each time, Walsh's voice would waver or fade or stop. He would say: "This isn't very interesting, is it?" or, "I'm sorry. Did I miss your question?" I would assure him hastily that I was very much interested. I truly was. When you interview some people you can ask all your questions at once, put the machine on "listen" and read a book. But I learned not to take my eyes from Walsh. He needed me. I had to be totally, undistractedly present so that he could be.*

*He talked about the Jesuit theater, about the empty world of Andy Warhol, about the full world opened by Teilhard de Chardin. His voice is louder and stronger as he talks about the Society of Jesus and its need for the fine arts. You're not immediately aware of it but his voice has raised pitch and he is starting to plane. You feel you are being lifted, somehow. You must watch, grip your chair seat, and listen tight. He says, "The long, cold regime of science is breaking up," and he breaks each word by slamming his hand edge down on his desk. "We're going back to the fine arts to help us become full human beings again."*

In the beginning there was a good deal of disapproval from the Old Fathers (as the elderly priests in the order are referred to) because of the word *dance*. That word certainly didn't fit into a Jesuit program of training, particularly for novices. But gradually they've come to see the results and to understand it a little. I don't feel their resistance any more. When the men who've been taking my classes become professors and administrators and Old Fathers themselves, I expect their attitudes about the fine arts and dance will be much different.

For the last three years there have been regular classes three times a week for the juniors and novices. I also teach dance at the University [St. Louis] and have a number of the philosophers and theologians in those classes. I've not been able to take all those who wanted to come because the rooms at the University are too small. If you get about sixty in your class you can't do much.

I think the reason for the sudden interest in movement started when they turned the altar around facing the people. There's an awareness that movement counts for a deal more than it ever did when the priest just simply had his back to the people. Gestures too. A gesture has to say something, and has to fit the words that you're saying. Movement influences our self-image and body image. If a person is confident in his movements, he is *self*-confident.

We do exercises which are a combination of a ballet barre, modern dance movements and some modern jazz movements. They are designed to loosen the body and relax all the muscles. It's nothing but fancy *gymnicum* — with music, and not very fancy music at that.

Dance has different advantages depending on what group I'm teaching. With the novices it tends to be therapeutic. When you're living in close quarters in the community you can really get on one another's nerves, especially during the Long Retreat and times like that when a lot of tensions can build up.

*You studied under Maria Ouspenskaya, for years the leading lady of the Moscow Art Theatre and in the United States the leading model of the "Stanislavski Method." What on earth was she doing in Denver?*

I think she had tuberculosis.

*Did she die there?*

No. She went to Hollywood and set up a studio on Sunset Boulevard. She died in Hollywood. She burned up in bed. She had been smoking.

*What do you owe her? Looking back, what did she mean in your life?*

She was a very short, little woman with black, black eyes that could be absolutely horrifyingly vicious, and she used to just terrify the life out of me. She would petrify me into doing things that I never could have possibly done otherwise. My strongest recollection is of myself with the cold perspiration sliding down the back of my spine. Now I've never had this with any other person in my whole life. This was a regular thing with her. She never once said that anything I did was any good. Never once.

I had been taking private lessons twice a week from her since 1928. Then in 1930 the Depression got so bad that my father told me "that nonsense" had to stop.

I imagine he was paying something like three dollars an hour. So it was probably six dollars a week, that meant about twenty-five dollars a month. So it amounted to . . . What? — Anyway, when I told her I couldn't study with her any more, she hit the ceiling. She said, "Why?" I said, "We can't afford it." She said, "You keep coming. Keep the same hour." So, for the next two years, I still went twice a week and she never charged a cent and she still never said anything I did was any good.

Then, that last summer she was all set that I was to go into professional theater. She always had a summer job at Elitch's, the oldest summer stock theater in the United States. She got me a job there as a juvenile that summer. That was my one professional season. I had bits in a number of plays, wherever there was a kid. I think my most important role was the young boy in *Ah, Wilderness!*

That's one reason why I owe her so much. I learned the Stanislavski technique of acting from the ground up, not just theoretically but in practice through and through. I feel she gave me an understanding of the theater that I could never have had from any place else. It's like somebody learning painting from Leonardo da Vinci, being in his studio every day watching him work. You learn in a way you'd never learn in a classroom where you are with sixty other people. You know what I mean? It was a gradual and intense kind of instruction. It ended up by really being part of your being.

She gave me such security in the theater that I never had a moment's fear of discussing acting as an art with any actor or any director any place in the world. You knew the thing as thoroughly as they did, and you knew that you knew it.

She didn't want me to become a Jesuit. But after a couple of terrifying scenes, she seemed to think there was nothing she could do about it. She probably sensed — because she knew me very well — that it was something bigger than myself. I guess she figured it was something bigger than her too.

*Did you correspond with her after you entered?*

No, because in the novitiate we couldn't correspond with anybody.

*While studying with her you apparently acquired the habit of mind of an actor. The habit of mind, as I see it, is what ultimately characterizes one as a person. Yet, even with this actor's cast of mind you considered assuming still another habit of mind, that of the Jesuit priest. Didn't you go through some terrible struggles with yourself in the Society?*

I've never had a moment when I didn't want being a Jesuit. From talking to other Jesuits, I think this is unusual. In any case, I was always thrown back into the theater. I always had the Christmas and Easter plays. During my regency at Campion I was up to my ears in dramatics. After regency, Father McGuckin, our director of studies, said, "We're sending you to Yale for dramatics." So you see, even though I thought when I entered I'd never see the stage again, I was thrown back onto it. I feel I've really had the best of both worlds.

*You were at Yale for four years. Do you remember your first day there?*

I remember I went into the "green room." There were all kinds of little groups sitting all over and complete silence fell over the whole place. They all looked at me. I was a Catholic priest and wearing a Roman collar. I felt isolated, different, and not much wanted. It affected me physically.

There had been Jebs at Yale before, but I was the first one ever to darken the door of that drama department. That's certain.

They came to accept me completely. I spent some of my happiest years there. It was just those months until Christmas — they were among the worst of my life. It was a big shift from the tertianship let me tell you.

*What made those months so difficult?*

Oh, a number of things. Since Yale is a professional school, many of the students had their Equity cards already. I had a lot of catching up to do. But it wasn't the work. It was the loneliness that was hard. There were hundreds of people milling about morning, noon and night, but I felt isolated. The Catholics didn't identify themselves. If it hadn't been for the Jews in the class, I wouldn't have stuck it out. They invited me to their homes for dinner. They asked me along when they went to see plays in New York.

*Didn't the fact that you'd studied under Maria Ouspenskaya interest anybody?*

I didn't tell them. In a situation like that you try to make it on your own.

*A director seems to have to become personally, intimately, even sometimes sexually involved with the people he's working with. Isn't theater today hazardous work for Jesuit priests?*

That's absolutely crazy. It's true there's a close identification between the director and the people he works with. You can't help but get to know each other very well. You're trying to create a new world with new people in that world. This gives you a special kind of knowledge of one another.

But I think this whole business of Lee Strasberg's — you know, having to go to a psychiatrist for eight months before he'll take you on, and his emphasis on experience, including sexual experience, is an inauthentic way to train artists. Jane Fonda didn't have to kill herself to play *They Shoot Horses, Don't They?* Art is not life to start with. Art is artificial. It's an arrangement of life. To show sexual intercourse on the stage is not art. It's just sexual intercourse. Art is not reality. It's life rearranged. Matisse says art is a big lie. If what you want is reality, you don't want art.

Just by reason of the fact that you're a human being, you'll understand a great deal about evil because you understand the possibilities of evil within yourself.

*What effect will the current show of nudity have on theater in general?*

It'll have a very good effect by demonstrating what art is *not*.

Claude von Italie said that the theater's become a religious experience because it's a communion service. Since we can't communicate any more on a spiritual level, we have to communicate on a physical level. So you go up on the stage, everybody, and have a big squirming dog-pile up there and feel everybody's body. At least you have a kind of physical communion. But what von Italie never says is how you feel when you leave the theater and walk outside and you're just as much alone, if not more alone than ever. You can't tell me that this is an aesthetic experience.

The greatest disappointment in *Oh, Calcutta!* for me is Kenneth Tynan. The really perceptive stuff he has done as a theater critic and what he was doing for British theater, and then to perpetrate this thing. I can't understand it.

*Will the university theaters start imitating the nudity on Broadway? Will the Free Speech Movement go onstage?*

Who knows? I suppose a school here or there will take a fling at nudity — like the University of Wisconsin's *Peter Pan* — but it will never last. It will be much clearer what art is and isn't when they do finish with all this experimenting.

*You did your doctoral thesis at Yale on the Jesuit theater. What is or was Jesuit theater?*

Martin Luther is really the father of modern propaganda. If you don't have television, or radio, or newspapers, or a large reading public, how can you reach the imagination of the people and capture its enthusiasm? Luther was the first to use cartoons to ridicule and satirize. He was the Thomas Nast or Al Capp of his time and practically laughed the

Church out of Germany. He was also the first to use the theater.

The Jesuits took up theater merely to fight Luther with his own weapons. But theater in their hands became something more than a propaganda device. Jesuits eventually had 250 schools across the continent of Europe and 350 court-endowed theaters at their disposal. (Jesuits also built the first permanent theater on the North American continent. This was in Quebec in 1640 and it opened with a play by Corneille.) They taught rhetoric and dance as belonging together because the courtiers they were educating were expected to speak and move impressively. The stage was a pedagogical aid, so theater was a functioning part of the curriculum.

For example, suppose in those days someone was going to present a tragedy. Since this was the time of the Renaissance he would draw his characters from classical mythology and would use classical Latin and Greek for dialogue parts. Since not all of his audience understood these languages, he would first present a preview of the play's plot line using characters from the Bible but chosen to parallel the classic figures. This *Vorspiel* was danced — in other words, ballet. This was how ballet started.

The same ballet master who choreographed for the Opéra in Paris, was also choreographer at the Collège Louis-le-Grand, a Jesuit institution. If you look through Somervogel's *Bibliothèque de la Compagnie de Jésu,* you will find over ten thousand titles of ballets that were choreographed by Jesuits at this time. Father Claude de Menestrier was the first person to write a history of the dance and one of the first to codify the rules for classical ballet.

*Why did they have to counterreform in Latin? Why couldn't they have used the vernacular language?*

I suppose it had something to do with the classical Renaissance training but it sure made trouble for the producer.

107

However, there were a few good spin-offs. The need to communicate abstract religious concepts in ways that were both clear and theatrically exciting led the Jesuits to develop skills in theater production. For example, Father Athanasius Kircher invented a light machine that would project scenery, ghosts, devils onto the set. He even found a way of making his projected images move. He was father of the "magic lantern," the first motion picture machine. Another theatrical development, typically baroque, was the use of fireworks. Jesuit theaters were regularly burned down as a result of some Jesuit scholastic's enthusiasm for lighting effects.

Some famous graduates from Jesuit theater are Corneille, Molière, Tirso de Molina, Lope de Vega, Goldoni and Calderón. Voltaire wrote to Dr. Bianchi in 1761 that the best part of the education he received from the Jesuits in Paris came from the "theatrical performances."

*In what sense are fireworks "typically baroque"?*

I mean baroque as in explosion, like Bernini's stuff — like St. Teresa of Avila swinging in ecstasy in his little church, Santa Maria della Vittoria. Like his great baldachinos in St. Peter's and his fountains all over Rome splashing, sparkling in the light, the water bringing stone to life by motion and sound. Have you noticed how drab and dead Rome is when the fountains are turned off?

Everything in baroque art had to be dynamic, everything action and explosion. This was the *Gesammtkunstwerk* idea of bringing all arts together for an authoritative, triumphant, final statement "all for the greater honor and glory of God!"

Few of the plays written in those days could qualify today as dramatic literature. Jacob Biedermann's *Cenodoxis* or Everyman is one that's lasted. It's still performed every year in Switzerland. People say there wouldn't be a Catholic in Switzerland today if it weren't for that play.

*Were these mostly Italian Jesuits you're speaking of?*

Italian, German, Spanish, English. You see we had the first chain of theaters ever in existence.

*Real theaters?*

Tremendous theaters. If you're really interested, all you have to do is get the *Oxford Companion to the Theatre*, and you'll find that it carries eight double-column pages on the Jesuit theater. That's practically as much as any other aspect of the theater gets.

The importance of the Jesuit theater is that it was the bridge between the medieval theater and opera. Grand opera is the culmination of the baroque momement, everything brought together — music, dance, set design, story — the whole thing. The Jesuit theater is the transition between the medieval, which included the miracle, mystery, morality play and the grand opera.

*The concept of opera was a Jesuit concept?*

It grew out of the Jesuit concept of baroque — inasmuch as you identify baroque and Jesuit. As a style of art it gathers together all art media with a strong emphasis on movement. Contrast the Medici Palace in Florence where everything is square with San Carlo's in Rome where everything has to curve and go up. It's explosion. It's total movement. No straight lines.

Reformers in the north of Europe were calling the Church the "whore of Babylon." Their idea of purifying the Church was to smash the stained glass, kick the heads off the statues. So you end up with the New England meeting house, absolutely chaste and sterile. But the Jesuits in the south of Italy and in Bavaria said, "No! This is Manichaeism and it's wrong. Beauty belongs to God." The Jesuit idea was to use all the arts in all ways to praise God.

Think of Tintoretto's paintings, everything on the diagonal, the most vibrant line you can have. Instead of everything being lined up like da Vinci's *Last Supper*, everything parallel to the footlights, all of a sudden everything is put on diagonals. The Spanish stairs in Rome are typically baroque. Everything has to have a dramatic approach now. Stairs all over, fountains all over. Light and darkness, terrific light and darkness. Back lighting where you can't see the source of the light, like the Scala Regia in St. Peter's where Bernini introduces perspective, one of the big discoveries of this time. Queen Christine in Sweden was so enamored of perspective that she had all her garden paths extended by putting false scenery at the end. And when it rained, the gardener had to go out and bring in all the scenery.

*What we are having today then is electronic baroque — the light shows and the sound agitation.*

That's a very good way of putting it. I'd never thought of it, but you are right.

What is a combine? The gathering together of a lot of stuff and then you put sound with it. Then you put light with it. Light shows. You get the noise as you walk into this glass house and you see yourself duplicated. In other words, you walk into the painting now. That is just what you did when you walked into a baroque church like the Assamkirche in Munich, one of the most beautiful baroque churches. You get totally bombarded from all directions. When you add the music to the bombardment, which is what they did, baroque music, you can see how this just swept everybody off their feet. Look at the terrific contrast between the severe, cold, Calvinistic, Scotch Presbyterian statement and the Italian or Bavarian statement, which had you throw in everything but the kitchen sink. But do it for the love of God.

110

*Who killed the Jesuit theater? What made it die?*

It had to stop at the Suppression in 1773 because everything Jesuit stopped — except in Russia. You know that the Bull of Suppression depended upon whether or not it was promulgated by the head of the country. They all promulgated it except Catherine of Russia. She protected them and this is why there's such a soft spot in every Jesuit's heart for Russia, and why we have the Russian College in Rome and why we're constantly sending Jesuits to Russia, even today. We managed to survive there till 1814 when the next pope came along and the order was reinstated again.

The Jesuits came back to an entirely different world, the so-called Enlightenment or Age of Reason, which had no time for the stage. As long as they had been training courtiers, there was a high premium on the fine arts. Now fine arts disappeared out of the curriculum almost completely. Jesuit educators now concentrated on training the intellect, neglecting the emotions and artistic talents.

*That was the world that the Society was reacting to. Is, then, the Society's history a matter of reactions? Beginning in reaction to the Reformation? Can you tell something about the times by what the Society is doing?*

*Always.* Because the Society has always had the same job to do — to try and bring Christ into the contemporary culture, whatever the contemporary culture happened to be. Today it's the same thing. How in God's name do we ever bring Christ to a world that thinks God is dead and is desacralized and dehumanized, and has all kinds of bad associations with a Christianity that isn't really Christianity at all? Now today we have to find a way of reintroducing Christ in his own terms. This is very difficult.

*The Society was summoned under a military metaphor to fight the Protestant Reformation. Is the Society in trouble today because it isn't being pushed by a hostile Protestantism?*

I think we've lost the image of the enemy, but I don't put the enemy where you do. We've never had such an opportunity as we have this moment, because I think what we have today is a world without hope, a world without mystery, a world that can't laugh, a world, above all, that can't love. We're living in the age of anxiety. Joseph Wood Krutch says that Freud's been the leading man in every Broadway play for the last sixty years. He *has* been.

You would think with the laser ray and Geiger counter and the computer and television and radio and cinema — all these things that have developed and blossomed in our time, you'd think this would make us the most secure, the happiest people that ever lived. Instead it's the opposite; you have nine million neurotics, one out of thirteen citizens an alcoholic, one out of every five marriages going on the rocks, a suicide rate among college students, according to a *Look* poll, up forty-five percent since last year; you have all these dropouts from society, going to psychedelia for some kind of way out, going to Zen Buddhism or some kind of mesmerism like rock-and-roll. It isn't adjustment to this life.

Take the movies. *Easy Rider, They Shoot Horses, Don't They?, Medium Cool, Midnight Cowboy.* Or take *Hair*, which is playing all over the world now in every possible language. What do they all say? REJECT! REJECT! It's a revolution with a big capital NO! They say *this is not a happy world*. This is not a world that has found the answers to successful human living.

Fellini's *Satyricon* is supposed to represent life in Rome in the year 2001 B.C. It's one long parade of orgies, homosexuality, violence and cruelty, but its despair and lovelessness and anxiety is no different from ours today. That's Fellini's point.

The only satisfying answer that can be given is Christ. He stands for what they're looking for. He *is* love.

The big threat for Sartre, the big threat for Camus is death. Life is *yes* faced by the big *no*. And man is trapped

*112*

between a *yes* and a *no*. This is Camus. Sartre says man walks alone in a loveless world with the only certainty being the certainty of death. As soon as you take Christ and the Resurrection out of the picture, there's no answer to death. We have no reason to hope. There is no reason to laugh.

Take Sartre's definition of man, man is freedom. With you being a freedom and me being a freedom, love is impossible. Sartre says hell is other people. Two freedoms can't get together without one having to sacrifice his freedom to the other. For Sartre love can only be some kind of a battle. Look at his chapter "Love and Masochism."

So love disappears from the picture and we end up with the big in-words describing our times. Waiting for Godot — waiting for some kind of an answer. Saul Bellow's "dangling man."

Tillich says waiting is the big descriptive word for our time. The other big word is *alienation*. I wonder if you saw the *New Yorker* cover showing a cocktail party, everyone standing on his own isolated little peak. In Antonioni's *L'Avventura* there's the same thing. People can't talk to one another, and in the background is this bunch of little volcanic islands sticking out of the water. So the isolated people and their setting symbolize human separation.

I owe a great deal to people like Sartre and especially to Ionesco, Nabokov and Samuel Beckett. They show us the world without the Resurrection, a world without hope, without love — you can't find love in Sartre. There's no love in these books. They don't really believe in love. I mean this quite literally. There are no love scenes in their books.

This shows how far off the mark they are, because from my experience of life I know there is love. If they have to cancel out one whole important part of human experience, they can't be right.

It seems to me that the artist today has to opt either for mystery or absurdity. The absurdist tries to create poetry by stringing clichés together, as Warhol and Ionesco have done.

*113*

Since he's taken God and the spirits out of life, he has no mystery. He resorts to ambiguity and other devices. A priest with his interest in mystery, in the spiritual, comes much, much closer to reality than the man who doesn't believe there is any mystery in life.

Andy Warhol's pop art is a true indictment of a culture that turns everything — human life included — into an assembly line of cheapness and uniformity. He reflects the drabness of a world without mystery. But I admire his honesty. The Stockholm art show catalogue of two years ago quotes him as saying: "If you want to know the meaning behind my paintings and myself, I'll tell you: *nothing*." And he's right. This is exactly what you get from his paintings — a spiritual zero.

The absurdists are experimenting with all kinds of substitutes for mystery — phony devil stuff as in *Rosemary's Baby*, black magic, hypnosis, astrology, UFOs, LSD — these are all attempts to have mystery in our lives.

Some absurdists use ambiguity for mystery. Who is the "Godot" that Didi and Gogo are waiting for? In Pinter's *The Dumb Waiter*, who is the mysterious stranger on the third floor who sends down the messages? Who is Tiny Alice — God? Satan? Nothing? We never find out. Does he mean God's a woman and is this Albee's ultimate slur? — like Baldwin asking, "Is God white?" It was the worst thing Baldwin could say about God.

*Is there such a thing as a priest-artist? Can a man make a full and excellent statement in both professions at once?*

I think the problem is one of the artist and his basic relationships. It's very hard for an artist to have a successful marriage, and I think it's very hard for an artist to lead a successful religious life. I don't think that the two ways of life are mutually exclusive, but because art is so all-possessing and so obsessive, it takes almost your entire energy. Yet

I've known artists to lead successful married lives and I think a priest can be an artist too. But it's a rare thing and a very difficult thing.

Abraham Maslow, the brilliant psychologist who wrote *Toward a Psychology of Being*, says we have desacralized all the texture out of living so that everything seems equally non-meaningful. He says we have to find some way of resacralizing the world. We need some kind of transcendence. You don't have to say "priest" in this question. You can just as well say "Christian" or "anyone who believes in transcendence" or who "believes there is more to life than just eating and begetting." It's most difficult to find a man who is a real first-rate Christian these days and a first-rate artist. You get either one or the other, not the combination.

There is a better chance of producing a Christian artist now than there has been for a long time. Throughout the nineteenth century, the Church was emphasizing words like "detachment" and "mortification" and the idea that the world was something to give up and resist. Now, since Vatican II, we're being concerned with this world.

The big problem had always been: How can a body have one foot in two worlds and amount to anything as a man? Camus's answer is you've got to live fully for life. If you've got any dreams about pie in the sky by and by, forget them.

Now this is new. We've suddenly come to realize that we can't understand what man is apart from Christ. Now we're saying, how can you possibly talk about man unless you see Christ as the human fulfillment of all man's greatest possibilities? This was why Vatican II kept stressing *human, human, human, human.* Once divinity joins with matter, which is what the incarnation means, matter can never be the same again and your life can never be the same again.

This is our faith today. This is what contemporary Christianity is. We believe that after the Resurrection, Christ took a new body and the body is us. He lived in us. If you want to find Christ today, you've got to find him in us.

I don't think you can understand life at all apart from Christ. If you believe this, and I do, why shouldn't this statement expressed in art be as valid as the statement of the man who doesn't believe?

*Hopelessness is a form of religion too. It's not Christianity, but it's somebody's religion.*

We simply cannot love any more. Well, this is what Christ means. He taught us what compassion was, what love was, and he gives us a reason for loving one another.

*If the Jesuits know this, they've failed to communicate it, and just Jesuits knowing it isn't enough.*

My feeling is that the Church has been dragging its tail. We waited on Vietnam. We came in when the peace cause looked good and safe. The same with the racial problem. The same with poverty, international poverty.

The Jesuits, if Christ and his values are the center of their lives, never had an opportunity like they have now. The way to resacralize a desacralized world is through the fine arts, is through communication. But first the Jesuits will have to be respiritualized. They can be just as lost and alienated as anybody else. I think the renewal, the *aggiornimento*, all has to begin with finding Christ in a great, great way. All the psychology and psychiatry in the world won't straighten out either modern man or the modern Jesuit novice. There's a danger of substituting psychology for spirituality. The only answer to the success mystique that has robbed this country of its soul is Christ.

The Jesuit artist's job will be the revival or re-presentation of mystery for a world that really no longer seems to understand it. It can't hope. It can't love. It doesn't even know how to laugh.

*You keep saying "Christ" but "Christ" is just a sound in my ear with many associations but no meaning at its center. I doubt it as I doubt words like* ballet, gourmet *and* art.

You're defining the problem for me. Many of the words we use to describe religious experiences are nineteenth-century words that have long been worn out. We say, in the Post Communion at Mass, "May we all receive our heavenly crown." What does "heavenly crown" mean today? Words like this give a phoniness and an unreality to religious experience. They're especially deadly now when the kids are demanding authenticity and don't want any junk.

I think what we're all going through now in the Society and Church is the best thing that ever happened to us. Because we will never get anyplace until we're driven to face and express religious experience honestly. It's crazy to talk about God in conceptual terms.

But I agree with you. You've hit the problem and all I can say is that it is the problem. We have to throw out haggard old terms that don't turn anyone on any more and find a fresh way to communicate Christ and his values today.

*The common enemy of growth is the cliché. We keep saying "as it was in the beginning." I remember asking a Spiritual Father in the juniorate, "How was it in the beginning?" He told me not to worry. But you have to worry if you say something again and again and again and don't know what you're saying. That's when you* should *worry, because then you're a machine. This is what I'm saying about the word Christ. It isn't enough to say the message is "Christ."*

No. But I can't say how it should be done. I only know that for myself the first thing I have to do is keep my own sense of Christ alive. You have to encounter Christ. The most important question ever asked was asked by Christ: "And who do *you* say I am?" Depending on how you answer that question, you live your life. You see, for us he is not just some-

*117*

one who lived once and died, someone you merely imitate. Our whole idea of reality is different because the dynamism of his Spirit charges and changes it. His living presence continues right now in the men and women I meet. Christ was limited by his own culture and times. He needs to live in us so that he can talk and, above all, love the poor alienated devils of our own day. Chardin talks about the "translucency of the universe" with Christ shining through. All we have to do is be aware of it.

*Artists are notoriously unstable people. How could you as an artist commit yourself to being a Jesuit forever?*

As an artist does, I always go to realities. I know that many men have been able to keep a permanent commitment, not just in religion but in married life. Love is always a risk. Unless you've got enough faith and trust to take a chance, I think you'll just end up a lonely, frustrated person, all by yourself.

I don't think any of my life makes a bit of sense outside of faith. Unless I'm talking to someone who will accept that my faith is a very real thing for me, my talk will sound like a lot of gibberish. Because I buy this business of a "calling" — that poor old beat-up word. A person *feels* his vocation, feels it because this was the thing he was particularly made for. He knows he could do other things, but where he is most really himself in a special way is when he is either writing or directing or acting or composing or choreographing or being a priest.

I was utterly wild about the theater when I was a kid. Theater was what I really wanted. But somehow or other there was this stronger pull that gave me more peace. After I petitioned for admission into the Jesuits, I prayed I wouldn't be accepted, because I thought that way I could in good, clear conscience give myself entirely to the theater.

Being an artist within the Society brings very special

problems along with it because the Jesuits since their restoration in the nineteenth century haven't given much encouragement to the fine arts. The artist always tends to be a little outside of his own society anyway. So if you find yourself with a group of men all charging off for a cause, and you want to charge off for the same cause too, but the way you want to go is different from their way, there just may not be a great deal of understanding and sympathy on hand for you.

*I believe that if a man can't work as an artist unless he's living in the East Village or Greenwich Village or any other art colony, there's something missing in him.*

I agree with what you're saying. If you have to bolster your image as an artist by living as a bohemian or with a group, something is missing.

*I somehow don't think the artist should require his community to endorse what he's doing. Why should the Jesuit artist expect his religious community to accept, endorse and favor him?*

Well, this worries me very much. Since the Jesuits don't have a living tradition of solid training in the fine arts, when an individual comes along with a *fair* talent, he might easily mistake his fair talent for a really special one. He might get along for some time posing as an artist or playing artist while not getting down to doing the hard, daily discipline that it takes to be an artist. Or he might think he was under-appreciated by his community when the fact is that he over-valued his own achievement.

If you're a real artist, your satisfaction has to come from what you do. You'd always like an audience to accept your work, but this can't be your motive for creating or you'll never come up with anything very good, I don't feel. It has to be your entire best for the sake of the thing that you're doing.

The artist within the Society has to come to a certain kind of adjustment if he's going to be happy as an artist. This adjustment has to be made in a context of faith.

One of the things that helped me most was studying Bertolt Brecht. Brecht has written, I think powerfully, about the Communist artist as a simple worker. He believed that the artist had just better settle for doing a day's work the way everybody else does, and that he'll get neither more money nor more consideration than anybody else.

You find out very early with the Jesuits that if you're going to be a prima donna about yourself as an artist, you'd just better leave. You can't fit into this context, unless you accept that he's going to be doing his things and you'll be doing yours. If you're going to want him to respect what you're doing, you'd better respect what he's doing too. Now I can't stand science. But when someone has got a new magnet that he's crazy about, the least I can do is try and understand what's got him turned on if I expect him to come and see the play I'm directing.

I have to say honestly, well — honestly as far as I've been concerned, there's been a great deal of giving on the part of the men and a willingness to go more than halfway. But this has not been the experience of other Jesuits who've pursued fine arts. Some of them have had a lot of trouble — I'm thinking about painters in particular.

But in the last ten years we've gone through a great transition as far as the arts are concerned in the Society. There are now at least a hundred Jesuit poets, painters, sculptors in the order here in the U.S.A. Three of the juniors who studied painting this summer took life classes without anybody batting an eye. In our time they would have sent you right home thinking there was something wrong with you if you even thought of such a thing. Now they've eased all of this.

What we're learning since the breakdown of the Age of

120

Reason is that you can't put all your eggs in one basket and can't put all the emphasis on reason. Systematic philosophy has not told us everything about man. There's a lot more to man than just a bare nous. He's got emotions that must be considered. If he's going to be a fully developed man, you'll have to really develop him totally.

They're realizing now that they have to have fine arts for communication and without communication it's like having a full barrel without a bunghole. They're also realizing that Jesuits haven't been fully rounded men. By suppressing the creative side of our men, we've turned out a lot of cold fish. They've learned that people might come to a Jesuit if they wanted a science problem resolved, but never if they had a human problem.

If the Society holds together, it will not be the enemy that holds us. An enemy might help, but it's not the central thing. What holds us together is the fact that we're all committed to Christ. It's what makes our vows have meaning. Without a love for Christ, "poverty" is something Johnson started a war against, "chastity" just means sterility, and "obedience" means slavery. Unless what we do is a gesture of love, an effort to give ourselves totally, I don't think the vows mean anything. The love relationship to Christ is the thing that keeps us going. If you take that out, I don't think there's really anything left to our lives at all.

I do believe in the Society and in the future of the Society, and I do love it very much. Jacques Brel's song to his homeland, Belgium, fits perfectly what I feel: "It may be the kind of landscape that nobody else would be attracted to — it's so foggy that the birds get lost when they fly over it, but it's my country and I love it." Ultimately, that's what makes me want to take part in this interview. It's talking about something I really love, no matter what's wrong with it. It might be a poor thing, but it's my own. I recognize there are things to be corrected, but my feeling about the Society is one of complete faith and love.

*John Culkin (with Marshall McLuhan)*

*Jesuits can do pretty much what they want
if they're not screwballs.*

John Culkin, S.J.

*A* Time *report* (*May 21, 1965*) *notes:* "*Man for man, the 8,600 U.S. Jesuits probably have less influence than the 261 communications-minded Paulist Fathers.*" *The fact that Jesuits are dumb as communicators grievously disappoints John Culkin, who believes the Society is fumbling a singular chance to make a distinctive, important mark in education. Culkin sees film and the electronic media as subjects of study in themselves, as media for teaching other subjects, and finally, since they comprise a system of equipment, instruments and forms, as teaching their very users. He criticizes the entire U.S. educational structure for being slow to see these advantages but particularly, sadly, and from a groaning heart, he criticizes the Jesuits for failing to seize the electronic media as earlier Jesuits once used the stage and the printing press to become the educators of Europe.*

*Culkin, who has his Ph.D. in education from Harvard University, is called "the Elmer Gantry of film media studies." He began staging film study conferences in 1963. His annual conference is now regarded as the patriarch of all such study gatherings. Conferences are attended by teachers or anyone else interested in making films. Over a three-day period they present films by children and films by professional producers. At the 1969 conference, for example, Frank and Eleanor Perry showed and discussed their film* Last Summer. Media & Methods *described the Culkin Conference style:* "*Cut the crap . . . create a relaxed atmosphere . . . communicate with each other . . . share experiences . . . have some fun, and the learning will take care of itself."*

*In 1969, Culkin resigned as director of the Center for Communications at Fordham University and started an independent organization in New York City called the Center for Understanding Media.*

*John Culkin is forty-one years old — "I have my old months, and my young months, and my bad years and good years." He calls himself "a clerical error."*

---

The first time I ever met Marshall McLuhan personally was about seven years ago — 1962. He said: "Father," he said, "er, I think the Jesuits must be in real trouble these days." Then he said, "Because they were founded on literacy." And wow — I saw it! Communication was the strength of the old pre-Suppression Jesuits as you indicate in your book on the Second R. The brilliance of Loyola to come along and grasp the revolutionary implications of movable type, and then to throw the energy of his new organization into that revolution making it work for him, that took incredible insight and genius.

*How does McLuhan connect literacy and Jesuit trouble?*

The Jesuit order grew up with print. Along with the rest of the world, it's shaped its organizations and schools, in a one-at-a-time, abstract, linear, fragmented, sequential way following the form of the printed line. According to McLuhan, for centuries the straight line has been our hidden metaphor. It was unconsciously used as a measure and model. It went unnoticed, unquestioned, and taken for granted as natural. There's trouble now because the electronic media have broken print's grip on everything. Radio, the telephone and TV have broken the printed line as a basic experience metaphor. Our traditional models and structures are shifting and breaking up. There's naturally going to be a lot of worried soul-searching going on.

*But the Jesuits don't own this problem alone.*

No, they don't. Most of our institutions are in trouble — well it's trouble for traditionalists. A lot of people find these exciting, wonderful times and see no trouble at all. But as Lyndon Johnson, Pope Paul, Grayson Kirk, Charles de Gaulle, and others found out, the old ways of running the business have had it. The tidy visual world which classified and categorized all of reality, including the people, is yielding to a much sloppier but much more humane way. We're learning to deal with people now instead of handling them.

It's interesting to note that the Reformation which broke up Christianity rode the fragmenting medium of print and that ecumenism is riding the electronic surf of radio and television. The need for involvement and participation has motivated many of the liturgical innovations which have brushed away the old vertical and linear styles to incorporate the laity in a liturgical experience. The media have also gotten into the act through the use of modern musical instruments and forms and through the evolving use of slides and films as integral to the liturgy. The God of Newtonian physics is dead. He was the big clock-winder in the sky who set the whole mechanism in motion. The personal God discovered through inner awareness and through other people is liable to be in for some very good innings in the future.

*Does the growing number of ex-Jesuits and the drop in vocations reflect the trouble McLuhan alludes to?*

I have no idea of the number of Jesuits who've left the order, but I was staggered when I heard that about three thousand men have left the priesthood in the past year or so here in the States alone. When you consider that communications takes all these enormous changes and makes people aware of them, that's trouble.

It used to be easy and quite uncharitable just to say of any Jesuit or any priest who was leaving, "Well, what was it — punch or Judy?" Another uncharitable thing we used to do was investigate whether the man was really crazy or not. Mental or nervous breakdown was the only alternative to the moral categories of defection and treason.

Many men, I believe, leave the Society and the formal exercise of the priesthood because they are disillusioned and frustrated by the poor way in which their service is used. Sacrifice is fine if something worthwhile results from it. Wasting one's time and energy is never worthwhile.

*I've been talking with Jesuits from New York to San Francisco about ex-Jesuits. They've expressed regret, good wishes, disappointment and sorrow, fear, and worry about men who've left the order. A few thought psychological disorders may have been involved in this or that case. But not one Jesuit accused an ex-Jesuit of moral disorders.*

Who wants to hold onto people who don't want to be held? The priesthood and celibacy, belonging to an order, these are mutual relationships. I was in Rome a couple of months ago doing a book on Fellini. I talked there with Father O'Keefe, a former president of Fordham. He told me the Vatican was just being deluged with problems from all over the world and lots of them had to do with priests who wanted to leave. I said, "Listen, why don't you just tell them to fill out a postcard and send it in and go? Why make them suffer? Who gains . . . ?"

Delay may keep some people from being hasty, but they're putting some of these poor men through a year or two of processing.

*Do you think the typical ex-Jesuit is able to cope with the competitive outside world?*

I really haven't been too close to the people who've left the Society. But a number of them think that Madison Avenue is just out there waiting for them. They have very unrealistic ideas about their market value.

*A psychologist in a firm that places executives told me that in the fifties many generals quit the army thinking they could get Omar Bradley's kind of $100,000-a-year job. The best job he could get for one two-star general was that of fancy night watchman at a big plant. He had charge of the dogs.*

We're used to saying that the Jesuit's training is a liberal education. I never bought it myself. There's nothing very liberal about it at all. It's highly specialized.

*From my experience in the juniorate and philosophate, it concentrated on heroes.*

Yes, but we have very few heroes to show for it. We're not very good at producing heroes. I've been reading a book called *Asylums*. It's about any self-contained society, whether it's an asylum, or hospital, the military, prison, seminaries . . .

*Marriages?*

Marriages, but only if you're both locked in the same room all day long. There has to be a lack of traffic with the outside world. In an asylum there's one group in charge and then there are the rest, the inmates. People in an asylum, the author says, invent the hierarchy of values and performances which fit them to survive within it. We're lucky if there's any congruence between the asylum and the outside world if we're ever released from it.

*129*

*Are Catholic schools "asylums"?*

We make them asylums. When McLuhan was at Fordham three years ago, we had twenty students who at their request were released from all course work, all grades — everything for a year. They were to be free to develop any of their ideas. They were very talented people, yet after about two weeks of freedom they came crying to be locked up again.

I was very hurt and upset by it, having fought the fight to give them their head. But then much later, on reflecting, I saw we had bred them in our schools so to depend on us that they couldn't fend for themselves on their own. We do the same to our scholastics. We keep them dependent for a dozen years, then ordain them and expect them suddenly to be priests and mature people.

I think I've been fortunate that my kind of work doesn't neatly fall into any of the existing work that the Society has done in the past. Right from the beginning, not really by desire, but because of the nature of my work, I've had to spend a considerable amount of time working in the real world. You almost have to use "real world" to distinguish it from the academic and certainly the seminary world. The Jesuits — to talk in purely pragmatic terms — get nowhere near the return they should be getting for their investment in people. It's about as ineffective a use of human talent as I can think of.

*Like the army?*

Well, the army gets what it wants. The army is a minimal achiever by design. But the Jesuit order isn't and that's sad.

*Did McLuhan mean to say the Jesuits were founded on literacy and are therefore stuck with it?*

They were founded on it and they've allowed themselves to be stuck with it. None of these things are irretrievable. And communication isn't the sole cause by any means though I'll be concentrating on it. If we took the Ignatian concept of *eloquentia* and extended it to mean an *all-media eloquentia* and then applied it in our educational system today, then we'd not only be educating but we'd be back in our original tradition. But I don't see this happening. We're *not* teaching communication. This is a failure we share with non-Jesuit and non-Catholic educators. But why should we share failures, stupidity and mediocrity? That's what's disappointing.

The Jesuits were supposed to be the light cavalry of the Church and all that sort of thing, supposed to serve troubled areas. We weren't to be just putting out brush fires, overnight stuff. We were expected to bring special insights and resources to situations that needed them.

College campuses are boiling up because of the ineffectiveness of colleges. The kids know what real problems are. They can't really sit around in philosophy class and get excited about pseudo problems. They've got unsolved real problems. Who the hell wants to sit around and try and solve problems that aren't that real? At least that you don't perceive as real. So to keep the class interested the teacher has to make classroom problems seem as real as real problems. But it always seemed to me that schools were for students. If students have unsolved real problems, that's where school has to begin.

Just run down the litany of currently talked-about things, like the war, drugs, poverty, environmental problems of pollution and things like that. These are very moral times, in that people are concerned with moral issues and not private moral trivia. Nobody's ever been more interested in talking about religion or morals than right now. Yet the Church and the Jesuits have either followed or done nothing. Jesuit Retreat Masters have been stressing a personal morality. It's been sex, stealing and lying and going to Church on Sundays. There's been no time at all given to social issues, to war, to killing people in large numbers rather than one at a time, to human worth. Few have ever confessed sins to a priest about these things.

I think the kids are quite right in saying, "If all you guys want to talk about is jerking off and birth control, go to it. They're not very important kind of things in the total spectrum. Man, I went to your schools and when it came down to what God wanted from me, he just wanted me to be sexually harmless. That's not much of an ideal in life, you know."

That's something of an overstatement, but not much of an overstatement in my book. If the Jesuits, as a group, are going to have meaning — well, now it's a buyer's market. It's not a seller's market. People don't want us. The kids don't want our absolution. They will want it less and less if we keep only being interested in absolving them from relatively small things. Whether they're even serious matters that need absolving is a good question.

What's happening today is that the media have just made it impossible to bring kids up in the dark any more and sort of say now this is the way it's supposed to be. Follow these steps to happiness and wisdom and wealth.

This is the first generation to have grown up with television. The TV set was waiting for them when they got home from the hospital and they liked it. They'll clock fifteen thousand hours of viewing by high school graduation. Their psychological intake system is programmed for the moving image. The latest in cinematic technique is served up daily on the sophisticated production of the commercials. The Late Late Show has much of the history of film waiting for them each evening. And there are films in theaters, in schools, and at expos. This generation also benefits from a maturing film industry and from the range of choices made possible through specialized theaters, 16 mm. distribution, film societies, library programs, and the independent and foreign film. It all adds up to a lot of images, in a lot of students.

The new media are turning out a new kind of student. They are plugged into the "now" and they want to experience it and be involved with it. Unfortunately, most of those in charge of the care and feeding of the "now" generation belong to the "then" generation. Traditional mediators of culture, like the family, church, and school, just aren't used to moving at jet-age speeds. They would be well advised to learn because much of the momentum for what is happening and is judged as relevant has already passed from their hands. Approval or disapproval of what is happening is considerably less important now than the willingness to understand.

What gets starved in the official culture now gets fed in the popular culture. Popular music, clothing, films, and dancing underscore this new concern with the person and with the need to involve all the aural, tactile, visual and kinetic elements of the individual. If all this sometimes goes too far, it may be because it has had to come from so far; that's the law for pendulums. If the official culture has stressed the outsides of things, today's student wants to explore inner space. The LSD thing is just a dramatic instance of the general desire to take the inner trip, to probe personal feelings, to experience as a total human being. Students mistrust formulas or verbalizations; they want experiences.

The kids are very sensitive to personal values. They want to learn how to get back and forth to each other — person-to-person and not station-to-station.

The neutral word "media" includes television, painting, music, sculpture, newspapers, magazines, advertising of all kinds, radio, comics, computers, plays, films, photography, opera, telephone, ballet, phonographs, tape recorders, speech, print and related combined forms of these media. I like the term because I can avoid tedious discussions about whether certain media are worthwhile art forms.

"Mediacy" is to all media what literacy is to print. Like all neologisms it has a quality of the precious and the unfamiliar about it. Like all new words it will survive only if it proves useful. All languages, English included, are mass media. The new mass media are so new as languages that we still don't know their grammar. If we could get kids using the media as ways of expressing themselves — this is revolutionary. This has got nothing to do with trying to make them better readers, although it does make them better readers. It does try to make them communicators, and that's a hell of a lot more fun.

*Let me string some thoughts. The Jesuits are in trouble today and going through organizational changes. Similar changes are shaking other institutions to the degree that they're founded on literacy. McLuhan thinks that the changes are caused by quake waves resulting from a fault in literacy. You believe that the Jesuits could survive and thrive if they extended the original vision of Ignatius to include the new electronics communication media.*

I don't see the Jesuits as having any great future as a corporate body and I come to this conclusion with regret and disappointment. The Society's failures have to be described in tragic terms. There need not be such terrible failures. They could make it. The ingredients are there. The tradition is there. The talent is there. But we've been in bad habits for a while, and also, we've had weak leadership.

*When you say as "a corporate body" do you mean the Society itself as a corporate structure?*

I don't really know exactly what I mean when I say those things . . .

*I mean leaving Fordham means you're leaving one of the Society's institutions. You're not leaving the Society itself by leaving Fordham.*

No. But I may, because both are suffering from the same kind of institutional malaise. The decision to leave Fordham was based simply on the fact that I couldn't get things done there. Almost no one in top administration has been there

*134*

more than three years and there is no leadership from the board. If you couldn't get a businessman to invest money in an organization run in such a fashion, I could no longer ask anyone to invest their lives in such an organization. We had four presidents in six years. Silly business. The one man who gave them some spirit and the ability to move was bounced on his head by the Jesuits. You can't have that kind of governance.

*Was there a lot of fuss over your decision to leave Fordham?*

It was a very quiet decision. I didn't make an issue of it. When my counterpart quit Columbia, it was a front-page story for the *Times*. That's silly stuff. I just wrote a three-line letter to the President, said, "Well, summer school is over and I think I could do my work better elsewhere. It's been nice . . ." — that sort of thing.

*Why did that happen? Is Fordham's problem a matter of keeping some buildings alive and warm?*

Sure. Again, this is a problem Jesuits share with lots of people. If you think the Jesuits have trouble, you should see Harvard's. We're much more careful about buildings than we are about people. Take Fordham Prep, for instance. Yesterday [December 1, 1969] we broke ground for a new three and a half million dollar building. Three and a half million for a building that's going to be empty in ten years! Now if we had taken that three and a half million dollars and put it into people and into educational reform or a place to feed and house people instead of putting up a bloody gymnasium, we could go somewhere.

*Is there such a thing as a corporate violation of the spirit of poverty? It would seem the Society as a corporation should take the same vows that its members take.*

*135*

Oh, it was beautiful, the Ignatian ideal. We were meant to be very independent people. Meant to be. It took some of the greatest Jesuit thinking in history . . . But it's a case of the founder and the original spirit going and then the lawyers coming in and taking over. Like St. Paul and the Gospels are two different religions. Paul is not a nice man because he was the first one down the road to say, "Now, see, if he were alive today, here's what he really would have done." Many of the things we're in trouble with today are a result of St. Paul, not of the Gospels. I've gone back to reading nothing but the Gospels, I don't read Paul any more, and none of the problems that are bugging the Church today are caused by the Gospels.

Now the same thing happened with the Society. As we became institutionalized, the insights of that smart man who founded the order were bypassed. What's happening now, with this whole higher education thing, and the lay board of trustees, Jesuits owning their own buildings and getting salaries and all that kind of thing, this is all a change. In my professional work, I travel first class. I always spent more money at Fordham than most of the other people because I earned more. And when I did things or hired people, I wanted to hire people that were right to be hired and pay them what they should have been paid, not have them take my vow of poverty. Because I think money is for giving away — I'm not a possessive person. But at the same time, I started to get very disheartened when there'd be meetings of the Jesuits and we'd be making our deal with the university. They sounded as though our stuff was being wrenched from us. But our thing should be: "Hey, boys, it's not our university. Let's talk about divvying it up." Something like that. "We don't care." But we got very possessive. If you're in the business to serve, you don't ask questions like, "Who's the owner here?" If you start asking questions like that, you should be legitimately challenged on whether you see your role as one of service.

*136*

*I was with Father Hesburgh when a reporter asked him whether his order owned Notre Dame. He said, "I think we owned it from nineteen hundred something through the Depression while we were still building it and losing money on it. Now, I suppose, Notre Dame belongs to the students, and the people of Indiana. We only help run it."*

This is true. To have put blood into it, suffer its growth, and then let go when the signs call for it takes a certain openness of heart.

There's a whole mystique about Jesuit corporate identity that impresses a lot of people. I'm not much in contact with the younger Jesuits, so I don't know if the Society is changing.

*I've seen a lot of young Jesuits and what I've seen looks interesting. I spent several days with one who travels around with harmonica and a blanket roll, writes noisy poetry for kids, works for the poor. He's making a new kind of regency.*

That's interesting. That kind of spirit is supposed to be part of what the Jesuits were all about.

This is what's kind of phony. At the time when many of the rather fundamental elements of Christianity are just out there — this nonmaterialism of the younger generation, also the emphasis on love and peace — and I know you can start pulling it apart by asking what kind of love and all of that, but at a time when authentic Christianity should never be more sellable than now, the images of Christianity and the Church are just plain silly.

I don't see that the Society as a group has had the kind of leadership to respond to these times.

*Do you think the Society is too big?*

No, because I don't believe there is such a thing as "Rome" — "Rome," that is, a single source of authority which has to pass on everything. I never believed that. Rome is what little people hide behind. It's too big if you think that the whole decision-making process is a series, too big if it's an organizational-chart kind of world.

My feeling is that Jesuits can pretty much do what they want if they're not screwballs. I've always acted on this premise. I was just lucky enough to have some very understanding superiors in my world. I found it much easier to tell them what I thought I was doing than to insult them by not telling them and trying to sneak it by. My feeling is that in the Society there has always been more freedom available than was either advertised or taken advantage of. That may not be everybody's experience, but I always felt it was. The fact that the freedom was not advertised or was not taken advantage of is another kind of commentary itself. We've often been brought up by some very small people. The leadership in the Society, as I've known it, has been pitifully bad.

*But didn't the leadership come partly from the example of the superstars?*

Sure. That's a kind of moral leadership. And in many ways, many of the superstars were the superpersecuted too, who were working against great obstacles. If the supermen can barely make it and if they die young through killing themselves, what can we expect for the less than super?

*Do you feel that you've been persecuted in trying to achieve your vision in education and communication?*

No. When I entered there wasn't much freedom around in the lower years. But by the time I got out to regency there was more willingness to experiment. A lot of us got our first taste of this. We were always fortunate, at least I always felt I was fortunate during the course of training, in having a number of great men as my teachers. It was a great thing

*138*

for me just to see the obstacles older men before me had to surmount. By the time I started getting itchy to do things, I had enormous freedom — by comparison is the only way you can talk about it. I had freedom to work outside of Woodstock, to travel. My only responsibility was to make damn sure when I took theology exams I did well on them.

When I got to Fordham, I wasn't tied into any departmental structure. I always did a lot of outside consulting and held my own conferences in hotels. I used to report to the chief man and say, "Hey, Chief Man, here I am and this is what I think I am good at doing, this is what I've done so far, and this is what I think I should do." I've never cost them much money because I was paying my way.

I could have stayed at Fordham and used it as a base, but I just couldn't go to my friends any more and say, "Hey, here's what we're going to do." Because if the trumpet sounds an uncertain note no one will join the cause. And once Fordham dumped its last president, it sealed off its growth for the future.

We're never going to catch up and be significant competitively with other universities in the existing disciplines. For example, we're never going to be a great science school. That's another thing: we should find out what we can do best and then really have the balls to hang in there and do that thing best. Maybe it's being just a nice undergraduate college or maybe it's running high schools.

*Maybe it's getting back to eloquentia?*

Maybe it is. Again, I don't just want to sing the communications song — but I think it is as important an area as we have. Morris Ernst recently said: "No culture can be much better than its mass media." I buy that. I'm not saying I could have done it. I'm less interested in me doing it than having it done. With their campus at Lincoln Center just by reason of their geography they could do something. With

*139*

proper management they had an opportunity to take a brand-new field as important as any other field.

I suggested that we incorporate communications separately, that I get my own board of directors. You can't let every part of the university rise and fall with the whole university. There has to be a way in which some people's mistakes aren't visited on everybody.

*Like Macy's. They leased out the butcher shop because they couldn't make money.*

I'm sorry to get this personal about it. But it's an institutional problem and I think it's important to name it and face it. I feel quite sure that I'd have been no happier at Columbia trying to suggest this type of thing. But I'm just talking in terms of the peculiar opportunities that this particular Jesuit institution had, and that the will is not there. It wasn't a question of money. It's something I find lacking across the board.

We're freighted down with a lot of real estate and everybody is sitting around asking questions about *what is a Jesuit anyway?* — that kind of identity crisis. And we're hanging around with a fifteen-year-long training course, and the time wasted — well, you know what it's like to be out cutting grass and chopping down trees and such at the seminaries. Unbelievable. The changes needed are so drastic. I think all the ingredients for solving these problems are with us. But as in the Church what they'll do is shilly-shally through the problem. They'll give in a little bit here and a little bit there instead of going right to it and cutting out all the intervening steps.

*Do you have a chance to talk with the young men in the Society about going into all-media communication?*

I have very little to do with the Jesuits as a group. Mainly because I find them less and less open to things than almost

*140*

any group I've known. That's just a description of my own experience. It may tell you just as much about me as it does the Jesuits. It's very difficult to work with the group that you belong to, you know. The prophet in his own country.

*Are other Jesuits involved in "mediacy"? It's hard to believe they're not.*

Oh yes. There's a fair amount of activity in it. Of course, in the Jesuits there are a lot of cycles. For a while everybody was in catechetics and sociology and that kind of thing. There's been a lot of interest in communication, but one of the problems has been we train people and don't have places to put them. Probably in the States, the most active Jesuit on campus, I guess, is Father Jim Brown in Detroit. He did his doctorate at USC [University of Southern California], and he's the head of the department out there. It's not a great department because it's in Detroit. If we're going to do something in this field, it's got to be done in New York.

All around the world if we trained our people — especially in the developing countries — to be the philosophers of the new communications, we could have an enormous impact. There are a few guys trying that. For example, Leo Larkin in the Philippines is in educational television. He just kind of owns the country. In the whole Philippines he's *the* man in this field.

*Does he figure in the politics out there?*

I don't think so. I doubt he would have the time to get too involved with that.

I guess Jesuits as a whole have been very open to studying film. That has developed within the last six or seven years. I'd say that in almost every one of our high schools there's somebody who's working in this. But in terms of people on the national level influencing opinion in this field and writing on this, I don't think they exist.

Jesuits get away with an awful lot because of the title. We're presumed to be considerably brighter. They think that, but in our day this wouldn't even be relevant for a large part of our population. Yes, we've got some superstars: a couple of Joe Namaths and Mickey Mantles in people like John Courtney Murray and Gus Weigel and Walter Ong. These are people with legitimate, hard-earned credentials by any kind of fair evaluation. So people tend to say, "Courtney Murray and Weigel and all those Jesuits."

Some men justify the Jesuit education, the whole fifteen-year megillah, because it produced a Courtney Murray. I'm not interested in these little occasional spin-offs. In what proportion did we produce them?

My own feeling is that the Jesuits are highly overrated as a group. I've always been embarrassed by it, by the people who did not know me, who right away chalk up a lot of strong points for my side because I'm a Jesuit. It's not a conscious PR job that gets them this. But, factually, when you ask what kind of image is out there, I think we're probably living on the perfume of a vase that's not that full any more. We have some strikingly good men but, unfortunately, in small numbers.

They've always talked about the possibilities that we have both nationally and internationally, that if we got our best men together on a problem we would have the ability to move with it — fast. It's still a good speech, but it's not executed.

We had a meeting ten years ago on the idea of getting the best people in the world in philosophy and theology and sharing them in some way with all of our institutions by video tape and film. Quite a simple idea. They are still having an annual meeting on it and they're no closer to doing it now than they were ten years ago. I'm a believer in two meetings — one for waltzing and one for closing. And if you're not with closers, you're wasting time. I've given good ideas that didn't cost much money to Jesuits and they wouldn't act on them. I took similar ideas to the "benighted" diocesan people and got them to spend twenty million dollars in eighteen months.

*In New York?*

In New York and around the country. These closed-circuit television networks that they've set up are the result of our work. So who wants to hang around giving speeches to people who don't want to listen to them if you can get people who do?

*You find you can be more effective by demonstrating from the outside?*

I find, too, that I can be more helpful to Catholic education by talking to education in general. Probably my role is somewhat that of a broker and gadfly. I'm a good salesman. I also can bring people from different worlds together to align them in common causes. I catch onto ideas fast, and through writing and speaking, I know I can communicate them. I'm a terrible administrator of things. I'm just now putting together some ideas on the whole preschool education especially involving the media and the art. It should be a concentrated effort to develop the sensory life of the child and the modes of learning.

McLuhan's thing about the Jesuits' being in trouble because they were founded on literacy, the applications of that idea are marvelous.

PHOTO BY T. MIKE FLE

*The Greeks thought* knowing *was like seeing.*
*The Hebrews thought it was like hearing.*

# Walter Ong, S.J.

*Walter Ong's statement offers a panoramic view of all other statements in this book. This is a book about changes in race relations, in the Church, in education and medicine, in society and in the Society of Jesus.*

*Ong is a change watcher and analyst. The statement over his name is the key to understanding many of the changes discussed in this book. He delivers a fascinating explanation of it in his interview.*

*Bernard Bergonzi in his review of Ong's book,* The Barbarian Within *for Blackfriars said: "There are few truly encyclopedic minds to be found in our intensely specialized world; but Fr. Ong's is undoubtedly one of them."*

*What can you say about an encyclopedia in a paragraph?*

---

I've never checked this, but my dissertation on Peter Ramus, the sixteenth-century French philosopher and educator, may be the longest dissertation that was ever handed in at Harvard — over seventeen hundred pages.

I worked in over a hundred different European libraries — I didn't realize that until I tallied them up afterward. I started in 1950, finished in '53, turned in the dissertation in '54. Two books from it were published by Harvard University Press in '58. They were *Ramus, Method and the Decay of Dialogue*, and *Ramus and Talon Inventory*.

One way of looking at these two Ramus books is to take them as studies in the history of the human mind. In a sense, that's what a history of education is because education is the transmission of knowledge from one generation to the next. The way you hand down what you know varies from culture to culture. If you can find out what's going on when people are being educated at any particular time, you can find out what it means at that time to be a human being.

*How did you get started on Ramus?*

I dedicated one of these two Ramus books this way: "For Herbert Marshall McLuhan who started all this. By "this" I meant he had first called my attention to Perry Miller's work on Ramus's influence in early New England. Miller was a far-ranging and profound historian of American thought. His work got mine started. Marshall and I were both at St. Louis University in the late thirties and early forties. There was a milieu in St. Louis at that time that nurtured noetic problems, problems of knowledge. Marshall lived over on McPherson Street, where some other young St. Louis University faculty lived, too. Slightly dotty neighborhood. Marshall likes to tell how one of the faculty used to grouse about the noise the bicycles made wheeling down the street. Another was known to meet his classes by coming through the window.

Marshall's first book, *The Mechanical Bride*, was published by Vanguard Press. I am pretty certain that only two people in the world reviewed it and I was one of them. Vanguard Press had just changed hands. The new owners didn't think much of the old owners' list and never advertised the book at all. Never gave it a chance. Marshall bought up a load of the remaindered books and stored them near Columbia University in New York City in the home of Bernard Muller-Thyme, a former colleague of Marshall's on the

*148*

St. Louis University faculty. Ultimately they became collectors' items. I'm sure they're all gone by now, because after *The Gutenberg Galaxy* there was a big demand for his old books.

*Do you and McLuhan keep in touch?*

Since those days Marshall and I have pretty much gone our separate ways, although the ways have often intersected. We had both been interested in medieval and Renaissance rhetoric, but I've become rather more of a specialist in that. We are good friends and I see his things regularly. But I haven't read everything of his by a longways. Because our interests do intersect it may sound strange, but I don't keep up with absolutely everything Marshall writes. Still, we're well tuned to one another.

*What makes Ramus important?*

I knew Ramus was some kind of bridge between the early Middle Ages and the modern world. I couldn't figure out exactly how. I had accumulated a tremendous mass of material and had done a lot of writing, but there was something at the middle missing.

Then somehow I came across the difference between the Hebrew idea of knowing and the Greek idea of knowing and in that moment everything fell into place. I realized that though intellectual knowledge has likenesses to all the senses, the Greeks were thinking of it more by analogy with seeing, whereas the Hebrews thought of knowing more as if it were hearing. We typically think of knowledge like the Greeks. The Greek word *idea* has the same root as *video* in Latin, meaning *I see*. We say "I see" to mean "I understand." We speak of ideas as images and *view*points. We describe them as clear, brilliant and dazzling. Our language is shot through with figures which "show" our visual bias. We're so immersed in it that we don't realize it's a bias — you know, like every-thing's wet if you grow up like a fish.

Once you have an alphabet that lets you represent sounds on a two-dimensional sheet of paper, and then develop writing by hand, and then, further, develop print, you almost can't help locking ideas into space. You tend to put an exaggerated value on surface as a means for storing and locating and con-veying information. You start drawing outlines, diagrams and systems. Eventually, after a few hundred years of this people naturally think that words were always on some kind of surface like paper, that they came from such surfaces and belong there.

I wasn't aware of how visualistic my own thinking was un-til I "saw" how the Hebrews regarded knowledge and "dis-covered" they were doing something different. Since the He-brews thought of knowing more by analogy with hearing, learning tended to mean listening to someone. They thought even of things as speaking, not only as showing themselves, but as declaring themselves.

*Yadha'* in Hebrew means *to know* in the sense of to know your way around. It means to have savvy. It is something that has to do with the human lifeworld and human behavior.

Knowing for the Greek means to be able to explain. It means to analyze, to take apart, to show the different pieces of. It's a very abstract knowledge. Our Greek visualist bias shows when we try to provide a rational explanation for ev-erything. This can't always be had and the attempt to set it up becomes more and more suspect the closer we get to the source of life. There is a kind of wisdom you cultivate in not being excessively rational.

*"Explain" or "show" also means to communicate knowledge. Then the ability to communicate knowledge must be an essen-tial part of knowledge.*

Yes, that's right. The Hebrews just didn't think much about explaining. It's notorious that there was no science among the Hebrews. They were event-minded. History-minded. People-minded. The ancient Greeks were too, by contrast with modern technologists, but by contrast with the Hebrews they show up as abstractive. Most early cultures were like Hebrew culture. The Greeks break with the rest of mankind here.

Hebrews were event-minded and thus were tuned in on sound because sound is the only sensory field that always indicates something is going on. Sound is current, that is, running. Sound is contemporary. Sound is transient and exists while going out of existence. Even in saying "existence," by the time I get to *-tence*, the *exist-* is gone. You can't stop sound or freeze it in flight. If you do stop sound, you have silence. What this all means, then, is that if you hear a sound, you are hearing something that's acting. Sound is an event in motion.

The fact that the Greeks and Hebrews thought of knowing in such different ways made great differences in the way they learned and lived. Today, when we want to remember a number of things, we make a checklist. We have dictionaries and reference books where we can "look up" facts. Even when they had the alphabet, most early peoples didn't do much "looking up." They "recalled" for the ear, as their preliterate ancestors had done. Verse meters or rhythms and rhymes were memory aids. In such a culture, you can easily see how age and wisdom go together. Old people got a lot of respect often because they were memory banks — human storehouses for information.

The great axis in my Ramus work is the shift from an orally oriented culture to a visualist culture. Ramus bridges antiquity and modern technology because he intensified and accentuated the visualist element in verbal cognition. What made this possible for him was the printing press.

A prominent feature of Ramus's work is the dichotomized outline. He'd take a subject like "dialectic" and divide it into "invention" and "judgment." Then he'd divide "invention"

*151*

into two more parts and do the same for "judgment." Then he'd divide each of the resulting parts into two more parts and so on and on. Ramus didn't know it but he was working out a crude computer flow chart. He dropped memory as a part of rhetoric because his diagrams and outlines are an elaborate memory system. That's what a computer is. It "remembers" data.

*It must have been awesome standing on the verges of such a vast sweep of human history. How did it make you feel?*

I felt awfully excited. I started writing. I put out quite a few articles about this before my big books appeared. I just couldn't hold it in.

*Some teachers say there's no longer any need to teach writing because film and sound will take the place of books.*

Writing is here to stay. The media never destroy each other. They reinforce one another. But they also interact and remake each other. This fools people. Many think a new medium is simply added to the old without any change in the old. This is the kind of person Marshall McLuhan likes to get at and does get at. Many people think that when you write you simply can put down what you talk. But no. You don't think the same way when you write. That's why people who talk with ease can find it difficult to write. Once you do write, however, some of your writing habits or styles feed back into your speech. People who write begin to talk as though they were writing, just as I'm doing now to a degree.

*I revise a lot when I write, trying to break clichés and searching for more exact language. These taped interviews are showing me how much my writing habits have influenced my speech. I sometimes sound like I'm stammering.*

*152*

When talking and writing interact, neither is the same any more. It's quite likely that peoples who know how to write talk more than the ones who don't.

Now our talk today is the talk of inner-directed people. We are social-minded, as earlier oral man was, but he couldn't think of any other option. Men had to be social-minded before writing because people came together precisely to talk and to hear talk. Talk was where the action was, where thinking was. People in an oral society are interested in events because early people didn't have science. We're interested in events, not because we don't have science, but because we've got so much science.

TV news reporting gives you a sense of participation largely because of the voice and sound effects. The picture generally supports the voice, not vice versa. Any studio man will tell you you've got to have the sound. A live picture doesn't seem really live unless somebody is talking about it.

*Remember when Apollo 11 failed to transmit pictures? People stayed at their sets anyway, listening to the astronauts talk.*

That's right. They have to talk up there on the moon. You can't read a weather map on television like you can read it in the papers. You've got to have somebody reading it to you. It's talk that gives you this sense of participation.

The reason for this is that sound unifies its listeners. Readers are all split up, but an audience is one group. "Audience" is a collective noun. There is no singular collective noun for readers and you can't form one because that's not the kind of thing readers are. "Readership" is not a true collective noun, but an abstraction.

*Editors and publishers, I notice, get shrill and up-tight about Marshall McLuhan. They think he's proclaiming the death of print.*

They are mistaken. Television and radio will help print. When print was invented, did it destroy writing? Just the opposite, and print is here to stay. Like writing is. New media do not cancel out the old. They build on them, reinforcing them and — this is what most people miss — radically changing their mode of existence and operation. But in their changed form the old media are stronger than ever.

In classical antiquity, people wrote a lot but they didn't read much. Once we got print it became necessary to have universal literacy. Everybody had to know how to write. Print didn't destroy writing. It forced people to learn to write. It interacted with writing. Now people began to write for print. The classical example of someone writing for print is James Joyce's *Finnegans Wake*. This has to be for print because with all his tricks of orthography we could never possibly get two manuscript copies that were even reasonably like one another.

*The film* Ulysses *had trouble with that.*

Of course it did. That's right. When man started writing for print his writing style changed. Even now when you write letters to friends which are not to be printed, there's an influence from print. Print didn't destroy the oral world, but it changed it. Our oral world is that of an inner-directed, chirographic people. Now that we have entered an electronic age, it is increasingly necessary for almost everybody to print. That's the typewriter. Television has to have writing and print in back of it. But neither writing nor print are what they used to be before the radio, the telephone, the phonograph and television. Look what we — you and I — are doing now in taping this interview.

What's going on here will produce a printed book. Electronic tape is supporting print. We're using talk and writing (for editing), and electronics and print. Yet the book produced will have been "written" by no one.

*Not in the usual sense of "writing a book."*

It will represent an interaction between talk and taping and writing and more talk and taping and writing and finally print. The only way I can characterize such a fascinating end product is to call it a "presentation." It's typical of our culture today.

*The writing after taping will be a more accurate writing.*

Yes. You can get a certain kind of accuracy with this. Right.

*Another difference is that you and I have different, perhaps conflicting images of the ultimate reader of this book. I might be thinking of a reader who's unfamiliar with Jesuits but open and friendly. You might be worried about a hostile reader. Your image could affect what you tell me. You'd tend to be more guarded, more defensive, more suspicious. I hope to avoid a conflict of reader images by having you address me instead of the tape, because when you address the tape, you are addressing your image of the reader and not mine. Of course, in order to address me you have to trust me, and I have to give you confidence that I can be trusted.*

Yes. The use of present-day media such as tape complicates our relationship to the ultimate reader. I am saying things to you to be taped in order to be typed out, edited, and printed. You are asking me questions in order to get me to speak in this complex. I know that what I say will have something to do with what ultimately appears on the printed page, but I am not quite sure in what way. So we cannot entirely avoid the conflict by our own personal friendship. No matter what, for our present purposes I am not talking really just to you. Still, friendship and our personal presence to one another can establish a tone.

*The Jesuits were founded in 1534 during the lifetime of Ra-*
*mus. Your particular studies should give a certain special*
*understanding of the changes troubling the American people*
*and the Society of Jesus today. Marshall McLuhan has said*
*the Society was founded on literacy and is therefore in trou-*
*ble. Is McLuhan right?*

Let me break your question in two. As for the Society being founded on literacy, yes, in certain ways. We have written Constitutions and we make a lot of them — so does the
United States of its Constitution. The British historian
Denis Brogan likes to point out that in the United States we
actually quote the Declaration of Independence and the Constitution in court, whereas if you quoted the Magna Carta
in England they would think you were crazy. The English
have a stronger feeling for common law, for the way people
talk and the way people do. But we, here, believe in writing.
Americans have the most literate culture the world has seen.
Comparably, in the Society of Jesus we specify that we cannot appeal to custom against our written law. This is rather
contrary to what had been a normal thing in canon law and
the religious tradition. It shows that we come from a very
chirographic culture. People in such a writing culture know
they can put things down in writing and that operations can
be conducted on that basis.

But early members of the Society of Jesus were also quite
oral because the old oral traditions of classical antiquity continued in our schools right up to romanticism. You never
tested a person in those times by asking him to write something. Testing was always oral. It was the Renaissance that
brought to the fore the old classical idea of the "rhetor" —
orator, the public speaker. Consequently, you have the stress
on eloquence which marks Renaissance and therefore Jesuit
education. Jesuits are writing-oriented and speculation-ori-
ented, but we're also activists.

Now the second part of your question, that the Society

was founded on literacy and is therefore in trouble. I don't know. Being troubled is part of human existence.

Fortunately, our tradition has always been that of adjustment. We've been very free-falling. We've never had any particular way of dressing. We are largely in education today in the U.S. but this was not our initial purpose.

The Society was founded to do whatever the Church needed done. We are becoming much more conscious of that now than we were, say, in the past thirty or forty years. We used to say it just as we've always said we were free agents unfixed in any special work. But now we're thoroughly conscious of it. Right now we're hanging loose in our activities and watching for major adjustments, though we do of course have to be true to commitments we have made to others. There's a lot of new programming going on now in the Society.

*The telephone company is severely based on written rules. Have you ever tried to get any information from an operator beyond what she was instructed to give you? Dealing with big companies today is more and more frustrating because the companies make sure there is no capricious deviation from their written rules by programming the rules into a computer.*

You always have to complement written rules. In the Society of Jesus the complement or counterpoise is the constant personal relationship between the superior and everybody in the province or the house that he's in. This is an oral thing. You do have direct oral communication all through the Society. This has always been cultivated and always will be. The Society is fathered institutionally in a literacy structure, but there's a conscious effort to complement the written Constitutions with things they don't have. We have the Constitutions, but the superior can dispense from them. We are founded on literacy but literacy is not the ultimate thing.

It isn't waved around as a flag, perhaps, the way it used to be. We are concerned that the flow of information from the members of the Society to superiors be kept open so that the commands of the superior are responsive to actualities of life. There is a great deal of talk about this, but it really isn't new, because the Constitutions provided for this quite specifically. One of the distinctive things in the Constitutions is that subjects are supposed to tell superiors if they have difficulties. There is more concern that this go on today, but that again is where the Society of Jesus is responding to the general structures of the society outside. Obedience is structured into that situation of lots of up-and-down communication.

*Two black Jesuits interviewed elsewhere in this book say that Jesuits in their spiritual training are sensitized to examine their consciences for subtle personal imperfections while remaining insensitive to gross social wrongs. Does a bias for self-awareness and introspection result from literacy?*

Yes. Inner-directedness goes with a writing culture. Before people knew how to write, they didn't think things out for themselves. There was nothing that corresponded to study as we think of it today. If you were to be in contact with the articulated thought of another person he had to be there, you had to be talking to him. Thinking was not the lonely occupation it became once we got writing.

People were examining their consciences long before Christianity — there were the Ten Commandments, for example. But you didn't have a stress on the examination of conscience as a reflectively controlled and directed activity, at least no stress that amounted to very much, before say around 1500. At about this time you do. Suddenly, you have all kinds of manuals for examining your conscience. There were lists of sins in the Middle Ages, but they were minor lists compared to the ones that came out at this time. The technique of introspection now became extremely developed.

The *Spiritual Exercises* show how deeply interiorized and inner-directed Jesuits are. The *Exercises* were to bring a man to make up his own mind all by himself in the presence of God. St. Ignatius cautions directors not to interfere with the one they are helping through the *Exercises*. Let him make up his mind. You can give him suggestions to think about but he is going to have to do the deciding.

But inner-directedness doesn't only mark the Society of Jesus. It's characteristic of everything that came out during that period right after the development of printing. It's part of Protestantism and the Protestant ethic, too.

*I have an optical illusion with the terms "inner-" and "other-directed." I keep wanting to think they mean introvertive and extrovertive or introspective and extrospective, as if "inner" were really "inward." I have to make a conscious effort to realize that inner-directed means self-directed or self-starting or self-motivated. Does the inner-directed person find it hard to socialize his thoughts. I mean, can he communicate?*

Oh, yes. Inner-directedness is not antisocial. By inner-directedness I mean an attention to oneself in all one's dimensions. This includes, very deeply, the social dimensions. The drive comes from within but moves out.

*Epictetus taught self-awareness.*

Yes. Epictetus was a Stoic, and Stoicism connects at certain points with the Christian tradition quite well. Of course, there's a lot of self-awareness in everybody all the time. No self-awareness, no human being. But the kind of stress that you get on it at this time is connected with writing and the intense literacy of the Middle Ages.

*Did people who lived before print and writing have personal prayer?*

Prayer was always to a degree personal but in significant ways not so personal as it became later after writing and print really took hold. Prayer was much more communal. The thinking was more communal. In human cultures before writing you didn't have individual thinkers who figured things out alone. All men's thought had to advance more or less at once. And prayer was likely to be felt as something that was done within the community.

Much that was later interiorized remained somewhat external, in certain ways. In the early books of the Bible, you have a ritual of purification, for instance, for touching a dead body. No one was exactly guilty of wrongdoing here, yet this contact was an impurity something like that of sin. Quite external, and yet it had to be treated somewhat as sin was. Then much later you get to where Jesus tells people that the things that come out of the heart are the things that dirty man. You see? We're becoming more clearly interiorized by this time. Exterior behavior counts, but largely because it connects with interior consciousness.

Anthropologists talk about the difference between a shame culture and a guilt culture. In a shame culture the pressures are more external, in a guilt culture they're more from within. Today, we're other-directed something like earlier man. We tend to measure ourselves by what other people do. But it's not a question of unreflective conformity so much as it was earlier, because we still have our inner-directedness. We study other people consciously, whereas the tradition-directed man simply conformed without any particular study. David Riesman has spelled out much of this very well in *The Lonely Crowd*, where he explains the tradition-directed character, the inner-directed character, and the other-directed character. These occur that way in roughly temporal sequence.

*Was there more of a chance for dialogue before writing and print were developed? I'm referring to the Buber kind of I–Thou dialogue, the attempt to reduce false images in communicating with others. I believe we get many of our false images of each other because of our visual, therefore surface, orientation.*

The frames of reference are so different. Human relations are human relations, so undoubtedly individuals related to one another very warmly from earliest times. They certainly could not, however, be as articulate about their relationships as we can.

Dorothy Lee did a study some years ago on the concept of the *I* among the Wintu, an Indian tribe. Every human being says "I," but when the Wintu says "I" he feels himself significantly in context with many other people. We don't so much. In early oral culture, a man couldn't ever get quite as far away from other people as we can. Privacy is a modern invention. Earlier cultures had very little privacy. In a tribal culture it might be a we-you relationship rather than an I–Thou. There is some of the I–Thou there but it's very socialized.

A former student of mine who came back after a couple of years with the Peace Corps in Nigeria told me about the linguistic isolation of the people she lived with. They couldn't talk to anybody if they went thirty-five miles from their village. People beyond that distance all spoke a foreign language. What she missed most for herself was privacy. Everybody knew all the time what she was doing every moment of the day. The only way she could be private was to go to her little hut, and there wasn't anything in there, nothing to do.

There is no word in ancient Latin for what we today call a family, that is, a husband, wife and children, who are felt as a unit, with everything else in the whole world outside this unit. The word *familia* in Latin means a household.

*That concept of* familia *is still strong in Italy. It also includes animals. I have a paper written by a seven-year-old*

*Italian child taking his toy dog to the doctor. He asks his aunt, "Who will pay?" His aunt says, "You will." "But I have no money," he says, and she answers: "But it's your dog." Then he answers, "The dog is not an outsider. The dog is one of us."*

*Familia* included all the people that worked in and around the house, the hangers-on, everybody. There was just no way for a family in our sense — husband, wife and children all alone — to have privacy. We don't have the old kinds of extended family structure much in America any more except among our poor.

*In my first letter to you a long time ago, I asked whether dialogue might not take the place of eloquence as the objective of a Jesuit education. We need the dialogic person much more than the eloquent person today. Eloquence, today, seems almost a selfish luxury. You wrote that it would take too much in the space of a letter to answer. Can we talk about it now?*

I don't remember your asking me that question but I think that to a degree what you suggest is true. What we are developing now in the Society of Jesus is people who are good at dialogue. Today you have to use dialogue. This is the typical modern approach. On the other hand, I think you can exaggerate the irenic possibilities of dialogue. There is a certain point where you have to put your cards on the table and say, "This is where I stand."

*But that's the point when dialogue truly begins. So long as you hide your cards you're faking or masking or bluffing. All these tactics prevent dialogue from happening. I don't think of dialogue as having irenic possibilities because you can end up enemies. The dialogue in marriage may lead to divorce. The dialogue in the Society may result in an ex-Jesuit.*

162

But dialogue is open. When you contrast dialogue with rhetoric, the rhetorical man doesn't have an open mind. A man who is defending a criminal in court doesn't have an open mind. He maintains his man is innocent, and the prosecutor maintains he's guilty. The rhetorical stance is not an open-minded stance. It is the stance of a person who has taken a position. Now the favored stance today is an open-minded one. However, we have to start from a position, and it is completely fraudulent to maintain that you have an absolutely open mind when you start. But you can have a relatively open mind. The dialogic approach means you don't know where you are coming out. You stand to be modified by the other man; he stands to be modified by you.

*Community life is probably the deepest source of problems for the Society right now. Is this true and is it related to what we are talking about?*

Yes. Yes, it is. It comes about with the younger people. They are the ones who chiefly have the problem. The Society's structures were ordered largely to earlier writing-and-print culture, but our younger people have grown up in a culture that is much more oral. They look more for a kind of warm community. In the older structure there was a great warmth, but it was restrained. Everybody was doing his particular kind of work in a very firm structure of behavior, having meals and common reading at a certain regular time — for we had reading aloud during many of our meals — the litanies and common prayer together. You felt a great sense of community because you knew that there was a personal bond uniting the individual to the superior and in that way to the others through the superior. There were personal relationships among individuals too, but you didn't have the feeling that it was necessary to get the whole community together and talk things out all at once. Now that's the kind of thing that young people come with today. It's the way in the colleges, too.

*But older men, too, complain about the absence of community feeling. By "older" I mean men about forty.*

In my experience, it's uncommon for a man in a higher age bracket — say over sixty-five — to complain in quite that fashion unless he picks it up from the young and recognizes the need for it now.

Forty is about the breaking point, I guess. Those around forty have been caught more than others in change. The forties probably feel it more intensely than the very young do today.

*Some of the forties I've talked with don't even live in the community as I knew it to be.*

The Jesuit tradition in the United States has been far more communitarian than in most other places. Our communities here are generally larger than Jesuit communities in Europe, and our activities used to be much more community-oriented.

There's a curious dialectic in evidence today. Some people who talk about community also talk about "doing your thing," and really don't live in communities. It's very strange. I suspect there may be some compensatory mechanism at work there, as there has been in similar situations in the past.

*Some Jesuits have some married couples as friends. Some find their friends in student groups and some find their friends among the lay professionals they work with. My point is that a community is where one's heart is and their hearts are with their friends.*

I'm sure I exist in a great many communities. I feel close to all sorts of in-groups, besides those in my own classes and student groups. And I trust many feel close to me. But my real home community is the Society of Jesus and the Jesuit

*164*

community at St. Louis University. I draw on it for other communities.

*Whether McLuhan is right or wrong about literacy, the Society of Jesus is indeed in some kind of trouble. There is a shifting of things. Changes are being made and if those changes are troublesome — that's trouble.*

That's right.

*What do you think the trouble comes from?*

I think many troubles in the Society of Jesus and the Church and in the civil order all come from the same thing. Human society is going through a reorientation process because of the technologizing of life. Technology affects not only the physical world but also our mental world. Because of technology, we're overwhelmed with awareness. In our day technologized man knows where all human groups are all over the world. He knows more history than ever before. He is torn by feelings both of unity and diversity in the human family. He has discovered that earlier living structures were rather provincial.

So far as you can say one thing about the changes disturbing the world, that's what you'd have to say. This is something Teilhard de Chardin used to point to. Earlier people didn't know where the rest of the human race was. We do. And once in a while some of them are on the moon.

*When you say "provincial" are you referring to tribal differences?*

No. I mean provincial in the sense of limited. People think of Emerson in Concord and how he was in touch with his past. But he was in contact with only a narrow band of the past. We're in contact with a past of all human beings all over the world, in a depth that was unimaginable before. The Vietnam situation is connected with this. A technologized society like ours can no longer believe that any group of people are complete villains. This was quite easy for Americans to believe in World War I. The Kaiser and the Huns were real villains. Or even World War II, the Japanese. But even in World War II men had difficulty in believing Hitler or Nazism was as bad as it was.

*Or that there was any villainy in our own men.*

That's right. Now this is the problem in Vietnam — one of the many, many problems. The Viet Cong can more easily believe that we are total villains. I suppose many of them really do. Just as we used to believe of those we fought. But they don't have our technology. And this is the kind of tension we're getting. You see everybody in a technologized culture is trying simultaneously to relate to everybody at once.

There's a dialectic in this. Because we live in the large structures provided by technology, by television, for example, we deliberately make structures which are small to complement this. So you will see Jesuits working with little groups.

We're in trouble, but I don't see that the Society of Jesus is in any distinctive kind of trouble. It's the trouble that the human race is in. If Jesuits weren't in this kind of trouble too, then we wouldn't be with it.

I don't want to sound smug about this but because of my work the things that are going on now somehow haven't surprised me too much. I've felt the need to make some adjustments, but a great deal of my adjusting has simply meant to push along on lines I'd already started on.

*What things are "going on now"? Could you specify one or two things?*

Oh, I suppose existentialist thought, personalistic philosophy and intergroup and interpersonal relations, minority revolutions, outsiders becoming insiders. Things like that.

*166*

*Some well-known priests have been leaving the ministry. When this happens, does it affect you?*

Yes, this affects me. It affects everybody. I cannot judge the individual's own motives, but one of the ways it affects me is by knowing the shock this sort of thing inevitably causes and the tremendous hardships it imposes on people in the Church. The more prominent a man is the more that sort of thing ordinarily affects us.

You can't talk about these things much because you have to be charitable and you don't know what individual problems are. When you do know, your knowledge is confidential, not yours to disclose. Consequently there is relatively little public talk in the Church about defections. There is some, but considering the number of them, it's always struck me that the amount of talk is quite limited and often guarded even when it pretends to be "frank." In general I think this is a good thing. One respects an individual's privacy, and especially his privacy before God. But, nevertheless, this kind of thing concerns me because of the blow it is — you have to speak frankly — to the faith of a great many people.

*Maybe they're requiring people to stand on their own faiths, and not on images of strong people.*

Yes. People now do have to stand more on their own feet. They have to interiorize their faith, live in God's presence personally. We should have been doing this all along. So what happens is that people are being put to a test today that they were not put to before. But it's not good to put people to a test just to put them to a test.

*It may not be a scandal. A good jolt may be just what some of them need to settle their convictions. I think they have a chance to become more authentic people.*

167

Yes, but it still shakes them. Jesuits are very inner-directed. We are supposed to stand on our own feet. Examine our own conscience. This is in all Catholic spirituality, but it's been a special mark of Jesuit spirituality. Today we are in an other-directed society. I think Riesman, in *The Lonely Crowd*, had this right. We look to other people and are constantly trying to get support from them. This is one of the problems of all younger people today. But there may not be that much support for you in other people. You just have to face this fact. Just because you want to talk things out, doesn't necessarily mean that you get the kind of support you need.

Younger Jesuits speak much more readily about religion than we did earlier. Probably not more, though, than what was done in the early Society of Jesus. But their support has to come both from the inside and the outside.

Many of the younger people — not all, by any means — find it hard to be alone. But unless you can be alone, you don't have anything to say. This is one of the paradoxes of human existence. You don't know what it feels like to be me. I don't know what it feels like to be you. We are completely isolated from one another, in a sense, but this is the only situation in which communication is possible.

*It is only when you understand what silence is that you know what sound is.*

That's right. Sound emerges from silence. And not vice versa.

*You've been able to get a lot of foundation money for your work. But you still live in the community and take your support from the Society, is that true?*

Of course. And when I'm on a grant I don't live in any high style. I use grants for what they are given for — specified work. Meanwhile I practice poverty like anyone else. Occasionally, I have quite a large income other than grants, and this income I always simply turn in to the community. And that's that. My life isn't materially affected at all by the kind of income I get from, for instance, visiting professorships and lectureships. That's all community money, for our corporate apostolate, for work for others. Your apostolic value, though, is not a matter of how much money comes through your activities.

The only things for which I have to ask superiors for money are ordinary personal needs — clothes, occasionally books, sometimes a supply of offprints of my own articles, medical or dental attention, and so on.

Poverty has to maintain itself in fresh forms, but some religious today are naïve in not recognizing that many practices long standard in their way of life bear quite clearly witness to poverty. I was mentioning to a layman recently our experiments with smaller communities. He asked, "Isn't this some kind of luxury? Living together in sizable groups is a way of living cheaper." The practice of living in large communities at the site of one's work is one quite evident way of practicing poverty or of trying to practice it, though not necessarily the only or the best way. Any businessman is perfectly aware of this. Small communities may be useful. But we should be more aware than perhaps we have been of what our various ways of living have already been saying.

*Do you have a secretary?*

I have a student who works for me part-time. Many religious in the past have had secretaries when their apostolate required it. St. Thomas Aquinas, I know, had one — one who couldn't type though. We use secretaries because we need more technological help. Certain kinds of work can be turned over to individuals who have particular skills. Other work can be done by machines. There will be more and more of this, but I don't see that this creates any really new difficulties in the practice of poverty.

*What do you think of Jesuits working on secular campuses?*

Except for serving as visiting professors I feel that by and large teaching by a priest on a secular campus is not as effective as working in our own institutions. Your presence is minimized. Our institutions tend to maximize it. I've taught on a lot of secular campuses, you know. However, there are many exceptions to this general rule.

*Dan Berrigan says Jesuits go into a school and accept it on its own terms and never think to challenge it. He feels there are times when they ought to challenge those structures.*

He's right. We get lost. You don't amount to that much. One trouble is that a priest permanently on a secular campus may get occluded as a priestly witness — though not if he is a Father Dan Berrigan doing his highly apostolic and highly visible work. It's one thing to be Berg Professor of English at New York University and have your name listed in the catalogue ahead of everybody in the department, to be lionized for one year. Everybody knows you're there as "our Berg Professor." You're the star. (There will be another star next year.) But it's another thing to go into a department, to live there ten or twenty years and maybe lose distinctive witness value as a priest and religious. In a Catholic institution the milieu helps sustain your identity. There can of course be other ways of managing elsewhere.

Faculties of high schools, colleges and universities in the United States are populated by hundreds — perhaps thousands — of Protestant ministers who have left the ministry or are relatively inactive in it. No one even knows that they are or have been Protestant ministers. Ministerial dedication can grow invisible. This happens a little less easily to Catho-

170

lic priests because of the structure of priestly dedication, especially celibacy in the Catholic Church, but it can and does happen.

*When you lecture in secular institutions, do you ever wear a necktie?*

No, unless clerical dress is prohibited by civil law. In circles where I move I am known this way. Other priests and religious may find their cases different.

Some say that a Roman collar distances you from people but my experience has simply not borne this out. After all, it's not a spectacularly different form of men's dress. I've taught as visiting professor at secular and state universities all over the country and abroad, and it is certain that in many cases a Roman collar made it easier for people to relate to me. High definition often adds appeal, and especially today, when costume is often favored over dress.

So I would constantly have to explain why I'm wearing a necktie. And I don't have time to explain why I'm wearing a necktie.

*When I was in the Society there was a hero group, some very brilliant men were destined to become the Jesuit philosophers and theologians. They got the best teachers and got their prime time. Lesser students were given the clear and distinct impression that they were not qualified to philosophize because they were not professionals. One of these very elite students, now an ex-Jesuit priest, told me he had had straight A's from kindergarten to law school and all through the Society. But now at age fifty he feels he wasn't educated. He had learned all the required structures charted by all his schools. Now he's trying to find himself.*

This is very real, I think. That attitude towards the heroes in philosophy was a real problem. It was not due to a defect in the philosophy itself, but to a lack of openness, a somewhat narrow idea of what philosophy was. I think we suffered from that a great deal. The philosophy taught at St. Louis University when I was studying it there was very good. It could have tied in with even more things than it did tie into, but it didn't because many of the people teaching it had a very specialized idea of what philosophy was. Precisely one of the things that it could have tied in with is the thing in your interests that makes you like the work of a psychologist such as Piaget.

I don't think our problems were any greater than those in any other kind of educational system. In many ways less. I hit St. Louis University when St. Louis Thomism rose to its first crest, quite vigorously historical and structurally sensitive in the hands of the good teachers. What I learned studying philosophy at St. Louis University made my work on Ramism possible and has given me a permanent edge over many colleagues around the world. The advantage of the kind of philosophical training we were given was that if you got it, if you studied it, you knew the central intellectual tradition of all Western culture.

But you didn't really know that was what it was unless you knew a lot of things outside of philosophy too. So you had something which was a wonderful, tremendous asset, provided you could open it up. That's just what many people then failed to do. Others succeeded. Today philosophy is beautifully open here, and I think strong at the same time. One of the most brilliant students I've ever had — she was offered around fifty thousand dollars in fellowships upon receiving her B.A. — told me that perhaps her biggest advantage in the Department of English at Harvard over other graduate students was the philosophy and theology she got at St. Louis University. So many graduate students in other fields need to get into philosophy in their work and prove to be complete innocents. They have no firsthand knowledge of central features of their own intellectual traditions.

*What difference do you see between learning and education?*

We use both those words in various senses. When you say "education" you imply involvement with another person. You can say a man is "self-educated," but then you make him into two people — *he* educates *himself*. A self-educated person is his own leader. But when you say "learning" you don't think about another person being there. It's thought of as an activity that originates within the individual.

*I wonder whether education might look into the person and his individual capacity for development, whereas learning has to do with a certain tradition or with systems and abstractions that have to be acquired?*

We do have that distinction too. Education involves a personal relationship, whereas learning is a transaction between you and a body of knowledge, which is a *thing*.

*Learning, therefore, would be more prominent in a print culture, because you do have structures of knowledge collected in books et cetera.*

Right. It would. There is a distinction in French between *l'enseignement* and *l'éducation*. *L'enseignement* is just teaching, instruction. *L'éducation* is the total development of a person.

*Are you satisfied with the Society's own training curriculum as it now is?*

It's undergoing such tremendous change that nobody quite knows where it will come out. You can never be satisfied with any structure of education, because every structure has advantages and disadvantages. As society changes, the disadvantages begin to get greater or lesser and you have to make

*173*

adjustments. There is no perfect way of educating, that's the first thing.

There were many advantages in the way in which we were educated in the Society of Jesus. Everybody had a common store of knowledge, and therefore shared a common background. This was why you didn't need the amount of personal discussion that you have in the Society today. You already knew a lot of things that were in the other people's minds. You could go off with assurance, developing your own intellectual community. Also, remember that the Society saw to it that many of us received advanced degrees in secular schools, too.

The problem with the older system was that for many people it was too closed and too provincial. It wasn't necessarily so, because many people kept an open mind to things outside and were able to develop. The difficulty today is, that with the wide variety of knowledge which Jesuits have to have, the common core is likely to suffer. I think we will have some kind of real problems here regarding the feeling of identity around a core of shared knowledge.

*Jesuit* community *will suffer?*

Yes. I think one of the real reasons for having meetings and discussion groups is the diversity of the knowledge content of our minds. We need this kind of personal unity more than in the past. It's a new way of acquiring a community sense.

*So that the Jesuit image of "I" is changing?*

Yes, it is somewhat.

*If you feel you have a common store of knowledge with other people, isn't that "I" different from the "I" you have when you all have different kinds of knowledge?*

*174*

That's right. There is a sense of "I" and a sense of community in both cases. But the way in which the two are structured into one another is quite different. Let's see if we can spell that out. Earlier, our sense of community was maintained by a certain number of rather formalized activities, which were, however, deeply interiorized by the individuals. That was important. They were interiorized because you did them out of obedience, an obedience which was not merely external but humanized and interiorized in faith. You made the formalized activities yours. I'm referring to things such as an exact daily order, the common refectory reading. These things may not always have been the most appealing in the world, but you were doing them out of obedience and you knew that others were doing the same thing that way too.

*And in silence there was a very taut closeness about it.*

Yes, the silence is important. Although we communicate with words, real understanding lies in the silences in between. So silence, the right kind of silence, is a deeper kind of communication than speaking. Human speech is defective. "The word of the Lord remains forever." This is exactly what the human word does not do. The human word is, of its very nature, evanescent. Silence for us remains. It is something enduring, and consequently, it is in our silence too that our communication is like God's. It is like God's in another way when we speak.

*Also you had one set of rules of behavior. In a context of silence you could see deviations and attitudes toward that rule. Through these you got to know a lot of people and their slightest differences.*

That's right. Extremely well. You knew their personalities. We had stories that were always told about personalities in the earlier days of the community. Such stories are not told so much any more because there isn't a very clear-cut norm against which you can measure the deviations. Now this is not only in the Society of Jesus but in the world at large.

*I saw an article lamenting the loss of the eccentric in England. Do you think the eccentric is on his way out?*

To a degree, yes. Because the eccentric is *in*. Today, you see, you have to be an outsider to be in. So any kind of deviation is standard now.

Until recently our training had firmly external structures which were deeply interiorized in the mature religious. Those firm external structures included the heritage of scholastic philosophy and theology. Given this formalized intellectual heritage, you had a good base for developing later on, provided you could open it up. Of course, as we've said, not everyone succeeded in relating it to things outside itself. Some did. Some didn't.

Today the "I" and the "we" is somewhat different. We didn't use to talk about the "we" very much. Now we talk about it a lot. We talk about community. We try to hold people together less by a formalized structure and more in talking about being together. In primary oral cultures men did not self-consciously talk about being together. They were together because they didn't have any alternative. Today, we talk about being together. We program our social side. We plot our togetherness in our secondary oral culture, the oral culture coming after print.

I think we've really discovered something here in our conversation. The generation problem in the Society of Jesus is felt more intensely than in many other places in human society. The older Jesuits have great difficulty in adapting to this other-directedness. Not all of them, because some understand it and go along with it. But some find it hard.

We're going to have to adjust to other-directedness. Some

Jesuits nostalgically try to detect little drifts back to older patterns, but there's no going back. On the other hand it's a mistake to pretend that we're going to get along just by working things out in discussion groups. You can go so far with this but then somebody has to make the decision.

Earlier Jesuits would not have consented to this kind of interview such as we're having now. We would not have opened up our somewhat private affairs for other people to read in a book. Not that there was anything to be ashamed of. You just felt that some things ought to be kept private.

*Families had more secrets, too.*

Yes. Now everybody discusses everything. So this is not peculiar to the Society of Jesus. The whole Church has opened up this way and so have other institutions in the larger human society. This is the trend toward other-directedness.

*There seems to be little formal concern for* tactus — *regulations governing touch in the novitiate.*

I think there was a great deal of sense in rules regarding *tactus* in the context of our training.

*It just occurs to me that* tactus *and silence work together. Silence without* tactus *could have been wild!*

That's right. *Tactus* and silence work together to isolate the individual. Yes of course. This is interiorization. It threw the individual in on himself. But in the context of a community, interacting.

*This seems to have achieved what sensitivity sessions appear to be striving for. The leaderless sensitivity groups flounder. Have you been to any of these?*

No. I haven't had much urge to, frankly. However, I'm pretty close to this sort of thing and have a pretty good idea of their purpose and how they work. It's super-other-directedness, of course, but, as you say, it doesn't work unless you have someone to program it. Which means that you may have someone operating on other people. Often such leaders are just getting people to verbalize the way they want them to. They almost have to be geniuses to do anything else. There aren't that many geniuses around.

*John Glenn Gray in* The Warriors *discusses how soldiers threatened by death in battle are comrades rather than friends. You don't utterly reveal yourself to a comrade and it's not expected that you do. But you may still die for a comrade. Gray believes it's the strong fear of death that makes the relationship. Remove two comrades from that context of war and they wonder how or why they ever got along together.*

There are some analogies in the Society but there is a difference. One of the problems everywhere today is that with the extended irenic structures in our technological culture it's hard to keep close to the fact of death. Unless you're neurotic. It sounds strange to speak of irenic structures, with all the violence we indulge in and advertise. There's a paradox here. Most other cultures could not tolerate our shows of violence: not enough irenic counteragents.

*When you say "irenic structures" do you mean forces working towards peace?*

I guess irenic is a little less positive than peace. By irenic structures in society, I mean largely the forces suggesting that life can be lived without a great struggle. Except in sports, we deinstitutionalize antagonisms, officially that is. Even amidst violence, cooperation overwhelms us. The coop-

178

eration needed to build one air-conditioned skyscraper, put on one TV network show, run a modern city or university for one day, is virtually incalculable. Not to mention the moonshot.

*Why are they "structures"? Are they attitudes?*

I'll try to spell that out. For example, all academic education used to be polemic, roughly until the romantic movement. A German Jesuit teaching in Xavier High School in New York recently told me joshingly — but he meant it too — "These boys here all want their teacher to be their friend. When I was in school everyone knew that the teacher was your enemy." But he was a purely ceremonial enemy. The same teacher who was your enemy in class could be the man you went to afterwards with your confidences and who was very sympathetic and understanding.

The old *Ratio Studiorum* for Jesuit schools used to encourage competitive learning. It calls this contest method *aemulatio*. The idea wasn't original. The *Ratio* just took what all education all along had been doing. The contest or competition has been identified as typically Jesuit, but it is no more typically Jesuit than using Latin in the schools used to be.

In the *Ratio Studiorum* of the Society it says that the boys are not to be allowed to bring their daggers into the classroom. This shows that the ritualized violence of the classroom not only reflected, but also sublimated the real violence outside of school. Now, today, according to a more recent general trend in education, you shouldn't pit pupils against one another but simply pit them against a standard. We're supposed to take all the personal contest out of learning. Don't let students feel they're competing with each other. That's one aspect. Another is the pupil-teacher relationship I just mentioned. The relationship now is supposed to be one of understanding and there's no real struggle involved in it. Student union negotiations and student arbitration boards are also irenic structures.

These things are good, don't get me wrong. I'm not saying you shouldn't have irenic structures. You should have all that you can. I wouldn't favor going back to the old style of education. On the other hand, despite irenic tactics polemic is also here to stay in one way or another. Every Marxist knows, as every Christian should know, that life is a struggle. There's always a polemic going on at some level. Some people rise to the top in General Motors or in the SDS, and others don't. Life is still competitive, but today we're encouraged not to see the polemic aspects of society.

*And yet they are all around us.*

They are. We don't ritualize polemic — again, except in sports. So it may hurt us more. Our education system today tends to mute polemic in its formal structures. We're Deweyites. So polemic asserts itself informally in demonstrations and confrontations — which themselves are now institutionalized, of course. But unadmittedly.

*All right. I understand "irenic structures" now. Are Jesuit communities breaking up because the men don't feel drawn together by the threats of a hostile world?*

I had begun before to say how the irenic structures in our technologized culture distracted us from feeling we were under the threat of death. Yet all Christians are called to martyrdom and *are* under this kind of threat, really. We should be. We should be ready to die for Christ. But since this seems rather remote today, the feeling of comradeship, not only in the Society of Jesus, but in the Church suffers from an illusion of security.

Comradeship, though, is not all we have in the Society of Jesus. There's also friendship. But the revealing of oneself has been structured strongly to superiors though not exclusively so. Your superior is to be personally interested in you. Of course, so are other individuals, too, but there's a very specially open channel of communication between the individual and his superiors. Here in one's openness is where the love is expressed. This is one way you know there is love among the people who are your companions. They have the same relationship to the total community through the superior.

But there is a great deal of this basic relationship of comradeship. We're all in the same boat. Many difficulties of the Church come from our somewhat falsified irenic structures. Our technological culture is more irenic than any that went before it; just the same, human society isn't really as irenic as we make it out to be.

*Your bibliography as of 1968 lists over half a dozen books and 276 articles. Of course it doesn't mention classes and lectures. How much time of your day goes to work?*

This is almost as bad as a question in the worst questionnaire I have ever received. It asked, "How much time do you spend thinking?"

I don't know how many hours I spend working. A lot of my work is thinking. In actuality, work and play are not entirely separate. Certainly not for me. My work is varied: teaching, counseling, ministerial activity such as hearing confessions or preaching, celebrating Mass — the liturgy, *leit-ourgia*, the work of the people of God — serving as consultor for scholarly foundations and inner-city work. All this as well as writing. I need time for private prayer, so I get up early, and for just being with people. That's not work. My reading is largely work in that it's purposeful, though at times in a random, relaxed way.

*What do you do for fun?*

Besides work? Work can be fun even when it's hard. I practice random recreation, I suppose. An art gallery, theater, or symphony once in a while. Occasionally I go out trout fishing. There's a place about an hour and fifteen minutes from our residence at St. Louis University. I'll go there maybe five or six days a year. Slosh and climb around the stream all day. Flies only. I don't do other systematic exercise like playing tennis. I tend to run upstairs and I guess I use up calories that way. I used to feel guilty about not doing systematic exercise. Being inner-directed I thought somehow I was supposed to. But I got over that. I don't see why you have to. I'm rather against systems, you know.

*Do you enjoy eating?*

I'm always hungry. I suppose I'd get fat if I ate all sorts of stuff. I could eat a lot more than I do. I skimp on fattening foods.

*Dan Berrigan was the first Jesuit I'd known who knew something about making food. He said he'd learned it living in France.*

Marshall McLuhan tells this story on himself. He and his wife frequently had Wyndham Lewis as a dinner guest. One evening Lewis called about an hour before dinner and asked what was going to be served. Ham. And what sort of wine? Marshall mentioned some popular table wine and Lewis said, "Well, I'll come another night."

I don't make an art of cooking, nor an issue of having food prepared this way or that way. Yet I suspect I know something about food from my father. He was from New Orleans. He wasn't a big eater but he was extremely demanding regarding the quality of his food. And variety. Any and all domestic and exotic dishes, arcane even. Mother was less demanding, but perfectly happy to venture anything. My brother Dick and I are completely omnivorous. Dick is like my father. If he sees a menu and there's something there he's

182

never eaten, he gets that. So do I. The only reason I've never eaten rattlesnake meat is that somehow I've never yet had the chance. Dick ate it first chance he got.

*I once tested children with herbs. I found that where children were afraid to try spices that were strange to their culture it was because their fathers were very cautious — meat and potatoes people.*

Overprotected. My father would have regarded that as very vulgar and childish. Meat and potatoes. Extremely timid and very fearful. I mean really. It isn't human. For man, eating demands maturity, the ability to assimilate and enjoy a variety of things. It's a way of learning to like all the different people who prepare and eat these things.

*I believe that a person's attitudes about beginnings, his openness to adventure and novelty and innovation are formed in early childhood and largely through eating.*

Oh, I agree. That was an important part of my training actually. I didn't know it at the time. But I believe it was.

All my life I've been interested in learning processes. This is tied in with an interest in art and doing things that would turn people on. I guess too, I'm a kind of spoiled biologist. I feel very rooted in nature and I am interested in growth processes. Wherever I am I'm constantly noting the terrain, the kinds of trees, the birds. It was that sort of thing — a part of romanticism — that used to be pretty completely absent from Catholic thought generally and from the central philosophical teaching at St. Louis University, although it is included there now very much. My whole intellectual career, from one point of view, has been the establishment of this connection between the romantic process-oriented, nature-loving side of knowledge and the structured side of knowledge. And neither of these seem to me sufficient unto itself. But I guess if I had to choose one, I'd choose nature.

*Did you see English as a field where you could combine both the romantic and structured aspects of knowledge?*

I guess when you shake it all down, I felt it this way. I had majored in Latin as an undergraduate. At one point, although I loved the language and literature very much, as I still do, I simply despaired of ever knowing as much about an ancient poem as I could know about an English poem. You just don't have that amount of information coming to you from it. But for my intellectual life and purchase on present actuality and modern media, I couldn't do without Latin.

*I should have said "language" instead of "English."*

All right. I'd answer yes, here too. I'm interested in language because it's the meeting ground of these two: process and structure. I guess you could put it that way, though I've never put it that way before even to myself. People in English label me philosophical. The people in philosophy seem to feel I'm philosophical but I think some of them tend to resent me because I don't do it the way some of them do. I'm constantly being misclassified. Or I'm asked to classify myself and I don't know how. Some people think I'm an anthropologist or a sociologist or a philosopher or a theologian. Occasionally, a professor of French. In principle, I'm a professor of English, but in my own way. I don't particularly see why a person has to first classify himself and *then* do something. I've been told I teach and practice Onglish.

*I have a feeling now at the end of these interviews that you're lonely.*

That I'm lonely? I don't think I am.

*184*

*There's a certain tone that runs through the tapes that sounds like loneliness. It might be fatigue. I understand you've just given fifty university talks as guest lecturer for Phi Beta Kappa. Or is it that inner-directedness is a lonelier condition than other-directedness?*

Well if it is I don't mind it. No, I really don't think I ordinarily give that impression. In fact most feedback I get tells me the opposite. I have believed that others find me friendly and sociable, at least to a normal degree. I hope I've not been wrong. But I feel that I can support loneliness, with God's help, when it's called for. We all need a little loneliness to be human. And to be Christian. Spiritual life demands isolation as well as community. Our faith is communal, but we are also alone before God, each of us. I suppose I have a lot of inner-directedness, that could be what gives you that impression.

Now you don't want to trust me too much here because I'm talking about myself, and first of all, I've never said this to anybody until you brought it up. But, when you think of it, my inner-directedness might look like loneliness. Writing is terribly lonely, as you know yourself. I'm trying to write a book to be read by thousands — so everybody get out of the room! But I don't feel oppressed with loneliness. If people do think I'm lonely, then I'm not: their concern has cured me.

*Are there areas of your work, say in Ramus or communication, you'd like to see others carry out and extend? Areas you don't have time yourself to do?*

Yes. The whole business of sensory perception is badly neglected in psychology, strangely enough. The implications of sensory perception and the phenomenology of sensory perception need a lot more investigation. Speculative theology, too, could be advanced by such investigation. Our understanding of the Word of God as Word is underdeveloped. And so are other central related doctrines, such as the Trinity and the Incarnation.

I have carried forward some of the leads from my Ramus books myself in *The Presence of the Word*, published in 1967 by Yale. Others, K. G. Hamilton, or Frances Yates in her fascinating book, *The Art of Memory*, have fed leads from the Ramism books into their own original research. Just recently, a French-Swiss institute for research and innovation in education, projected a study in learning aimed at trying to find out why we teach what we do and why we teach it the way we do. This calls for tough research into intellectual history and into shifts in priorities among the senses. All of this connects with my work on Ramism.

It was twelve years ago that my books on Ramus came out. When you publish a book, you think everyone reads it the next day. Mere vanity. Ideas take time to get around. But it's encouraging if at some point others find your ideas useful for their own thinking. Scholarly writers need encouragement. It can be a lonely business.

*What kind of a human being*
*should we let scientists*
*make in their labs?*

# George Shoup, S.J.

*When George Shoup, S.J., finally goes to work in 1975, it will be like stepping out of a Trappist cloister into a furious light-and-sound bombardment of angry, public controversies. He expects that controversy will be an inevitable and continuing part of his career, something he'll have to learn to live with.*

*Fortunately, Shoup, who is thirty-three years old, has intellectual and personal resources for coping with such troubles. He is the Kennedy Foundation's first Medical Ethics Scholar. He is a priest. He has a doctorate in cell biology and is now getting his M.D. from Yale Medical School.*

*This present interview may test Shoup, for he discusses the Pill and abortion, sex education and SIECUS [the Sex Information and Education Council of the United States], cost-benefit attitudes toward life and health, mongoloids and their value to society, the absurdity of keeping some people alive, the selfishness of the American Medical Association, the Catholic funeral racket, kissing nuns and ex-Jesuits.*

*Shoup handled all questions, not always gracefully, but honestly. His answers were personal — Shoup-to-me, not institutional; no looking over his shoulder for censors, no fear. Rich with Philadelphian accents. There's feeling and care in his talk. Sometimes you have to wait while he sorts out his mind, throwing words right and left, and some of his paragraphs are word-jams. It must be because there are so many*

191

*George Shoups — Shoup the doctor, Shoup the political humanist, Shoup the Jesuit priest — all trying to talk at once.*

---

Who's going to live and who's going to die?

Who should be allowed to conceive and give birth to children and who should not?

What kind of human being should we let scientists make in their laboratories?

These are the big moral decisions that will confront the conscience of the next quarter century. The pressure to solve them will come from the population squeeze. The decisions should not be made by scientists alone, nor by lawyers alone, nor moral theologians alone, nor cost accountants alone. They are such complicated decisions that it takes a community of disciplines to handle them. But time is running out. They must be discussed now. They are not being discussed because the medical, moral, and legal professions today can't or don't want to communicate with each other.

So this is what a medical ethicist is: it's somebody trained to deal with both the ethical and biological considerations of life and death. I'm a medical ethicist.

My own special interest is in ethical problems connected with genetics. For example, today it's theoretically possible to keep two people with muscular dystrophy alive to the point where they can reproduce. Now, if two parents abuse and cripple a child, society will take the child away from them. But two people with muscular dystrophy will inevitably reproduce a crippled child. Should they be allowed to reproduce?

I say it would be better if they did not reproduce but I wouldn't forcibly prevent them from reproducing. I wouldn't want a law to stop them. Maybe, although they are handicapped, they see some value in their lives. I may not see it because I haven't got their handicap. Genetically or biologically, I don't like seeing them reproduce. But I don't think I have the right to say that they should not reproduce because I don't like it.

Have you ever seen a Tay-Sachs baby? No. A Tay-Sachs baby looks normal until she's about six months old. She looks much like a beautiful doll. Her skin is generally pale and translucent with a healthy pink color. She has long eyelashes and fine hair and her body measurements are within normal limits. Then sometime between the sixth and twelfth month the symptoms begin to show. She becomes irritable and abnormally startled by noises. Mental and motor deterioration sets in and the child increasingly loses contact with the world. Ultimately, she becomes deaf, blind, and totally paralyzed. Even with the most devoted care, she will seldom live beyond the age of three.

Again, should we prevent two Tay-Sachs carriers from marrying or, if they marry, should we require one to be sterilized? There are people who want such laws now. They're saying everybody should be tested before marriage for certain recessive genes. Also, the language of some proposed abortion laws could be interpreted to apply to such cases. A law like this would be an enormous infringement of personal rights. But in a population squeeze personal sexual rights may have to yield to community rights. That's another kind of medical ethics problem we have to solve.

Today we can diagnose at least fifty inborn errors of metabolism which, when combined through two carriers, cause death in early childhood. The ethical problems are how and why and by whom are defective children aborted or their conception prevented.

The fact that your body carries a certain genetic error is good information to have about yourself before you're married. If you programmed that information about yourself into the dating computer, you might avoid meeting the wrong person, genetically speaking. It's up to you as an individual

*193*

to decide what you're going to do about it. But if they make compulsory genetic testing a law, tomorrow's Romeo and Juliet will be lovers who carry matched chromosomal defects.

Body-part transplanting is a rich problem area for medical ethics. Suppose I have ten patients waiting for a kidney transplant. I only have a couple of kidneys in the hospital. Say one patient is the president of a big corporation and one is the mother of five kids. Who has more value? Who gets the kidneys?

The decision will ultimately be made according to the values of the decision maker and this is what frightens me: that science, or the medical profession, may be the sole determiners of values. I think we need humanist values in there too. We may even have to have some kind of jury system set up in a hospital to decide whether any particular baby should be killed or not in the uterus! As things are today a couple of doctors can decide everything. Suppose a married man wants to be sterilized. Right now it's usually just he and the doctor who decide. What about his wife? What about a psychiatrist? Shouldn't they and others be heard from?

*Were you serious before when you said lab-made man will be an ethical problem in the next twenty-five years?*

Maybe sooner than twenty-five. This is science fiction ethics — genetic surgery and engineering. Theoretically, it's possible to take a cell from my body and grow it up into another complete human being — cell cloning. Given that possibility, will we make *slaves?* Will we make *fighting men* to wage our wars? Medicine could make gigantic advances if it could experiment on living human beings. Think of all the drugs that could be tested. Society prevents such tests now, of course, but if we can produce human beings in the laboratory we could create our own supply of experiment subjects. Is that what we want to do? We breed chickens now for their

*194*

breast meat. Should we breed human beings to be sexual objects or baby-sitters or space pilots?

We've only recently isolated the gene for the first time. A team at Harvard did it. It was brilliant Nobel Prize type of work. Now that the gene is isolated we may be able to correct genetic errors, say by using a laser beam or by letting a virus carry chemicals into the deficient cell. The techniques have to be worked out but eventually we'll be able to correct diseases that come from mixed-up genetic messages such as hemophilia and diabetes.

When the Harvard team that isolated the gene made its announcement to the press, one member of the team said, "We don't have the right to pat ourselves on the back. Some people, under the guise of aiding humanity, may think it's a good idea to phase everybody into the same sort of skin color, eyes, hair type, height and personality. We may have loosed more evil than good on mankind." I think he was overdramatizing, but he makes the case for medical ethics. It's the medical ethicist's job to appreciate what he's doing as a scientist, but at the same time act as watchdog for future man. If the scientific world can project what's going to happen genetically fifteen years from now, theology and law has to think that far ahead too. We know where the problems will be. We should start writing and talking and working on them now or there'll be chaos when they suddenly start falling on us. Fifteen years ago I remember John Thomas said we should be reexamining our ideas on abortion. No one did anything about it. Now the bishops are milling around, bumping into each other because they don't have their answers worked out.

*Do you think medicine is tending to make human beings with fewer differences?*

I think, yes. Now I don't know that that's a conscious thing. It certainly seems to be going on.

*The Kennedy Foundation's announcement says you are expected to "provide a bridge between the disciplines of law, divinity, philosophy and medicine." How were you trained for this kind of service?*

I studied theology and philosophy as a Jesuit. I have my Ph.D. in anatomy from the University of Colorado Medical Center, where I did work in cellular biology. I've had some philosophy of law and will probably get more. Right now, as you know, I'm in the med school at Yale.

*Suppose the scientists accept your medicine but reject your ethics? How can you be sure they won't interpret your concern as a Vatican attempt at supervision and control?*

I'm not a Vatican infiltrator or tool or spy. I don't in fact represent the Vatican or the Catholic Church or the Jesuits, if by these terms you mean a moral system that's stubborn, frozen, and locked up in the natural law. That's the way things used to be but it's not so any more. A lot of scientists' negative attitudes go back to the Vatican's own negative attitudes toward science. These are the sources of some of our communication failures today. I'll just have to show them some things have changed and other things are still changing. In time they'll see I'm trying to be right. I can't do much more than that about other people's prejudices, can I?

*May I quote you as saying that the natural law is dead?*

In part that's what I am saying, at least, the old natural law. Vatican II and Teilhard de Chardin opened things up and gave us a new understanding of Christ's human nature. The psyche sciences came in through the opening and gave us new understandings of man's human nature. Modern communications spread these ideas around to the people.

Our total image of man used to be a collage of superimposed images taken from philosophy, theology and biology. Our philosophy said man was made of body and soul, his body subject to death and decay, his soul immortal. Our theology gave the soul priority and so we addressed ourselves to saving it. Our biology said man's life began with conception in the womb. Man's body had certain specific organs. Their functions determined their nature and prescribed their duties. He had eyes to see, sex organs to procreate with. To use any organ in a way that didn't express its specific function went against the nature of that organ. It was immoral to frustrate nature.

*But man's intellect was also regarded as part of his nature. Wasn't it frustrating nature to ignore or suppress his reasoning if his reason told him there were occasions when he had to frustrate or redirect or circumvent some lesser biological organ?*

Yes, I think you're right. In the case of contraception we often did frustrate the mind in order not to frustrate certain organs. That's what I mean by a narrow, mechanistic interpretation of nature.

I can remember as a little kid my father, who is a urologist, arguing, "We're trying to get this couple to have children. I can't test for fertility without semen. Why can't we get this man to masturbate so I can get an adequate sample?" Now that's an example of the narrow biological way we interpreted natural law then. The specific function of semen was to fertilize the ovum. Today, most moralists would say go ahead. I would certainly say go ahead.

Rome used to squelch everything the Scripture scholars tried to say. Now the scholars are relatively free. Today, moral theologians are going through what our Scripture people were going through thirty years ago, only more so.

Scripture was studied by comparatively few intellectuals. The disputes seldom filtered down to the people. But when you talk about contraception, premarital sex, mortal and venial sin, fertility tests and so on, you're talking about something that concerns the man in the pew. Our old classical moral texts with their neat hierarchy of mortal and venial sins is meaningless to most people today in this personalistic and existentialistic age. Of course, the changes shock the conservatives who like everything to be neatly packaged, but human life can't be categorized that way in tidy vacuum-packed boxes.

*Aren't the behaviorist sciences trying to determine man's nature so they can predict his movements? Isn't this a kind of search for natural law?*

Yes, it is. The behaviorists are using different instruments. They'll deny they're making a strict definition, but in effect people use their findings as if they are definitions.

*I believe an understanding of natural operations is important for the artist and communicator, but it's important to keep our image of nature open for observation and discovery leading to new insights.*

The concept of a natural law is all right if you keep open to changes in nature. Psychology and psychiatry are at the root of the changes in moral theology. They've taught us much about factors that may limit man's freedom. Before psychiatry, man had little understanding of subconscious drives and motivations. Psychiatry has shown we are less free than we thought we were. It's also made more freedom possible since we're capable of knowing ourselves better and hence capable of better self-mastery.

*I caught something you said before I'd like further comment on. Did you say that during a "population squeeze" — were those your words? — personal, individual rights might have to yield to society's right?*

Yes, they might. In Judeo-Christian ethics, the great stress has always been on individual human rights, on personal rights. I think we're coming around now to stress more the rights of society and the obligation the individual has toward society. This has enormous implications, for example, in the population explosion; somehow or other we have to encourage people not to reproduce. Paul Ehrlich, the population biologist, says: "Too many cars, too many factories, too much detergent, too much pesticide, multiplying contrails, inadequate sewage-treatment plants, too little water, too much carbon dioxide — all can be traced easily to too many people."

*Haven't we always stressed the common good and our personal obligations toward it?*

Yes, that's in Judeo-Christian ethics. That's why we formed society — for the common good. That's the basis for putting criminals away. But when dealing with sex, or reproduction, or abortion, we haven't really looked at the obligation the individual has toward society.

*Do you feel free to write and speak about the Pill, abortion and such matters if your opinions don't agree with those of other Jesuits or with bishops?*

Yes, I feel free to speak and write about these things. As I said earlier, I'm not required to represent a fixed, centrally determined Catholic or Jesuit point of view. The whole purpose of speaking or writing about them is to get discussion, to clear the way for action. That's part of my services as a medical ethicist.

*199*

*How do you stand on abortion, then?*

Right now, theologically, I can't see any excuse for abortion. There are undoubtedly many biological and sociological arguments to be heard so I could change radically on that. There are Jesuits who do accept abortion, but it seems to me that we're still dealing with human life. I can't care what life looks like; if it's a human ovum fertilized by a human sperm then biologically it's human to me. You can think of all sorts of hardship cases that plead for abortion, but you can't build law on hardship cases.

*Do you think the State should legislate on abortions or should an abortion decision be left to the individuals concerned?*

I think the State should get out of this abortion business. It is each person's own responsibility. People should be educated, theologically, psychologically and philosophically, so that they know what a responsible judgment would be, but then what they decide to do is up to them. We should not try to legislate morality.

*But doesn't the State have the responsibility to preserve and defend life?*

Yes, it does and we want it to. But we're questioning human life now and we have to consider the *quality* of human life. During the war in Biafra, would it be right to allow an infant to be born only to have it certainly starve? I don't think so. We have some evidence showing that many children raised in institutions later show severe psychic problems traceable to institutional rearing. Is it right to let a child be born if it's inevitably going to grow up in an institution? That's one of the questions we have to discuss.

Paul Ramsey at Princeton finds in Scripture the premise

*200*

that it's through love that the human individual is made. So, Ramsey says, love and reproduction go together and can't be separated. He sees a problem with artificial insemination in that reproduction is separated from love. He argues parents don't love their child merely because he exists. They love him because he's a product of their love. Now, also, if I clone a cell of my own body and produce another child I'm separating reproduction and love.

*Would Ramsey also say that the child reproduced after rape could be aborted?*

I presume he would. Technically, the Catholic Church has already approved of abortion in rape cases. We were always supposed to get rape victims to a hospital within three hours for a D&C. Why the deadline of three hours? There was no scientific basis for saying there hadn't been a fertilization within that time. And, by the way, the Church also officially approved the use of the Pill in the Congo when nuns were being raped. They did so on the principle of unjust aggression. It's a simple argument then: once you allow something, it can be allowed.

*What has to happen to make you change your mind about abortion?*

First of all, I want more discussion of what a person is. A person is more than just a group of living cells. This is why we need more humanists to get involved in this argument, more philosophers. I don't think we can just leave it up to medical or scientific personnel. If we argue for abortion on genetic grounds as the scientist would, I think this is dangerous. We're in great difficulties. But again, they are the only ones who are making the decisions. We certainly need more people asking, *what is a person?* That question has to be rethought entirely.

*201*

*A humanist, you feel, encompasses a variety of disciplines?*

Right. Doctors have humanistic feelings and inclinations. They appreciate music, art and literature, but they don't know how to apply these tendencies to practical problems. Often physicians don't seem to see their patients as full human beings. They'll refer to "this heart case" or "liver case." He's not a case. He's a whole man, a full human being who happens to have a sick heart or a bad liver. We're now being taught that the more we know about a person, the better the medical service we can give him. Where does he come from? What's his background? What are his fears, his other problems? This all ties in with psychosomatic medicine. You can push most of this information to the background while you're treating a patient, but it has to be there influencing you. For example, you can't let yourself get angry with a patient just because he's angry with you. His anger may help you understand some important fear that's disturbing him and affecting his health. Good doctors have always done this in the past. But I think the fact that it's now being taught in medical schools is part of the revolution being brought in by the young.

*You said before that some of the proposed abortion laws contained language that could be applied to genetics.*

I forget what I said but I think we have to watch abortion laws so that decisions regarding abortion don't later harmfully inhibit other work in genetics. The abortion laws today will be the establishment's law tomorrow. Do we have the right to determine the life values of the generations that will follow ours? Don't we today reject many values established yesterday? There is such turmoil over the value, meaning and dignity of human life at the present time, why do we want to freeze any particular value judgments now by making them laws?

*Last January, a group of women representing women's liberation interrupted a Senate hearing on the Pill. They resented men convening to make decisions that would control the lives of females. How do you feel about their demands?*

I'm strongly in favor of women being involved wherever they want to be involved. It would be my understatement of the year to say we certainly need their help in dealing with problems of reproduction. I could see why the Pentagon might refuse to seat women at tactical staff meetings, but maybe this is what the Pentagon needs. I just simply can't understand why women weren't part of the Pill hearings in the first place.

*Are you and Ned Cassem the only Jesuits in medicine?*

No, there's a growing Jesuit interest in psychiatry. Ned's in psychiatry, you know, and there's James Gill who works with adolescents in Boston. Angelo D'Agostino's in private psychiatric practice in Washington, D.C., and teaches at Georgetown. Lou Padovano entered the Society as an obstetrician and gynecologist and is in residency now at Columbia-Presbyterian in New York. There's Art Reilly, and there are a number of men in the Middle West and the West Coast. I think medicine definitely is a direction for the Society in the future.

*When you work in a hospital, do you identify yourself as a priest?*

You mean by wearing a cassock or Roman collar? Some men do and some don't. Here at Yale I don't wear a collar, but I identify myself as a priest on many occasions.

*Do you believe that's important?*

Yes, I do, for my own identity's sake and as a witness of Christ among others.

*Did you find your priesthood a handicap in graduate school?*
*What did the grad students think of your professional celi-*
*bacy?*

They started not trusting me. One reaction was that I had
to be odd in one way or another. They certainly can't understand celibacy. Then they were always trying to match me
up with somebody. Like at parties they were always trying to
get me to dance, or they'd want me to play bridge and there'd
always be a single girl at the table. After a while, it became
a joke and they quit. Then they argued that someone with
my education and genetic background ought to reproduce.
I'd say, "At least I'm not helping the population explode.
We need more celibates in the world, more nuns and more
priests!"

Lots of science research people, especially the older ones,
see they could probably have done better as celibates. I know
some who certainly love their lab more than their wives.
These are enormously dedicated people. The way they work
is fantastic. They'll think nothing of setting up a cot and
running an experiment continuously for three or four days
and nights in a row, getting up every four hours during the
night to check on something. The family vacation might be
attending a convention. The time away from home, the problems and tensions drive a lot of them up on the rocks. Their
divorce rate is very high and there's also a high rate of alcoholism. In one of the hospital labs, a technician told me that
I and another person were the only men in the department
she hadn't slept with. That meant fifteen or twenty men!

*Maybe she was putting you on, George. She might have just*
*said that to shock you.*

I don't think so. I found her attitude pretty common.
There's a lot of tense feelings in research labs.

*Have you definitely ruled out marriage for yourself?*

I'm for optional celibacy for the diocesan clergy. I know that I myself cannot be a diocesan priest. I'd go insane without the Society. And that means celibacy for me. In other words, if a Jesuit wants to be a priest and also to be married, then he can be a secular priest. That's my opinion. Others disagree with me. They think that you can have married religious communities. To my mind that's far out. For me religious life means celibate community life, not a commune. The Society is a religious order. The vows have, with the possible exception of poverty, deep meaning for me. I may omit poverty because I'm not sure I really know what it means in today's world — nor am I really sure anyone does.

I think it's important for priests not to be isolated from women. It's important for them as it is for all men to be comfortable in the presence of women. Women are half the human race — more than half. If I've met a woman several times and feel I know her, I always kiss her hello and good-bye. It's something we do in our family. There's one nun I've met, a sincere religious, I guess she's several years younger than I am. She gave up school this past summer and volunteered instead to take care of a nun who mentally was almost a vegetable. Anyway, I saw her a couple of times this summer and each time greeted her with a kiss. But the other day there was a conference for contemplative nuns at Woodstock. She happened to be attending with a group of other nuns. When I went to kiss her hello, she stopped me and said, "Oh, I just prefer shaking hands."

*Might it have meant something different to her?*

Well, I don't know. I think the meeting was more public for her. I also realize some people are brought up differently.

All sorts of people get upset about priests marrying nuns. You hear our guys say that the last person in the world they'd want to get married to is a nun. A lot of it's half joking, of course. But basically, you have two idealistic and dedicated people. They're naturally attracted to each other. It makes a lot of sense.

*You were very definite about not wanting to be a diocesan priest. Why is that?*

I couldn't be a diocesan priest because I need a mob of people around. I like community life. I do enjoy that. So there is a structure to my life. I can always come back to where I'm living and can find solace there. I admit it's different from the married person's solace. But a lot of guys who've left to get married don't realize that married people can be just as lonely as we sometimes think we are.

A man may feel lonely in a community because he isn't fun to be with. He feels rejected because he *is* rejected. I sometimes feel a little guilty about this, because you do tend to stay with the people you know best. That's a human thing. But then where does charity begin? I find a tension here myself. There are some people you don't want to go out to dinner with come hell or high water. If you go out to dinner you'll ask those you were out to dinner with last week, too. You can always excuse yourself by saying I've worked hard all day and I want to relax and not make the effort to be kind toward someone you don't particularly like.

I know and I keep in touch with many ex-Jesuits. I think a big, big problem with many was loneliness. I don't think some are going to be any happier outside than they were in. Some of the men felt lonely because nobody seemed to care what they were doing. But I didn't see a lot of giving on the side of those leaving. They didn't seem to care what others were doing either.

*Ned Cassem, the Jesuit psychiatrist we mentioned earlier, teaches classes of graduate nurses how to create a context in*

*which suffering man can die a dignified death. Cassem be-*
*lieves that general hospitals and terminal-care homes neglect*
*their responsibility in this sad matter.*

I'm in one hundred percent agreement with Ned. He can
make a very important contribution to medicine here. What
Ned's saying stems basically from a theologic or philosophical position. This is where the priest-doctor differs from the
doctor. Doctors are trained to save life at all times, at all
cost. And they'll try to do it. They're good this way. But
sometimes this is unfortunate. For example, they'll keep
somebody alive on machines long past the point when duty
and common sense tells them death would be more honorable
and dignified. As far as I'm concerned we ought to turn off
these machines. I'm not advocating euthanasia but I cannot
see taking "extraordinary means" to preserve the life of an
old, old sick weary person: cardiac massage, for example, on
an eighty-five-year-old man, or even I.V. feedings in some
terminal cases.

In moral theology we say you're not obliged to take extraordinary means to preserve life. It means great expense,
a rare, serious operation, the use of very special equipment,
the kidney machine, for example. But the sooner we can get
rid of that term, the better because Catholics and doctors are
hung up on it. The term changes meaning. Thirty years ago,
an appendectomy was considered major surgery. Even I have
a six-inch incision scar from when I was six years old. But
you can hardly see the scar from the incision they make today.

*They go through your navel with a buttonhook now!*

A mongoloid boy was born at Johns Hopkins about five
years ago. One of the frequent complications in mongoloid
children is pyloric stenosis for which abdominal surgery is
rather routinely performed. There is a high mortality rate

from operations on mongoloids but loss of life is usually due to cardiac defects and this kid didn't have any. So it was a simple operation. His parents didn't want him. They consulted their priest who said, "No, you're not obliged to take extraordinary means to prolong his life. He's going to be a mongoloid. It might be better to let him die." The professor of pediatrics, Dr. Robert Cooke, went to the courts and the courts couldn't interfere. He then wrote to the cardinal and someone in the cardinal's office sent back a snotty note saying that he was interfering in a purely Catholic matter. The hospital managed to keep the child alive for two weeks. Dr. Cooke told me it was heartbreaking. He got to the stage where he wouldn't go to see the baby any more. He had the residents report to him. He told me, "Here I am training my residents to preserve life and the Catholic system won't let me do it."

I can understand the feelings of parents not wanting a mongoloid child, but in this case I believe the doctors were right in trying to keep him alive. I may change on this, but I believe a defective child, say a mongoloid, does have value to his family and society.

*Don't you expect too much of people when you expect them to suffer defective children for the sake of society? If it's good to have mongoloids, why not also polios? And if disease is good, why try to prevent it?*

I'm not saying it's good to have mongoloids. I'm saying that since we actually do have them, they are human beings and hence valuable to society.

I'm against the cost-benefit approach in deciding who's a valuable member of society and who isn't. People ask, "How much is he worth?" — I'm against that kind of question. They're deciding worth by how much money he has. This value attitude is unconsciously at work in the way our society regards problems of the aged, the derelicts, and dropouts, the physically handicapped. Human life itself is a value to be treasured. All sorts of money is being spent on heart and kidney transplants to the neglect of care for the aged and the mentally retarded, because some people believe the aged and mentally retarded are economically less beneficial to society. Transplants are better business. If you transplant a heart into a forty-five-year-old man, he can continue being productive. He's a labor asset. He even has sales and promotional value for the medical profession. The expense of saving his life, in other words, will be paid back. Since I don't think scientists alone should have the power of deciding who's to live and who's to die, I also don't think economists alone should have that power. We should try to alleviate suffering but in the Judeo-Christian point of view suffering has value. Also, we believe life itself is worthwhile, everybody's life, not just the strong, the rich and the young.

*In New York, the 1969 AMA Convention was disrupted by some young doctors who accused the convention of smug and callous attitudes toward the poor. One sign deriding the Hippocratic oath went, "Hipp-Hipp-Hipp-o-Krit." What did you think of all that?*

I'm certainly on the side of those kids because they drew public attention to problems that need exposure. The medical profession needs this kind of pressure put on it because its patterns have to be broken.

One of the professors in public health told a class that one of his proudest achievements is that before coming back to Yale to teach he practiced pediatrics for fifteen years without ever joining the AMA. The place went crazy with applause. The AMA's image today is bad. It deserves it and should do something about it. You'll find few organizations with as many fine men as members. But their corporate image is disastrous. Their neglect of the poor in this country is atrocious. Literally atrocious.

Medicare and Medicaid are basically good pieces of legislation. There have been abuses and red tape problems but that doesn't mean the laws aren't basically good. Yet the AMA fought these laws to the bitter end. AMA is overly concerned about maintaining the prestige of doctors. It shows a lack of concern regarding innovative, efficient and modern means of improving health delivery services, especially to the poor.

Nurses are highly skilled but not permitted to function according to their ability and training. Much of the doctor's time is taken up with things a nurse could do, and much of the nurse's work could be done by aides. Maybe the doctor does things with more sophistication. A lot of doctors are afraid to let their nurses do more because they don't want to lose control of medicine.

I think there is presently a great hope in the medical schools. Yale, for example, is deeply involved in studying methods to improve health delivery services, new approaches to community medicine, public health and holistic medicine. I see radical changes coming up when these classes now get out into practice. A lot of people are skeptical. They say, "They'll start running for money just like everybody else." But I can't believe that some of these reform attitudes they show here won't last. Some of it has to stick.

The doctors are avoiding some really horrible situations in our society and are bringing up all kinds of excuses for doing nothing about them. Probably some of their defenses are correct, but the fact that we're tenth in the world in infant mortality is hard to defend or forget. The infant mortality rate was 12.8 per thousand births in white suburban Detroit. In the inner city it jumped to a 60.3 infant mortality for every thousand births. Our national average is now 29.6. But it's either Sweden or Switzerland — I always forget which — that has 11.3 per thousand, the lowest in the world.

A big, freakish thing that happens in this country is this

"crib" death thing (doctors object to the term), sudden, unexpected and unexplained death. A child is put to bed at night. He's perfectly healthy. When his parents wake up in the morning he's dead. This may happen anytime during the first six or seven months.

One theory is that they get an upper respiratory infection which sends their temperature skyrocketing and kills them since there's no one there to cool them off right away. They go into acute respiratory distress and die.

My brother has four boys. The youngest one was running a bit of a temperature at dinner time. My brother Paul and Kate were supposed to go out that night to some meeting, but Kate decided to stay home. Paul went to the meeting alone. The baby's temperature just kept climbing. Kate was wrapping him in cold towels to bring his temperature down. Just as Paul walked in the baby stopped breathing and turned blue, just like that. Kate yelled and Paul came running upstairs and began mouth to mouth resuscitation. He didn't know much about how to do it. He remembered reading about it. The man next door was a naval officer. He came in and took over. They rushed the baby to the hospital and at 2:00 A.M. he was released. His temperature was down and there were no side effects at all.

*How many crib deaths a year in the U.S.A.?*

Estimated: 15,000 to 30,000. In France, they account for twenty percent of all infant deaths.

*Cassem says that the more intense a patient's suffering, the more difficult it is for the patient to distinguish between his need for physical relief and his need for human spiritual comfort.*

I agree with that. Jimmy Mallon, S.J., who spent much of his time as a hospital chaplain, only called on patients after dark, because that's when people wanted to talk. They were alone then. We're so afraid of being alone. It shows by the noise level of our society. Kids can't get into a car without turning the radio on. We're afraid to face ourselves, I think. I can see this in the Society too. There are Jesuits who are just running, running, running all the time, getting out of our houses.

*Why don't priests go into the funeral business? I don't mean as a business but as a Christian service. It seems very natural that priests should manage the entire funeral. This is a very, very sacred and important time, not only for the person dying but for his family with him.*

I can see what you mean. Right. Too many priests look on a funeral as "another job." There is too little expression of what death means — a unique human and religious moment. The new liturgy is a big help here but there is little effort spent on explaining the meaning of the new liturgy for funerals. If it's anything, Christianity has to be a religion of hope, a religion founded in the Resurrection and taking its very meaning from the Resurrection. Does the average Christian ever hear anything about the Resurrection except on Easter? The usual sermon is on sin, financial reports, charity drives, Catholic newspaper drives, birth control, et cetera, none of which even comes close to the heart of Christianity.

*Graham Greene has a short story about a boy who's told if he masturbates three more times he'll certainly die. As the story ends, the boy is heard in his room saying a fervent Act of Contrition. The story has pathos and humor but it's about cruelty toward children.*

Oh, I agree with that. There's all the difference in the world between innocence and ignorance. There's just no excuse hiding information from kids. I don't care what they ask, if they ask a question about sex I try to answer it.

*Jesuits operate about fifty high schools in the U.S. with a total enrollment of about forty thousand boys. If you were responsible for the sex education program in these schools, what would you teach about masturbation, homosexuality, virginity, premarital sexual experiences?*

In each of these matters I'd teach all known scientific facts and problems. I'd explain the psychology involved. Sex isn't everything in life and neither are the Sixth and Ninth the only two Commandments. I'd try to get them to see the value of virginity and human love and marriage. They ought to recognize and understand sexuality within the context of their full personalities. I'd also explain abortion, contraception and menstruation to them. And I'd explain the need for population control.

A Dominican nun teaching sophomores in New Haven asked her classes what they'd like to discuss in religion. She expected interest in sex, but was amazed at the number who wanted to talk about contraception, abortion and premarital sex. She called and asked if I thought it appropriate to discuss them. I said, yes, of course discuss them. They probably know something about these things already or they wouldn't have brought it up. Accurate information drives out misinformation.

In high school classes for girls, I would describe all the available contraceptive devices: namely, the Pill, condoms, diaphragms, spermacidal jellies, I.U.D.s or intrauterine devices — "the rings, the coils and the springs," as they say in med school. I'd point out the advantages and disadvantages of each, the modes of operation where known, and then what moral issues are involved. Once a person has honestly ruled out selfishness and still finds a true need for contraception, then, to my mind, the moral issue is resolved. The only moral issue I myself see in using the Pill has to do with its possible — I emphasize possible — side effects. There's still some evidence that points to the I.U.D. as causing abortion. The egg gets fertilized but cannot implant. The so-called morning-after pill also seems to operate by causing abortion. An abortion machine is not a contraceptive.

SIECUS, the Sex Information and Education Council of the United States, is a controversial organization because it's misunderstood. Some people get angry with it, but I think their fear is falsely founded. They're afraid that sex education will lead to promiscuity. We've used their materials at Woodstock. I've read most of their booklets and think it's a good service. I think it's most important not to flinch at hard discussion of these topics. If we avoid them the kids will stop believing us.

At Misericordia Hospital in Philadelphia, a nun doing her residency discovered that female Negroes working at the hospital were scared to death of male doctors and particularly white male doctors. She offered to run a Pap test for cervical cancer and was amazed at the response: 125 to 130 women came in. Four immediately had to be operated on. All of the women who had the test had never ever been examined before. I think the Pap test ought to be explained in high school. At least by early college, girls ought to get into the habit of having regular checks every year. I think girls in high school ought to be shown how to feel for abnormal growths in their breasts and instructed what to do when they're found. They shouldn't just sit around and wait for trouble to happen. The same is true for convents. I've asked any number of nuns if they've ever had a Pap test. They say, "Oh, my God, no!" I guess they think it would be immoral.

I wonder how priests and nuns handle marriage courses if they themselves need sex instruction. There's an absolute need for sex education in convents and seminaries. No one can freely choose celibate life without knowing his or her sexual drives and needs and the meaning of deep personal human love. Many nuns and priests are ignorant of basic biological facts. In too many convents menstruation and its possible side effects such as pain and depression are ignored, never mentioned even to friends or superiors, as if it doesn't exist. I could go on forever on this point and my voice tends to get shrill I get so mad. I think it's cruel and very wrong to impose suffering on nuns and priests by keeping them ignorant or afraid of their personal sexuality. Of course, as sex education becomes established in high school and in the grades and as parents themselves learn to explain sexuality at home where it's really best handled, there'll be less need for sex education in convents and seminaries. What they need there now is remedial sex education.

*Do you ever feel that being a Jesuit may handicap you as a doctor?*

Not at all. It slowed up my studies in medicine for a while. I had asked to go to medical school in 1962, and the provincial then said no and sent me to graduate school instead. He didn't see any need for Jesuits being doctors. That was seven years ago, but even for then I think it was narrow. It was Edward Sponga, our next provincial, who brought the whole subject up to me on his first Visit. It's an example of what a brilliant provincial and administrator he was. He didn't call us in alphabetical order and he didn't have any notes in front of him. I had to introduce myself, of course, since he didn't know who I was. But at one point of our talk he asked was I still interested in medicine? It meant he had read through my file. I said, yes. He said, "Well, let's see if we can't get something worked out." He asked me if I was interested in psychiatry. I said I wasn't. I started talking about medical ethics and he saw right off the necessity of getting people involved in this field.

215

*How did you feel when Father Sponga left the Society?*

Enormously depressed. We lost a great leader. I felt very much like I felt when Jack Kennedy was assassinated. I felt lost and didn't know where to turn. I was at Woodstock, it was during the summer, and there were very few of us around. We sort of clung together. You don't want to see lay people at a time like that.

He left on a Thursday night. All the personnel at the provincial's residence were out at Woodstock on Friday to a funeral, and they didn't get his letter until they got back at two in the afternoon. Then they called an emergency session of the consultors in a motel, Holiday Inn, in downtown Baltimore. They thought it might be forgery, somebody playing a joke. They finally called his mother and found she'd received a letter too. They felt it had to be true then. It was announced to us about ten — a sign went up on Saturday morning. I just couldn't believe it. If I read that sign once I read it twenty times that one day.

*You said before you didn't want lay people around when you first heard the news.*

I didn't think lay people could understand. I can see why many of our guys left but can't always explain it to other people. It's very difficult for the parents. In many cases it was best that they left, but parents can't see that.

*How do you feel about Sponga now?*

At the time we all felt he had let us down. Now, I guess, I wish he had done it differently. He could have resigned as provincial first, and then got out. It's sort of a hang-up I have with law. I don't mind priests getting married. I like to see them be able to get married validly though.

216

*Is the Society accommodating itself to all the changes going on in the world?*

Today, yes. There's no doubt about it today. If you'd asked me that question as recently as five years ago I would have hesitated because I wasn't so sure then. Today anyone can do just about whatever he wants. Of course, if it's far out, he talks it over with some people first. There's a lot more freedom and we need freedom, we need the elasticity to adapt.

PHOTO BY GEORGE H

*I'm thinking of writing an article
for* Playboy *on the vows.*

**Paul J. Weber, S.J.**

*Paul J. Weber, S.J., was ordained a priest on June 4, 1969, at the age of thirty-two. He is important to hear because he is a middle-of-the-road Jesuit. He illustrates how far leftward the road has cut since Vatican II. A middle-road Jesuit twenty years ago was usually not as candid and free, nor did he show as much warmth.*

I wouldn't doubt that Weber was the "most elected man of the year" in any school he's ever attended. In the novitiate, he was manuductor, in the juniorate and philosophate he was beadle. He was elected by all the scholastics to represent them on the Missouri Province Board of Consultors. At St. Louis University, the student congress elected him to represent them on the Graduate Studies Board. It's not surprising that Weber's university work is in political science. Some scholastics and young priests say he is being groomed to be a superior. If they're right, we can conjecture what the future Society will be like by watching Weber's decision making.

Weber sat in on part of my talk with Ted Cunningham. He heard Cunningham call the Society "racist" and listened to him belittle Northhouse, a ghetto house where Weber was working. Weber told me later, "When I played team basketball or football, the one thing I couldn't afford was to let somebody get me mad. If I got mad, I'd stop thinking, and if I stopped thinking then the plays couldn't work."

I'm not as close to the ex-Jesuits as I feel I ought to be, but I do have a couple of very close friends with whom I correspond. When I go to New York I stay with them. But I have strong negative feelings about men who formed boy-girl friendships while they were in the Society and left it to get married.

I think the friendships that a man has while he's a Jesuit have to be integral to his life. In other words, if you promise you're going to lead a celibate life, don't cheat. Now, I have some very close friends among women, among Sisters, students and so on, but I hope that they're always honest and where they're not honest I try to make them honest or stop.

If a guy decides he can't lead a life of celibacy and leaves, OK, *then* he should find himself a wife. It would really bother me if I fell in love with a girl, left to marry her, and five years later realized that I still wanted to be a Jesuit. That would be terribly unjust. I just couldn't put a woman through that no matter how much I loved her.

I don't really buy this self-fulfillment through love bit either. It's like I'm going to fall in love, then find somebody to fall in love with. It just doesn't happen that way.

*An ex-Jesuit told me: "Once I saw that I could fall in love, then I was open to fall in love." He went out and did it.*

I can fall in love. Hell, I've been in love in the past, you know. I'm sure I will be again. I'm certainly open to it. I just hope that the loves that I have are honest loves, love in which I'm not cheating on my present commitment or deluding them in someway. I'd always be very careful about that. Like in counseling, you can get yourself all hung up on girls if you want, but it's not necessary.

*Do you have a good image of marriage? I don't mean of other people's marriages, I mean for yourself?*

Oh, yes. I was almost engaged before I entered the Society. But, well, it's just one of the prices you pay.

I come from a terrific family. Six boys. Two girls. This is probably one reason I feel I can leave it. Obviously my folks fought — the whole family is quick-tempered. I mean I know what it is. But it was a beautiful marriage, and though I've given it up I don't fear marriage.

I'm thinking of writing an article for *Playboy* on the vows. I doubt they'll want it but I may try. I'd like to describe the vows as a type of protest against the materialism of our age in which our advertising milieu says "consume, consume, consume, consume." For me to consume and respond to every need I'm told I have is a degrading and antihuman thing. I don't want to become what manufacturers and advertisers want me to become. I want to be myself. By my vow of poverty I'm saying, "No. I'll consume what I need. I don't want a lot of created needs." As for the vow of chastity, I'm reacting against sex without commitment because raw sex isn't what gives full human happiness. Love and commitment give a person happiness. Chastity opposes the exploitation of sexuality. My obedience is a protest against everybody doing his own thing. I don't want to just do my own thing. I want to do it as part of a community. We make joint decisions and do something together.

*What does your family think of all the changes going on now in the Church?*

I came into the Society from Cascade, Iowa. Around home I associated with farm people a lot. Changes don't shake them. It's an all-Catholic area. We had eleven girls in my eighth-grade graduating class and five of them joined a convent. Sharp girls. Dated a lot and that sort of thing. They're still in, fighting for changes. My folks like the changes, think they're terrific, not threatened by them. They have a faith that smells of the earth. It's a beautiful thing. They love jokes. They drink their liquor and they go to Church. They're good people.

*223*

*They were German, I guess from your name? Were they farmers?*

German with a lot of Irish. My great-grandparents came over as farmers. We started out very poor. But my dad worked hard, bought his own automobile business before the war and worked his way up. He made some money during World War II — baling hay. He had a hay-baler.

I worked on construction for two summers after high school. I did idiot work. After high school I went to Notre Dame because of the football. I majored in commerce. Couldn't stand it.

Then for one summer I sold cars, new cars and used ones. I sold cars because I thought I was going to go into my dad's business. I don't mind selling things but I hate forcing them down people's throats, and often that's what selling automobiles really is. A man would come in with a wife and two kids. The kids need shoes and he wants a car. He wants a hot car. If you don't sell it to him someone else is going to. You want to tell this guy, "Look, buy your kids some shoes." Which I did sometimes, and he'd go and buy his hot car from someone else. He's not about to listen to you. He doesn't listen to his wife. And he wouldn't listen to a doctor either.

The whole experience just made me feel I could do something more worthwhile in life. I couldn't see any purpose in it out there.

*I've seen the young Jesuits are a lot freer in their feelings toward women and also toward other Jesuits. The attitudes are more personal and natural.*

This is true. I have a lot of very deep friendships in the Society. If I withdraw from these friends, it's because I've become wary. You become close friends in the philosophate, then you go on to teach in different places, one guy goes to Korea, one goes to Omaha, one guy goes to Campion, and so on, and you don't see them for three years. This hurts. So the temptation is to say, "Well, I just won't get that close to people the next time." But I think that's cheating. You have to love one another enough, that's part of the friendship, pain is part of it too. You have to be willing to give out, to belong and be with, and also to be away from, to miss each other.

Voltaire once said something which impressed me very deeply, both in its distorted understanding of the Jesuits in his time and the danger it warns us of today. He said that the Jesuits are men who come together without knowing each other, who live together without loving each other, and who die without mourning each other.

I meditated a long time about that. Really, because loving and getting to know a person is painful and dangerous. Like this ex-Jesuit friend in Japan now. He's building an atomic energy thing over there. He's an engineer. I don't think I cried when he left the Society, but I probably would now because now I'm a lot freer with my emotions than I was then. It pained very deeply. We'd been through a lot together. He wouldn't respond to letters. It really hurt him too to leave the Society. He had to cut things off.

That happens everytime somebody leaves. Each time it's a little harder to get back to work. It's even harder to wake up and get out of bed the next day. What do *you* feel like when your brother dies? You don't want to do anything, you know. I remember sometimes as novices when somebody left it was a kind of insult. Somebody no longer believed in what we still believed in. There's more to friendship than that.

*I always hated the surprise of hearing someone was gone. When I left I went around and I told people I was going.*

I do too. Nowadays, it's pretty much a communal decision. They talk to people. I think it's a much better way of leaving.

*We were whisked out as soon as the release papers came in from Rome.*

At night or during prayers or sometime like that.

*Where do you expect to work after theology?*

I'm very much interested in the Church in a violent society. All through the Mass we talk about "give us peace," "peace be with you," "give us peace in our times." We've got to go beyond the prayer type of thing and get down to how we're going to operate in a political situation. I'm interested in practical politics. How you get things done. I look at the Church as an organization. As a political scientist, I prescind from dogma.

However we handle the population problem, we'll soon have to handle the problem of people being crowded together. When people are crowded together you have situations which bring violence. A lot of violence is caused by fear.

By trying to solve the problem of violence, we have to solve other problems that are both racial and ecumenical. Once people of different faiths learn to work together at problem solving there's time enough to solve the theoretical differences.

Violence cuts across racial differences because it hurts everybody. Whites are guilty of commercial, political and institutional violence; blacks cause riots. Blacks are sought for crimes on the street, but the most serious crime is white, organized crime which infects our political power structures; the Mafia is a far more vicious threat to our culture than street muggings.

All right, what can the Church do about violence? Look at the advantages of the Church. One of its strong points is its organization. Very few organizations in our world can talk to as many people as the Church can — not just the Catholic Church, but the Protestant and Jewish too. It can muster a lot of votes, so it can talk to the government. It itself is a gigantic consumer and can speak to millions of members who are consumers. So it has some clout with business.

What is the strongest white presence in the ghetto outside of the government? It happens to be the Catholic Church. That presence isn't measured by the number of people who come on Sunday. It's much more measured by the people in trouble who call you first, who need some help and know that this is where they're going to get it. When the black people want to pray, many will go to their Baptist or spiritualist church. But when they want help they'll come to the Catholics.

*Their churches are not service churches?*

They're much more preaching churches. Now, I don't think Catholics give enough service. We don't know how to serve without being patronizing and paternalistic. But we can learn.

Here is an area in which we can use the leadership of the bishops, because it's a kind of nonthreatening area. That's why I want to use this approach. I think we need authority in the Church. But I don't think the bishops know how to give good, authoritative leadership. If we get into this area which doesn't have a lot of hang-ups right now, perhaps we can begin to exercise leadership in a good way.

*Can the Society's organization be used the same way as the Church's?*

I don't like the word "using" — I'm not using. I'm *operating through*. The Society has a couple of advantages. First of all, we're relatively independent of the bishops. We're free to move around and talk and write without getting a lot of flak. Another advantage is the support we can get from the Jesuit community. I get a great deal of support, I get both intellectual stimulation and the friendships I need to do my work. The Society keeps me human. It's my family. It checks me from doing nutty things, from going way off.

I have very conservative tendencies. It's a help just being in a community where there's such a fantastic diversity of interests and personalities. You'll see what I mean when you meet Ken Feit who's coming in later. We think quite differently on a lot of things, but he keeps coming up with ideas I haven't thought of. It's men like that who keep me alive.

I don't consider myself a liberal, and I'm not a conservative. I'm a classicist. A classicist is one who sees the value in his own roots, and in the Society's roots and traditions in the past, and accepts those that are valid, and yet who likes improvements, who likes to change what's bad, to experiment. I'm a fence hanger, in some ways. I like alleged improvements to be spelled out so that we have a clear idea of everything that's going to be involved in a new idea or a new kind of work.

I'm not trying to radicalize people. What do I mean by radicalize? Let's talk about it in some terms of resistance of one form or another to the establishment or the system. You have to have an establishment or system before you can have a radical opposition to it. An atheist has to have theists so he can see what he's not believing in.

I'm very much more interested in seeing what the establishment can do, and how it can be used and manipulated for good ends — not the people in it, but the establishment, the way of operations. For example, resistance groups are not going to overcome the problem of poverty or violence in this country merely by biting at the heels of the establishment. Resistance groups are necessary to keep the establishment thinking and moving and feeling the pain of being bitten, but ultimately, it is the establishment that's got to move, that has the resources to solve these problems. That's where I feel my role is: helping it move by interpreting the bites of the frustrated, angry and disappointed radicals.

People like us have got to keep the pressure on the government, on ourselves, on business, on wherever the power is. In the racial thing, we've got to pressure the poor and the blacks to keep coming to school, keep getting educated and keep getting jobs. Now turning on this day-by-day pressure is not something that grabs headlines, but it has to be done.

It's not the "in" thing now to work among the blacks, because on the surface we're not always that welcome in the ghettos. But whether we're welcome or not, if we can do a job there for the people, not in a paternalistic way, but in a very real way, we go on.

*Successful organizations don't run on superstars but on a collection of average guys who work together. Is this true of the Society of Jesus?*

I think this is probably true. There has to be a man in every organization who can do a good, solid job you can depend on day after day after day, who isn't afraid of creative ideas and creative people, but who, first of all, can make the ideas work and can organize people so that they can work together in such a way as to bring out the best in each individual person. I back away from using the word "stable" to describe this quality because it suggests other people are unstable and that's not necessarily true. I don't particularly want to be called a great stabilizer, but it takes just that to make an organization work.

*As a young, middle-of-the-road American Jesuit, one who understands and appreciates both the radical Jesuits and the Old Fathers, where do you think the Society of Jesus is going?*

I'm troubled by the future of the Society. A lot depends on whether we lose our nerve, whether we keep thinking it's something worth fighting for, living for. I don't know how most people are going to go on that. So I have a certain amount of fear. But when I look at the number of men we have who are just tremendous people and who are young and highly intelligent, I just can't see how — if we keep our *esprit de corps* — we're going to fail.

At the same time, Jesuit survival is not going to depend just on Jesuits. We're going to have to be relevant. I think this is a much more important consideration. We're going to have to keep looking outward to see how we can work with and help people outside. If we don't do that, we'll die.

PHOTO BY DON DOLL

PHOTO BY GEORGE RI

*The Society of Jesus
should make a public apology
for being racist.*

# Theodore
# Cunningham, S.J.

*I've never been called a "nigger"
in the Society.*

# Barthelemy A.
# Rousseve, S.J.

*Ted Cunningham is a forty-two-year-old black Jesuit. He entered the Society in 1952 and was ordained eleven years later. Cunningham's talk is quiet, easy, smiling talk, organized in well-developed paragraphs. The warm, musical sounds and the flashing, crinkly-eyed smile are dangerous for they may lull you into feeling that God's in His heaven and all's well in Cunningham's world. But, in fact, quietly, smiling and rational, Cunningham ought to be shocking the hell out of you. He is telling you that American Jesuits and all white Christians everywhere are deeply rooted racists.*

*Some of his views are institutional black caucus platform views. The extent of his love for whites, it sometimes appears, is limited to not wanting them murdered. We worry, listening to gentle Ted Cunningham: if this is what's going on in the mind of a Jesuit priest, what are the ghettos thinking?*

*Bart Rousseve is from New Orleans. He followed his older brother, Numa, into the Society of Jesus in 1959 at Grand Cateau, Louisiana. He was nineteen years old then. Numa left the order after ten years and is now married and living in New York. Rousseve has his M.A. in English from Washington University in St. Louis, and is now studying theology at Boston Theological Institute.*

*Rousseve and Cunningham have never met. Their only communication has been on paper where each has had a chance to comment on the other's transcribed interview. Rousseve reenforces many of Cunningham's feelings about racism. But Rousseve is younger and he's from a southern town culture. He thinks these two facts may explain why he and Cunningham differ.*

*Cunningham asks: "Can a Jesuit think black?" Rousseve answers: "Shouldn't he be thinking human?"*

*The quotation over Bart Rousseve's name illustrates the subtle, but hurtful spiral of black-white relations toward mutual respect. Rousseve explains ruefully that in the Society Italians may be called "dagos" or "wops," Poles may be "polacks," Germans "krauts," but blacks are never "niggers." He longs for the day when blacks can get their insults like everybody else.*

---

TED CUNNINGHAM. A reality that first struck me when I walked on the streets day after day as a teen-ager during World War II was that I never saw an Uncle Sam who had a brown hand and a brown face. He was always white and pointing at me saying, "We Want You!" I began to analyze the things that I thought America was, and I didn't see myself represented as America.

I began reflecting upon my grade school and high school, what it had taught me America was, not showing me anything that was black in Uncle Sam, or showing an image of the black person that wasn't what I considered myself to be, or an image of a black person's success which I knew I could go way beyond.

*Were you a good student?*

TC: Fairly. Mainly B.

236

TC: **No.** I went through the public school system in Omaha. I was out of school for a year between high school graduation and college. In that year I became a convert. We had a kind of Oxford Movement going on at Creighton and Omaha University. Most of us — twenty of us in the two colleges were not Catholic. But by a year or two after college, two-thirds of the group had entered the Roman Church, through good intellectual fist fights, not from the persuasion of any one person, not any one book that we had read.

I wanted to become some kind of instructor or priest. I graduated from Creighton University in 1951 with my A.B. in philosophy. My parents didn't favor it, but I entered the Society and became a Jesuit novice the following year. Because of the philosophy I'd had, I was able to cut a year in the juniorate and a year in the philosophate.

I'm at Creighton University now, teaching Afro-American art and culture. In two semesters I try to develop what black culture is, who its creators and movers are . . . some of the social problems that sociologists are unable to see, how they are hindered by their scientific tools from reaching black-culture, aesthetical problems, philosophy : what man is.

We use music and show its history as seen by three or four different writers. We listen to jazz, we see its development, we hear the artists talking, we read about them, we have films on them. What influences the musician? What's he trying to say?

I'm using *Blues People* by LeRoi Jones. It requires a re-evaluation and rewriting of some of the history they know and that I was taught. I'm using DuBois's *The World and Africa* to present another understanding of Africa, not simply as a land partitioned by Europe but seeing the rise of capitalism as very dependent upon slavery and ivory and exploitation of the African continent.

I spend a lot of time on communication. We discuss symbols and symbol clusters, speech and sign languages. We see that black people who've been in certain cities, say like Dayton, Ohio, a long while, have a distinct culture that's evident in the symbols and symbol clusters they use to communicate with each other. Their symbols are different from those of the white community in the same city.

I was in Africa in the summer of '69. I was mainly interested in how they were teaching African history and African literature. At Dar es Salam in the university, I talked to a fellow who will be chairman of the department of literature next year. Going through the syllabus, he showed me four courses in Shakespeare were being taught, but no courses with black writers, either Afro-American or African. So you see a neglect of reading their own writers, of teaching children their own writers, teaching children familiar things in a familiar background. Instead of that they were going to the damp, cloudy atmosphere of England and making their children memorize Shakespeare.

Last year the university offered me a new job, special assistant to the president. Instead of teaching, I'd direct and develop a black studies program across the board in the curriculum. How could I ever begin a survey in black philosophy when one man in the department says only St. Thomas is to be taught and that there was no possibility of teaching DuBois? Who will teach this kind of curriculum? Once the teachers were brought in, would they be accepted by the institution? There are both laymen as well as Jesuits here who are so far out of it that they'd accuse us of teaching heresy or something. I might give it a try for a year or so. But I don't want to take a job that's simply going to try to correct all the mistakes that were made because they didn't get the right advice in the first place.

When I entered the Society I wasn't thinking of civil rights as something that would concern me as a Jesuit. I wasn't really thinking of operating in that area. It wasn't until I got to theology that I really got to see I should be involved and saw that the Society could be involved too. I shouldn't say I wasn't at all involved in civil rights before then. I was a member of the chapter of CORE in St. Louis, got kicked off a few field buses, sat in at the White Castles, the Admiral. But I wasn't asking the provincial to get on a bus and go down South. I see guys doing it now. I saw individual Jesuits getting involved, like Markoe and Twomey. But an institution isn't involved until it spends some money, and it doesn't think of itself as involved until it does spend some money.

*Do you find racism present in the Society of Jesus to the extent that it hinders your work?*

TC: A large institution, such as the Society of Jesus, is so much a part of the American scene and of American institutions, that it can't help but breathe in racism. It's in the air. If it's institutional racism we're talking about, then it certainly has to hinder my work because it's there and always has been there. I wouldn't think of staying in the order or leaving it because of civil rights matters. If I leave it will be because of personal matters. But after a while you can't separate the two.

*Black studies help create black identity. You are a black Jesuit. Which is most important to you — your blackness or your Jesuit-ness?*

TC: When it's a matter of deciding between whether I do something as a Jesuit or do it as a black man, the Jesuits lose out. If the two ever come into conflict — "Who dies, mother or child?" — I haven't been in this kind of conflict yet, but if the Society forces me into it, any decision I make would favor the black cause. I would see that that would be the Christian thing to do and that the Society wasn't really a Christian organization.

Can a Jesuit think black? We had our second black priest

*239*

caucus just on this one point. We had a sensitivity session lasting two and a half days to try to figure out whether the priests attending this conference could think black.

BART ROUSSEVE: What does "thinking black" mean? For me, I am black, it means having shared the *experience* of an oppressive system, of being cut out and isolated because of one thing about me which is only part of me, my skin color. That's not "thinking," it goes deeper, a lot deeper.

The inability to "think black" means not being able to sense, in someway, what this experience means to those who've had it. If a man can't think black he's dead, and whether he died because he was killed or because he refused to take hold of life does not matter. We've got plenty of living dead in this country, people who turn off to each other, to themselves and to God — that is being dead. And there're both white and Negro dead — the skin only covers an identical death.

Hopefully, Jesus' dying and rising again has made it possible for a man to think human. A priest, after the model of Jesus, works at being "all things to all men," and essentially at being himself, since that self is *freed.*

TC: The ability to think black means that I can go into a white institution and come out thinking as a white person might think, but at the same time continue to think black. It's this ability to feel and think and sense as a black person that will allow me to be effective in a black community.

Can the Society of Jesus be the kind of institution that will let a black-thinking man enter and come out still wanting to think black? Or must it try to convert him into what they are calling today a "Negro," someone who has been white-washed, unwilling and unable to think black, but who exists and thinks along the lines graphed by the present institutions in America.

As a Jesuit "Negro," he is now valuable as "our man" in white middle-class America. He may be a good mathemati-

240

cian, a good sociologist or good chemist. But he is no longer valuable to black people, and no longer able or willing to think black. The "Negro" Jesuit can't be a good chemist or sociologist or mathematician in a black area helping black people. The "Negro" Jesuit is crippled so far as work with blacks is concerned. The "Negro" Jesuit is only able to work among and with white people.

*But suppose that in working with white people he's then better able to interpret the problems of the black?*

TC: Yes. Okay. But what I'm saying is then he's no longer able to think black. I'm not saying he cannot be an effective worker, I'm saying *where* he can be effective.

I can explain what I mean by "thinking black" this way: I worked on the French Revolution for my master's thesis in history. I did an analysis of a single crowd scene as described by five different witnesses. One scene was reported by a continental writer, who selected facts and details that would interest a person living on the continent. A second account was the same crowd scene with the facts altered slightly as selected and interpreted and understood by Republicans living in France at that time. The scene changes a third way when interpreted by a Royalist, and changes a fourth way when reported by a Royalist who had escaped and was living in England. The same day, the same building, the same people involved or maybe other people now highlighted and some of the original people dropped out, this is the fifth scene as told by historians in the Cambridge School.

All we are talking about is what? An editorial policy. When I say "thinking black" that is what I am saying: thinking black is an editorial policy. When I think black I select and highlight and understand and interpret things from a black's point of view.

BR: Every man does have a viewpoint. And this becomes a hobble when a man cannot see that his is only a viewpoint and not the whole picture. Then that man is imprisoned and dying. Unfortunately, the system of education in this country, by its methods and content, works against developing a broader view, stifles creativity, and generally cramps the human spirit. In school we should "produce"; "learning" means "teacher or textbook says — students repeat."

TC: When I editorialize, I write my report to favor the institution I'm working for and the one that holds my money. Living as we do in America, we can't help but write history to favor the capitalistic system and we do this without even knowing we're being capitalistic. It's simply the way everything is, the way we look at it. It's what we grew up in. We don't look at it as a possible step towards another political system that could evolve and be lived by other men, say, two hundred years from now. We think this one is working and it's always going to work. Our form of government is good and it's always going to be good.

A person who thinks black thinks about facts that will alter present conditions towards a better black condition. That's what I mean by thinking black.

So when I talk about thinking black I'm not just talking about people who are colored, but about someone who is thinking: "What can I do to change institutions that are subjugating black people?"

Now this certainly does not exclude the white who understands institutions, whose heart is in the black movement, and who perhaps realizes he can't be a leader in the black movement but has to be content to give an idea here and there, and has to help find people to be black leaders in the area.

BR: What's so all-fired hot about being a leader? One of the institutions to be changed is that the only worthy place for me is telling them — whoever they are — what to do, where to go from here, et cetera.

TC: But when a community begins to say who will and who won't live in it, what ideas it will accept and what ideas it will not accept, it's going to be very difficult to talk with this community if you're not the right color.

*Don't you just have to look at it in the way, well, as mission-ers once had to: wait and hope that by service gradually you'll be accepted. You don't give up.*

TC: What I'm saying, however, is that the white mission-ers in the past have accepted their own institution and this very institution is now being criticized at a level which can really shake it down to a very few men perhaps. If the Chris-tian Church wants to correct itself, I'm not really sure what's going to be left of it. That's really what I am saying. I don't think the Church wants any kind of radical change in Chris-tian institutions that's going to shake it in this way.

*You don't feel that the Church wants to radicalize itself by becoming Christian?*

TC: I think a missionary would be willing to go out and teach and preach and baptize and never really talk about the house he came from, whether they are Christians or not. He will accept, work with, and try to achieve goodness for the people he is baptizing. Back home, he's looked upon as the missionary sent to the pagans, the fools, or as white priests are called in Omaha, the "nigger Jesuits" because they live at Markoe House: "They're missionaries to the niggers, while we carry on an intelligent institution called the Uni-versity."

Now until the house or institution back there that sends the missionaries out wants a radical change, I don't think a sign of Christ is going to be seen in the world. I don't know if these institutions are really Christian. They are institutions and they are ongoing, "good," feasible institutions, but I think we're going to have to begin Christianizing them. Maybe the youth in the country or maybe the black people are going to force this radical change in the Church.

BR: One of the fundamental mental frames of the missionary in the West conceives of people to whom they were sent as cultural defectives, that is, as incapable of receiving the Good News until they have been "educated," until they have accepted the homeland's values. Thus, the Aztecs were savages, while as a matter of fact they had a far more sophisticated and refined culture then did their "deliverers." Similarly, in some parts of Africa, in this century and in China, et cetera.

Missionaries too often care so little about their people that they don't learn their language, much less try to understand how they think — *why* they think that way being out of the question. When Jesus was asked whether true worship would be in the temple at Jerusalem or in Samaria, he answered that men will "worship in spirit and in truth."

TC: The Church is caught up in an identity crisis in this matter. The Church and the Society of Jesus, too, should make a public apology for being racist institutions. They could make clear that their racist actions come from being in a racist situation. Their confession would not only be a great service, but it would give them a chance to act as Christians.

BR: I really don't care whether they apologize or not. But Church and Jesuit institutions and individuals, if they are honest about believing Jesus, must begin *now* to change themselves first (there's plenty of resistance here) and then institutions so that the Papal Social Doctrine, all seventy years of it, gets off the paper and onto the streets and, especially into the hearts of men and women.

TC: At our time in history, in these United States, the black is now coming of age psychologically. He has had a crippled self-image and is correcting that. Growing out of this new psychological maturity is a consciousness and a vocabulary which gives voice to a black thinking.

He's like a person who has just been hired, say, by NBC and is told, "This is the way you pronounce this word and this is the way you think about this word." And the black now goes home and he eats and sleeps with his new words and his new ideas and his new thinking. It's the way he, and friends that he wants to influence and bring along, now want to think. And so black thinking is the creation, really, of a new power system.

Economists recognize that there has to be some coming together, some systemized way of gathering strength, from which to be able to bargain. The black doesn't have it now, neither psychologically, economically or politically. But as blacks develop this habit of mind, this thinking black, they'll come together and so form a basis for arbitration with the white power structure.

I think this is the way *some* people are thinking and the way they see it going. But I can't say that every black man on the street thinks this way or even understands the movement.

BR: If you want to know how the black man on the street feels about the movement, ask him whether he likes Carl Stokes as mayor of Cleveland. Like most "men on the street," he is not interested in thinking about "the movement"; what he wants is results.

*You can't discuss black thinking without black language because no one thinks without language. So a man's ability to talk black is evidence that he can think black. But if he talks only black he's in a ghetto. If a Jesuit can learn to talk white without losing his ability to talk black, isn't he going to be of service to both black and white communities?*

*245*

TC: If we both want to accept him, yes.

BR: What's so important about acceptance? The important question is what kind of services can such a "bilingual," "bi-cultural" man offer. What is the implication of your being of service?

*You can't control your own acceptance anyplace.*

TC: Now that's another thing you always have to ask. I can't say that if he can think black he's going to be accepted, if he's also a priest and also a Jesuit.

I can't say what the blacks will need five years from now, or want and accept.

*Has the priesthood helped you get to your own black people?*

TC: I don't know if people who aren't Catholic know about the priesthood. The priesthood can't really be a sign of Christ to people who don't know who you are, what you are and what you do. The neighborhood wants to know where your wife and kids are. They're just curious. I can't really say we're bringing Christ to the neighborhood. That's the way Jesuits would look at it, not the way the neighborhood sizes it up.

*Nor can you predict that if he is neither a priest nor a Jesuit. As a human being he may not be accepted by a community.*

[*Paul Weber, S.J., whose interview appears earlier, has been sitting in on the dialogue for some minutes now, smoking a pipe, listening. He takes the pipe out of his mouth.*]

PAUL WEBER: That brings up a real good point. I sometimes feel that we at Northhouse have been too well accepted by the community in which we're living. They don't want us to pretend that we're black or any of that stuff. They just want us to be ourselves. Most of the kids we work with are just coming into the middle class. Many, not all, have brothers and fathers employed. They're very interested in getting ahead, and they very much accept us and what we are. Maybe we have a real role here, whereas the street corner guy is leading a subculture of the unemployed. We can't get to this subculture.

We don't get negative feedback about our work at Northhouse or Sophia House. We get some from a few black militants, but in general, even they like what we're doing though they may not like us personally. Okay. So, when you talk about the black community, maybe there's a great section of the black community that *will* accept our presence and our services.

*Some of what you call "thinking black" strikes me as racism. The White Citizen's Council thinks white this same way.*

PW: I think the point you bring up is an important one. I get extremely frustrated very quickly when people tell me I'm racist and can't point out why I'm racist.

BR: An up-tight reaction is often proof enough for some people — and they write you off. Why does not such an accusation ever appear to you as an invitation to show yourself a Christian? Why do you feel that the accuser must show cause?

This sometimes is just what black people call "rapping." It's just this thing. You must look beyond a tremendous amount of obscenity and vulgarity that goes into it. But it's really saying, can you accept me even though I talk like this? Even though I give you a hard time, can you still deal with me? If you can't deal with me when I give you a hard time, you're not worth dealing with.

That's the way black people treat each other on the corner. This is how we do in the ghetto all the time. You curse the person's parents and you tell him about his clothes, you talk about his family, and his sisters, and his brothers, and his shoes, everything. All this is saying, "What kind of man are you, eh? What are you? Come on, let's see. Let's have a little verbal sword play." Of course, not everybody does this. This is soul people I'm talking about.

*The way Ted used the word racism is not the way we're used to using the word. We've been calling Eastland and Strom Thurmond and Bilbo racists — we know we're not Bilbos or Eastlands.*

TC: Some of us are not.

BR: But are your attitudes fundamentally different? Your actions are, of course, but you're in a different culture, too.

TC: Recently a black militant said, "The government pays our senator for not growing anything on his property. Is the government also subsidizing the worker who would work on the property if it grew things? It is not." Then he calls the government racist . . .

BR: Because the government directly assists a system which is openly racist. Unintentionally? That's no excuse.

*I resent being called a racist. Racism is a thing of the heart and mind and I don't find it in myself. I don't call anyone nigger and I don't think that way. You're talking about institutional racism or corporate racism.*

TC: I think, however, this is what the Kerner Commission's Report is trying to point out. If racism exists, where does it exist? What are these institutions that continue to initiate

248

and carry on very true racism, maybe not in their primary policies, but in their secondary policies.

BR: If you participate in that institution uncritically, you participate in its racism, since you are part of that corporate entity. You are thinking of racism of commission. What about racism of omission — not less of an evil, I assure you.

TC: The stamp of "good American" is being given to these institutions. Even being an "equal opportunity employer," even that tag doesn't say that a corporation is not racist. They'll hang a big sign out front saying, "Our door is open to everyone." They mean this. They have people in the personnel department whose job it is to carry out this top office policy. Yet, in the summer of 1964, three industries in St. Louis asked me to find them comptrollers with three years' experience. They said, "Our doors are open to everyone." These are racist policies. There is no such thing as a black comptroller in the St. Louis area with three years' experience or a bookkeeper with four years' experience.

BR: This kind of stuff is a time bomb these companies are putting in their own boiler rooms.

PW: What you're saying is, "Where are you going to get the three years' experience?"

TC: That's right.

*The "equal opportunity" policy is deliberately racist?*

BR: Deliberate or unconscious, the effects are the same. People are generally uncritical. If A, B, and C do a thing one way, D goes ahead and does it the same way. As long as profits roll in, satisfaction. How many people really examine the long-term costs of present policy?

*249*

TC: It can be used by someone who doesn't want to employ Negroes. It can be used by an honest person too, who doesn't understand how racist this policy is.

BR: Take a look at established education. We have been growing mediocrity, and now the harvest — Nixon, Agnew, Carswell, Hicks, Westmoreland, and on and on . . .

TC: We have to understand that many people in Washington are from the South. They know how to write things to keep black people out. The equal opportunity policies look good until you see a company no more integrated in '66 than it was in '60, no more in '69 than it was in '66, and this company is still stamped as an equal opportunity employer.

PW: I was down at the police department seeing a sergeant down there. "Look at all these jobs available," he said, going through page after page of the help-wanted ads. "Why don't these people work?"
Where are you going to get the experience to take up any of them except the maintenance jobs? There's no way they can get in. Every ad says "experience needed." Or if it does say "no experience needed," it's for a car salesman and it's going to be out in Ladue. Who's going to buy a used car from a black salesman out in Ladue or University City?

TC: Nixon says his welfare policy "will help a man who wants to help himself and is willing to work." Then you hear that the sign of his "willingness to work is that he has been employed." But the person who has been employed is usually the blue-collar white person, not the blue-collar black person.

BR: What will this do for the Appalachian? Tell me that and then we will talk about blacks.

TC: What about the people who have never been employed? Secretary Finch of Health, Education and Welfare was unable to answer this. He was initiating a racist policy.

BR: Much of the present administration's "forward-looking" policy will draw a zero or worse when examined closely. I am frightened because the people want just this.

*You don't think Jesuit inner-city projects like Northhouse and Sophia House are important? If you had the choice of continuing or dropping them what would you do?*

TC: The choice has to come from the neighborhoods that the houses are in.

*And that's going to be determined by how practical they are?*

TC: I'm not sure how the neighborhood will make its choice. I don't think these houses are established to solve a national problem. Nor are they established to solve the problems of the Catholic Church, or the Society of Jesus. If you talk about the Society of Jesus and its black Jesuit novices or its national policy or its investment policies, I think you are talking about a much greater problem. Northhouse or Sophia House involves only a few men working with black students in the city.

BR: "Inner-city projects" without pressure on suburbia where most Jesuit students and alumni are living and without pressure on city hall is gradualism today and tomorrow and tomorrow.

*Ted, can I assume that you as a Christian priest are opposed to violent tactics?*

TC: As used by whom?

*Anyone, I suppose. Students against the university, black/white violence is what we should discuss now.*

TC: When we talk about violence, frequently we neglect to consider psychic violence. Therefore we have difficulty recognizing that shows on TV or the movie screen or even the car-

*251*

toons in the papers are violent. We can't see that the philosophy of a particular person heard in a classroom is violence. We can't see that the prejudice engendered by a society or the prejudice and belittling of human value of a person of color is not violence. I think these things are forms of violence in that they destroy people.

We have to look at the whole person when we think about violence, not only at blood being spilled, but also the psychic energy being spilled, the manhood being spilled, the womanhood being spilled, the child not developing and therefore being spilled, and in this context I think we live in a very violent society. But the press tells us certain things are violent and we focus in on those things and forget about other things that are also violent.

We would be very un-American, that is, unlike any American that we meet up and down the street, if we said that as Americans we do not agree that violence should be used by us to check violence. We do this all the time. This is an American characteristic of the American personality.

In our first black clergy meeting, we agreed to a principle of responsible violence, meaning that life, not property has priority. So in the kind of action that I would look towards in a new revolution, or a revolution that is ongoing, would respect this principle: that no one on my side is killed and no one on the other side is killed. Nor should killing be intended. But to bring the oppressor to the bargaining table something is needed. Therefore property goes up. This would be like department stores going up in flames, blackouts being caused in the city, telephone companies going out of business for a few days — this kind of thing. This is responsible violence.

BR: Talk like this of revolution is a bit naïve and certainly premature. When people discover what has been perpetrated on them they will demand change, or make it. But only when — if ever — they discover the truth.

*If people were in a department store and it were bombed, can you be sure that no one would be hurt?*

BR: This is really a useless question. Posing a hypothetically real situation does not really challenge a principle. And my principle is life and its increase.

TC: No one on my side. No one on the other side. It's kind of universal when you say either side. The intention is not to kill anyone. It would be against property.

*But in a department store? All right — if you bombed it at night.*

TC: It's not so much the matter of bombing a department store. It's to call attention to the act. It's a threat. So a fire would be more likely than a bombing. Something where you could control the situation and it could be seen as being done by someone who purposely does this. For example, five fires simultaneously, so the simultaneity and the five-ness, rather than, say, destroying a whole store. It's not that. It's to say that, this is being caused. Now do you want to bargain or don't you want to bargain?

BR: I don't believe in violence ever. But suppressed, oppressed, or a postponed anger is a terrible quick force.

*New York City is extremely sensitive to black anti-Semitism. I bring this up speaking of psychic violence. Jewish liberals feel especially hurt because they helped the black movement get started.*

BR: Did you know too there are black Jews in Harlem? Anti-Semitism hits them too. The New Testament is not without its diatribes against the Jews. Must we follow and act this way, too? A Jew is a man; I am a man.

*253*

TC: I think the reason for it is obvious. The main business street in a black neighborhood will usually be eighty percent or more in the hands of people who are not black. Many are Jews. The resentment against Jews builds up from childhood whether you have been mistreated by them or not.

BR: Any white man working in the ghetto, even if Irish or Prussian, is a Jew — read "money-grabber."

*Ghettos in Boston, I understand, are dominated by the Irish, those in New Orleans by Italians. Why isn't there a similar anti-Irish, or anti-Italian feeling on the part of the blacks?*

TC: Perhaps in those cities there is.

BR: There is. There are Jews in New Orleans, too. Just walk down Dryades Street. There *is* an anti-Italian feeling in New Orleans. "Dagoes" is the label. But Italians are not quite the same as the groups referred to as "the Jews."

*But the news is how blacks pick on the Jews.*

TC: I think that's the press's fault, the press highlighting one aspect of the situation.

*TV and the press give a distorted picture of the black movement. What am I to think of a movement that's led by heroes like Martin Luther King, mystics like Malcolm X, bad mouths like Stokely Carmichael and Rap Brown, high spenders like Adam Clayton Powell and the sensational Black Panthers?*

BR: The only way you're going to understand "the black movement" is to see it as a wide spectrum in which no one group stands isolated from the rest. The spectrum ranges from the Black Panthers to the Muslims and Malcolm X and SNCC, CORE, the Urban League and the NAACP. The

254

southern black movement differs from the northern movement. The rural movement is different from the big-city movement.

Malcolm X gives us the best example of the radical underlying unity in the black movement. Malcolm became the best among the Black Muslims, a saint, and like many saints, a heretic. He stands alone because of his deep respect for thought, and his personal integrity, his dedication to a vision, because he remained, right to the end, one of us.

Martin Luther King is a revered figure, but no one has been nor will be "the supreme leader" of the movement. It is true that black people suffer from a common oppression wherever they are and in this sense share a common bond which unites them all in soul, but Selma demands from soul something different than Chicago.

The Panthers grew out of an environment which lacked even the fragmented sense of identity from which Malcolm X grew. Chicago is a long way from Oakland however you cut it and from Montgomery and Atlanta too. Guns are big in Oakland because of what Oakland is — a physically violent place. Ask Hell's Angels, they come out of Oakland.

But Oakland is us and so are the Panthers. What the Panthers did is to take for the blacks the fundamental American right to the gun. For some very complex reasons, which I do not completely understand, this is "a threat to national security." Maybe it is because they feel black people won't keep "their cool" while carrying the gun. Or maybe that they may also hear the drumbeat that echoes "darkest" (Hollywood) Africa.

The Muslims and the Panthers and Malcolm X come out of the people on the streets. The Urban League and the NAACP are basically middle-class establishment organizations. Roy Wilkins and Whitney Young work within the establishment but their work is relatively uninteresting so far as the black people are concerned because it's undramatic and they are so far from it.

CORE and SNCC are closer to the people because they work with the people. The Urban League's major successes are in industry but these successes seem to have benefited relatively few people. The NAACP's major successes are in the court and these have reached a lot of people.

The Muslims actively created an identity for black people in Chicago and New York. They brought in Africa. And maybe this is more important than the work of the NAACP in the courts. It's at least as important as that, because it created a popular front. Stokely Carmichael, one of the founders of SNCC, came out of Harlem, and Muslim was big for him. It wasn't all, but it was big. He became active in the voting drives in the South which followed in the wake of the school decisions. Those things created consciousness.

The Muslims and Malcolm X have receded and the Panthers are big now because they're the most important for the young black people. The young people take the work of the NAACP as *done*. They don't identify with it because they had very little part in it. It's done on a different level than theirs, one that requires professionals. The work is tedious, intellectual and impersonal. That's why it's downgraded. Roy Wilkins and Whitney Young don't appear to personally suffer. But I know Wilkins does, and Young does, and those people in the NAACP and the Urban League really have to work and suffer. NAACP raised expectations but this was mainly in the South. It wasn't in the urban centers, and this is where the Panthers came from.

*Can you interpret or explain the Black Panthers' violent behavior in the courts?*

BR: While I was down in New Orleans a man was put on trial for killing his wife. Both were black. He strangled her. A white man who had killed his wife would have been guilty of a capital crime. But in the eyes of the court the life of the black isn't worth anything, so this man got five years on manslaughter and then a suspended sentence. A black life isn't really protected by the law because it's not considered important enough. And this is why the Panthers act up in court, I think. They show complete disrespect because this is what the law has meant to them.

They refuse to accept the solemnity of the common-law judicial system. This atmosphere oppresses the soul within them. Its apparent inexorable logic they expose as a sham. Julius Hoffman's emotions under the stress of Bobby Seale and the Chicago 7 have manifested openly what black people knew all along.

The Panthers don't want to be absorbed into that sham world. This is also why the NAACP and the Urban League are downgraded right now. Because they work within the system and the system is the enemy.

*A Brooklyn Jesuit told me that one day an old, old, black woman wished him "Happy Feast!" on St. Ignatius Day. She said, "I bet you wonder how I know it's a feast day. My mother used to be in the Society." It took him almost half a day before he realized what she was saying. Her mother had been a Jesuit slave! Did you know Jesuits here once had slaves?*

TC: In a general way I did. But I never investigated it. It's a matter of record and could be found out.

BR: It's an example of how much the Society of Jesus takes on the customs of its surroundings, usually with little critical attention.

*Can you be pushed to a point where you'll "confront" the Jesuits?*

TC: I've just finished doing that at Santa Clara. There were eight provincials there. I directed quite a few things to the Society, in fact many things they didn't want to print. I'm interested to see what some of the notes from Santa Clara are going to be. Everything that I said out there should be printed.

*I'd be happy to give you a forum if it's not.*

TC: I'll wait to see first what they're going to do.

BR: Confrontation has its time and place. When it comes I will be ready. The Spirit is in me.

The *Spiritual Exercises* of Ignatius too often reached only into the Jesuit's personal life. It had little to do with his wider, social responsibilities. Only recently have more than a few isolated Jesuits felt free to express their views in the public forum on race, politics and civil justice. They still feel less than free to act on their views.

As an institution, Jesuits are racist. Their institutions (schools, parishes, retreat houses, et cetera), though not always deliberately [racist], have effectively been closed to minority groups. These same institutions propagated the existing cultural mores and attitudes with little, if any, critical analysis. Very few of these institutions have yet confronted their own attitudes. A poll surveying attitudes and practices of Jesuit schools' alumni in areas of social and civil justice would show serious deficiency and, sometimes, real reaction.

As far as I can see, criteria for men applying to Jesuit seminaries have not excluded minority groups. But attitudes of Jesuit teachers and seminarians have made survival of seminarians from minority groups and white students from low-income groups very difficult. They've been taught that their language is "wrong," their manner out of place, their interests vulgar. In other words, Jesuits are often, I've found, very bourgeois. Since this generally means, among other things, conformity and uniformity, *chicanos*, poor whites, blacks *don't fit*.

I didn't want to be in "A" class, because what you had to do in "A" class was lick ass — maybe you don't want that in your book — but you *did have to*. You had to say the right things. And you could turn in a good paper but if you didn't make the right acknowledgments, that paper did not get accepted. In other words, it was not read for what it said.

*This wasn't just because of your color though.*

BR: No. No. This was everybody.

*It was an educational attitude.*

BR: Right. It's cultural too. Many people who came from working-class backgrounds did not get the kind of acceptance that a person had who had gone through a Jesuit high school and Jesuit college.

*One of the images presented to Jesuit scholastics is that of St. Peter Claver helping blacks. Work with blacks, then, is part of the Jesuit tradition. But the image of helping is associated with the image of someone who is dependent on help.*

TC: Father Schockley has a proverb for priests who come down to work in his inner-city parish in St. Louis: "You give a hungry man a fish today and tomorrow he's still hungry. You teach a hungry man to *catch* fish, then he begins to provide for himself." However, I may want him to remain hungry so he'll be back tomorrow.

BR: That's a pretty good picture of what "charitable" institutions and civil welfare efforts have generally been in this country, and that includes the Church, and the Society of Jesus, too.

TC: A person can live a thousand miles away and find someone else to give him that fish on my behalf.

This is how I see the institution of colonialism. This is how most black people see the institution of paternalism. The black man is beginning to understand the white Christian Church is caught up in this kind of paternalism. He is now pointing at various religious orders and at, say, the Vatican, as being this kind of paternalistic figure in his life.

*BR:* I see this partly as a general cultural problem. Colonialism was once seen as limited to the South. Chicago has always been against, and even worked against, segregation and racial injustice in Mississippi, Alabama, Georgia and Louisiana, while ignoring it in their own neighborhoods and institutions. New England began the Abolitionist movement while some New England shippers were banking on the triangular trade. The North sees itself as more righteous than the South but colonialism is all over and it's not only limited to whites.

*Do you ever talk with young Jesuits in the order?*

TC: Yes, I've talked with them. I try to answer their questions. I try to avoid just talking theory.

*Are they afraid to ask you questions?*

TC: No, they're not. They try to make parallel situations. Some of them have worked on the Indian missions. They'll say: "The Indians are poor, the black people in the cities are poor. Therefore, there's a commonness in poverty or there's a commonness in cultures, because both people are colored, both people are poor." They have been misguided, I think by their directors.

*Everyman's poverty, like everyman's grief is different.*

BR: We don't need more knowledge, we've got an overload. What we do need is to touch hearts, and failing that, to change customs or prohibit ways of acting. I'm in this work to touch hearts — deep.

*260*

*Were you ever made to feel uncomfortable, like an outsider, in any Jesuit community?*

BR: Usually. One can't help but feel foreign where no one shares your experience, speaks your language. Then there are the conscious slights, and put-downs and meannesses: "Being made to feel at home?" "I was reading Martin Luther King the other day . . ." "I met so-and-so last night. Do you know him?" (I must since he's black) . . . "He was so well-mannered and intelligent!" This kind of unthinking patronization is really hard to swallow without spitting it right back. I've seen Jesuits treat foreigners, especially Latin Americans and Orientals, with a really sick kind of condescension, too.

TC: Each house has a different tone because of the different people in it. There has to be a house breaking every time you move into a new house. When I was a novice I was older than most other novices and so I worked somewhat with my master of novices. I used to talk about how I might help some of the white novices get along with someone of a different color. I used to be annoyed at the overextended acts of charity, like someone waiting for five minutes holding the door open for me.

*That was typical in the novitiate. It annoyed all of us when we went through.*

TC: In theology, it was the first time I was ever with southern men from Mississippi, Alabama, Louisiana and so forth. By that time I had decided to forget about helping whites understand me and was more myself than I had ever been in any other house, not really caring too much about how my color might affect the feelings of someone else. I was too busy working out community relation problems twenty-five miles away in Topeka to worry about furthering some individual Jesuit who didn't understand blacks.

I'd play ball, say, at St. Mary's. When I'd slide into second I'd know that the guy on second, if he were from the South, would probably get out of the way. He wouldn't know but that I might get up and fight because I wouldn't allow some white to tag me. This became a sure way of scoring, whereas in the novitiate I would probably have talked to him after the game and said, "Hey, I don't mind if we play baseball rules in baseball." I would have made a joke of it, get him to see what maybe he was unconsciously doing — shying away from tagging me. But back at St. Mary's I'd tell the team, "Well, we've got a guy on first and with this southerner on second, we've got a sure third."

BR: I won't talk about insensitivity. That's on both sides and it's very subjective. But I want to point to the constant, deliberate slights: omissions, meannesses — yes, that's the best word. It's really little things as DuBois says, "We'd been so busy feeling hurt about the little things that we overlooked the big things like schooling and jobs."

Right after I got into the novitiate, I remember an incident during my first month. There was another novice from Ecuador, an aristocrat in his own country, and there was this *secundianni* saying in an undertone, "Spic. Spic. Spic . . ." It wasn't heard by many other people, but the Ecuadorian heard it and I heard it. I took that as an affront to me, too.

I've never been called "nigger" in the Society. But there are those little slights, like I'll ask, "Will you pass the butter, please?" Nothing. "*Would* you pass the butter, please?" Nothing. Then finally, the person next to me looks at me, one of those long meaningful looks, and passes the butter. Very slowly. Puts it down very meaningfully. Plunk! Those are the kinds of things. There aren't many but there are too many.

*Were there many Jesuits who acted this way? Was this typical behavior?*

BR: It wasn't typical. But it wasn't looked on as exceptional. There were very few people who did these things but when somebody did act this way it was regarded by the majority of others more as a breach of etiquette than as inhuman or antihuman.

*Were you ever badly hurt either accidentally or intentionally by anyone in the Society?*

BR: Yes. I've been hurt. "Badly?" That's relative, of course. I'd learned before I entered the Society to expect psychological oppression and injury. But being in the Society gave me opportunities to learn how to deal with it constructively. Nevertheless, finding among Jesuits — priests and superiors — the same attitudes of bigotry I'd learned to accept as ordinary "manners" outside the order was a real blow to my pious (naïve) view of the Church. It took me a while to get myself straight again. I think I've made it, but it took luck. It took loving care by God above, a lot of it. I hope I've made it.

TC: I don't really think I've been hurt. I can recall situations that could have hurt other black people but they didn't hurt me. There was more than one guy from the South who wouldn't speak to me in the four years we were together in theology, wouldn't even say hello, or good morning. That would have hurt some people but you know there were two hundred men in the theologate. You treated him as you would treat someone who'd walk by you and wouldn't speak to you in the city.

After a while I began to see what the Church was and what it would permit, what the Society was and what it would permit, and then I'd think that this kind of person might one day also be a college president. You can see what some of our Christian institutions are today when they're run by men who are functional or effective, but not necessarily Christian. Their Christianity might be simply their code of personal ascetical philosophy.

The southerners who wouldn't talk to me, would make their daily *examen* and say, "What did I fail in today? Oh, yes. I saw that guy again today and couldn't speak to him again, and that's a bad thing and I pray that I can overcome it and I must work on my kindness." But you know, that *examen* doesn't really correct anything. He'd get more from it if he used it to analyze his Christian position regarding people of different color. He may never even see this until he gets involved with them.

BR: I've been lucky. I entered the novitiate in '59. Kennedy went into office not long after and the mood of the U.S. opened up — Jesuits included. Dr. King was getting something big going too. So I was protected because I was black. It's very touchy to get at me. But the Spanish Americans, the *chicanos*, get this kind of thing and get it heavily.

*Do you feel that you have to be smarter than the average Jesuit in order to be accepted as a black Jesuit?*

BR: But definitely. And the joyous gratification some expressed when I *did* do something well! That said a lot too.

TC: Yes. I did too. But often it would depend upon the persons I was working with.

*Was it also expected that you as a black priest and black Christian had to show more personal goodness — faith, charity, humility and so on — than the white priest and white Christian?*

TC: I think this has been expected.

BR: Yes: "the savior of his race is here."

TC: I don't expect it of myself. I might have in the beginning, and may have been very conscious of it, but there were enough human beings, let's say, who haven't allowed this. We've been ourselves. That's probably what is necessary. You need to have friends. I mean Jesuit friends and non-Jesuit friends. You can't be in the Society and be a loner.

BR: You can see that I still carry some bitterness. Cynicism has become too usual a way of seeing the world. I must consciously guard against expressing this bitterness and cynicism. It helps nothing and it can eat away the heart. We've got to act independently of what "is expected."

TC: I was never able to use the words "Mother Society" or "Holy Mother Society." I'm not caught up in that mystique of thinking of the Society as being the best men on earth. They might have the propaganda going for them as that. However, it's just like the canonization of saints by the Church, there's politics involved, and there's money involved, so it practically comes down to who can muster the highest bankroll for this or that saint, and who has the right contacts.

BR: If a man were to wait on the institution's recognition of the work he feels God wants him to do before he gets on with it, he'll take it undone to his grave.

TC: The way saints now appear, for example, there might be eight hundred who are, say, people of religious orders, two hundred are the ordinary diocesan priests, and then finally there is one layman.

*I bet he's not black!*

BR: I see that bet and double it that he (she) is European!

TC: Yes. So as I see it it's a matter of who is writing about holiness and that's the way he sees holiness.

*But it hasn't bothered you then that Jesuits aren't the greatest bunch of men in the world?*

TC: It hasn't bothered me, no. I've never been too impressed with the idea of being a "community man." You leave the community too much. I don't know what a Jesuit community is. It's a Jesuit residence. Jesuits live there. I think throughout the training you develop your own style. You develop yourself. You become an individual. As a philosopher I used to walk over to Homer G. Philips Hospital. I ran into some opposition from the pastors of St. Matthew's who thought I was trying to take over their operation. They resented patients telling them that the "priest" had already been there to visit on Thursday, and therefore they didn't want to see him on Sunday too. No one said, "Don't do it." No one called me in to say I wasn't doing well in studies because of my Thursday trips to the city. Yet there was not institutional approval for what I was doing. While I was practice-teaching at Creighton during the summer after philosophy, one of the guys still there complained that the only thing I was doing at Creighton was hanging up my hat, that I was out in the black areas of town all the time, that I was too often off campus. I let them talk. I couldn't understand what I'd be doing walking around Jesuit halls all day.

I try to talk to people so they can understand their own goodness. Just two nights ago I was talking with a lady who is embattled in a little city across the river in Illinois. Near the end of the evening, I said, "Now would you give me a blessing?" She had never been asked that question before and she had never really thought of herself in this role before.

I think laymen and laywomen should begin to build up their own self-images and to see their own goodness. They should see that it's not only the people in religious orders who are canonizable. But this is the way the propaganda system has worked. It has made us think this way, feel this way. I think this kind of thing needs correction. Therefore, I don't go around talking about the great Jesuits all the time.

BR: I think if we don't look upon much of Church doctrine as propaganda we are closing our eyes and will soon have only deaf ears for God — who is still bigger than the Church which so loudly claims him. "Not all who say, 'Lord, Lord' . . ."

*I wonder whether those of us who do talk about the greatness of any society of men, and that includes myself, whether we're not, perhaps, clinging to some image of past glory because we're afraid we might be too weak and small to meet the agony of today alone.*

BR: Too true of us all. Note the ranting and emotional attempts to identify in any group of "converts," whether to Catholicism, black power, love, peace, and so on.

*Bart, maybe you should be out working in the black movement. Is staying in the order a cop-out?*

BR: Okay, maybe staying in the order can be a cop-out. Maybe you can sell out very easily by staying in. But, if you can maintain your personal integrity, you can deal with ecclesiastical, educational, financial and social structures on their [own] terms. You can go in their door, as St. Ignatius puts it, and come out your own door. Start on their turf and make them end on your own turf. That's not easy, but it's possible.

Although your questions didn't lead to this, I would like to mention there are some really great Jesuits. Louis J. Twomey, and Claude Heithaus, who was exiled from St. Louis University back in the forties. Some of the men I'm working with now in Boston and others around the country. I hope they — and I — can hold up and carry on. Others, also, whose names I don't know. Their anonymity itself tells a tale.

*What is Northhouse and how did it get its name?*

PW: Northhouse is a place in north St. Louis (hence the name . . . very creative!) where teen-age boys can come to study in the evenings. It was begun by a group of seven Jesuits three years ago in an old abandoned storefront. It's grown over the years and now has about twenty-five boys every night. Last year we helped place twelve of our seniors in colleges around the country, and prospects look good this year. We think it's a good beginning.

The Jesuit community that lives there does all its own cooking and fund raising. It works out its programs with the kids. We've learned from the kids too, perhaps even more than they have from us. We've learned a lot about the black culture that one can only learn through firsthand experience.

*I wish you'd tape these kids, their attitudes and images and so on.*

PW: Look, we're not generating any publicity for the Jesuits. We're not there for that. We're up there to work with the kids. I haven't written any articles about them. I haven't used the kids in any way and I don't intend to. If the kids themselves want to come out with something — yeh. Okay. That's the way I'd work it. If they want to make a tape, all right.

Once you're in a place like Northhouse you begin to see how people are exploiting these kids all the time. Sociologists come up and listen for a while and say, "You've got a neat accent. We're going to get you on tape to see what you can talk like" — like they're monkeys in a zoo or something.

*Do you think any blacks will come into the Society from Northhouse?*

PW: It's hard to say. We have a kid who got kicked out of home mostly because he wants to become a Catholic and a

Jesuit. He's nineteen or twenty. He's going to St. Louis University on a scholarship. Now there's a start of something here, but it would be a mistake to put a guy like that through the same type of training we went through. He doesn't come from our culture. He doesn't want to work in ours. Now what adaptations can be made for him in Jesuit training? I think we could open a program to fit his needs and his abilities and so on.

*If a young black said he'd like to be a Jesuit, what would you tell him?*

TC: I couldn't recommend the Society without great caution. I'd have to see what's going to happen to the black power movement in Christianity. So far, all that the Church and the Province has done was pay my way to the black caucus.

*Bart, would you feel right asking other blacks to join the Society?*

BR: Certain others, but very few. I'd have to promise them a hard road.

*What would you warn him against?*

BR: The hardest things probably would be cultural isolation and the insensitivity of some men. He might discover he was wasting valuable time and psychic energy trying to save his fellow students from their lack of soul, from their cultural deprivation and ignorance. He would have to watch very carefully what he says lest he be misunderstood and thus jeopardize his long-range effectiveness.

TC: You have to look at the work the Society is going to do, because that is eventually what the men are for. If the So-

269

ciety is going to be teaching in black areas of the cities, and needs black Jesuits to do this, then she will have to attract black candidates to the order and train them for this work.

However, some black leaders are saying, "You're more beneficial to us if you remain in the suburbs to teach." They're not asking for black Jesuits. They're asking us to remain as we are: a white Society teaching in white suburbia. We're already equipped with the language and the communication system to teach in white suburbia, though we may not have all the material that's necessary to correct racism there. Now I don't think it's necessary to have had white people living in the inner city in order to teach in suburbia. I don't really think we're going to have any blacks from there become Jesuits, because I don't think the Jesuit order is geared that way. Nor is the Church geared towards the black areas of its cities.

Ten or fifteen years ago there was the exodus that left skeleton buildings, Roman Catholic churches, all through the city. Where those Catholics now are is still very much where the Church is. When Jesuits talk about working in the inner city, we are not really talking about the Church, we are talking about missionary objects. People who are going to have water poured on them and be *made* Christian. This is what black people see. And we don't want that.

BR: We certainly don't. If the Church, if Jesuits really preached Christ in suburbia to the white middle and upper classes, we would have a much different set of race relations.

*You feel that inner-city work produces a kind of colonialism?*

BR: Basically, yes. The "master culture" discovers a problem so sends agents to solve it by palliation. If some changes happen to take place, well, these can be absorbed since they will be relatively few. That's the basic dynamic that takes place. This must change — and not because the Church will lose its people, but because only in this way will she honor and praise her Lord.

TC: I think so, and I think that's what many of the black people are saying. Keep your Christianity for suburbia; we don't want the same kind of thing we have been getting all along from the Church. Now, the sincerity of the Church through some kind of dramatic, evident signs of Christianity showing she is truly interested in the poor might change this whole role. But let's just pick *one* of the Christian corporations, the Vatican, say, and let's not talk about the Vatican as property owner in Rome, let's talk about the Vatican as owner of property in the United States of America, and in just two instances, Washington, D.C., and in New York City. When we face a black leader who says, "Tell us how the Vatican is returning money to the poor people in Washington, D.C., and in New York."

Then we're very embarrassed. We know darn well the Vatican is not really interested in the poor, not in this way. It is investing money to help these poor people by using things that seem to exploit them. So the Vatican is very much part of the machinery that's exploiting them.

*What do you think of James Foreman's strategy of demanding that churches in America pay reparations for their contribution to racism?*

TC: It's a good idea. A plan suggested by some Afro-Americans that's a little easier to carry out and more effective is the refusal to pay income tax in certain areas until the federal government implements promised programs, such as school desegregation. It's a matter of how Foreman's program would be managed, whether there'd be a cooperative effort or whether it would be helter-skelter. I wouldn't want six unrelated organizations each not knowing what the other is doing, one taxing the Methodists and not bothering the Presbyterians, and so on.

*271*

BR: The main purpose is to galvanize public opinion. In this Foreman has been at least partially successful.

TC: Five years ago I don't think black people could see this. Now even the illiterate black person is understanding that the Church is part of a system of investors that holds poor people down, and is not doing anything to correct this machinery of capitalism. That's the way they're talking. That's why a black manifesto says: "The Church owes us $5 million . . . $10 million . . . $20 million."

"What's he talking about? We don't owe him anything." — that's what the Christians will say. "We don't owe him anything. We don't have any money."

But the black's not talking about individual persons. He's saying: "St. Louis High, are you a corporation? St. Louis University, are you a corporation? Missouri Province, are you a corporation? Do you know where your money is invested? Is it invested in South Africa at all? Is it in a bank whose policy is to not give loans to black people because they're black? If that's true, then why don't you change your money from First National to Federal? And print it in the press? — *We are switching our capital from First National to Federal because Federal as a Christian corporation is doing a much better job of handling black loans in this city. Here are instances of successful black loans . . .*"

This kind of thing will begin to make sense to people who are always pointing to the Society of Jesus as being rich. Jesuits deny that. "We're not rich. We've got land but we're not rich." That's the answer that always comes back to the blacks. So they say, "Well, the Jesuits are hypocrites."

BR: How many deep-down good people of many colors have said just this to me, and I can only answer with my sadness. Jesuits aren't hypocrites as individuals, but they are very uncritical about what they are doing as a group. "That's X's responsibility. I have my work." I don't care if he is working in the inner city and killing himself at it; if he turns his back on the work of the provincial's or president's office, he is still betraying the very people he feels and does so much for. He betrays himself.

TC: The Jesuits aren't really hypocrites but I don't think many of them understand that the Society of Jesus is an investor. We should understand ourselves a little better, learn how people are seeing us, before we can ever be a Christian image to these people. We don't act like Christ. We simply act like a big institution that's very rich and that really doesn't care about doing more than baptizing a child and giving the child an education that whitens him, instead of allowing him to be black as he is.

BR: I agree. He's not allowed to be the person that he is. He must be "culturally enriched" and "upgraded."

PW: In other words you're saying that we're not consciously prejudiced . . .

TC: In part. That's what racism means.

PW: But our prejudice is more on the unconscious level. We do what we would not do.

BR: And the effects are the same.

TC: Condoning existing institutions. Allowing them to remain. Perpetuating them. By simply keeping step with the rest. Not initiating anything . . .

BR: Racism by omission. Where are the prophets today? Have we killed them all?

PW: There's a militant here who's accused St. Louis University of having investments in South Africa. A layman who works in the investment department says it's not true. "I wish it were. Then we could change it. But it simply is not true."

Now there was an accusation made without any foundation in fact. The militant said, "I'll bring the proof next time I come." But he didn't come back.

TC: But how could he prove it? What I am saying is that the Jesuits themselves don't know where their investments are. The point is, Paul, what about the other investments? What kind of a Christian marking would they be able to show? It's not so much that she doesn't have investments in South Africa, but where are the investments?

PW: Yes. That's a valid point. I see.

*In addition to that they aren't very visible actively helping the black banker. They aren't helping funding that's needed.*

BR: What they say is: "But that's a job for the federal government." With this kind of leadership, do we wonder why the U.S. is in the state we see today?

TC: We tried this past year to get the president of Creighton University to put three thousand dollars of the university's money into a credit union the black area was beginning. The University said no. The president didn't see any need in doing this, as the university's money was already well invested. If this kind of nearsightedness becomes public it could wreck him. I don't think anybody is going to tell. Only a couple of people know. But it's a dumb way to say no.

BR: Black people can indulge in an ironic chuckle as pollution — air, water, noise, garbage, crime — turns the whole country into a slum. We will have to update the image of the Four Horsemen of the Apocalypse, but they still come for the same reasons and do the same things only with greater efficiency. They won't be kept in the ghettos any longer. And how many opportunities have slipped through fingers grasping for wrong dreams?

TC: The only reason we have a Markoe House at all is because the present provincial wanted this kind of thing to happen. There were Jebs in Omaha who didn't want it enough in high places who could have stopped a loan. We wouldn't have had the loan if it hadn't been for Jim's cousin. Jim made the contact possible.

Our health center was started through after-Mass talks on Sundays with Creighton medical students about possible developments in the slums. We found this house, a nice, solid small home. We made one bedroom into a kitchen. We had parlors and an examination room. Then the med students began to develop programs. It's open Wednesday, from seven to nine at night. Inoculations, slide lectures, movies for the kids who come with their parents. Prenatal care on Sunday afternoons.

All this was done without the help of Creighton, but now that the program is operating, the president would like to claim this as a Creighton University program. I think the people would identify it with the people of the neighborhood. The program was set up by talking with people who had gone to Creighton's clinic. The med students and nurses had talked to the patients to find out what they wanted in a health center, in a clinic, how it should be operated, what they wanted to learn, what were decent hours. This is how they got the program going.

*What kind of support do you get here from the Society of Jesus?*

TC: *Per diem,* that's all. Nothing from the Society of Jesus as an institution. From individuals.

*"We have not a perfect world"* — *Linus* (Peanuts)

R. James Arenz, S.J.

*What do engineers think of Ralph Nader? Do engineers know how to deal with human problems?*

*As a priest, R. James Arenz, S.J., is committed to prophesy — to confronting his community with its antihuman wrongs. As an engineer, his professional community is made up of technologists who are involved in polluting our air and water, spoiling our land, who are blamed for designing TV sets that fail and cars that are unsafe. How does Arenz meet his commitment? In the interview that follows, Arenz describes his image of the priest-engineer.*

*Arenz's studies of hypervelocity impact helped insure the safety of U.S. astronauts on their moon trips. In his experiments, Arenz, who is assistant professor of mechanical engineering at Loyola University, Los Angeles, and a consultant at Cal Tech's Jet Propulsion Lab, shot metal particles against typical spacecraft structures at speeds in excess of seventy-five thousand miles an hour to simulate the dangers threatening astronauts should their spacecraft hull be bombarded by meteoroids.*

*During research on the mechanics of high-polymer materials, Arenz conducted studies of solid propellant rockets for the U.S. Department of Defense. He also helped improve designs for ballistic missile silos by studies of ground shock waves. Some Jesuits say that a priest who works for the Defense Department contradicts himself. They ask: "How can a priest promote war and peace at the same time?"*

---

I was born in 1924, in Iowa, and my family moved out to the coast when I was six. I went to Oregon State University and majored in aeronautical engineering. I expected to be involved in the research and design of aircraft or space vehicles.

For two years after graduation I did stress analysis, analyzing the way loads act on an airplane's structure so it won't come apart in the air. Then I went into aerodynamics for three years, predicting airplane and rocket performance. I was with the Douglas Aircraft Company in Santa Monica, California, for about five years.

Sometime after I got out of college, I began to get more interested in what my faith meant to me as a Catholic. I did some reading and thinking about it that led me to decide what my lifework might be.

I had been going exclusively to public schools. My first Catholic school was the Jesuit novitiate, which I entered in 1950. I had hopes of continuing in scientific and technical work, but I was willing to do whatever I was assigned to do.

The Jesuit order has several engineering schools, but none east of Detroit. There's a school at Detroit, one at Marquette, and then four on the West Coast. This year, in fact, St. Louis University announced it was dropping engineering.

I started engineering school again when I worked for my master's at the St. Louis University Institute of Technology. I continued for a doctorate in aeronautics from California Institute of Technology and I spent about half a year at the Ernst-Mach-Institut, a research center, in Germany.

Cal Tech was an interesting experience. The graduate students had plenty of questions about my attitudes on sex, but mainly their questions were theological.

*How could you, a smart man, believe in God — was that their attitude?*

At the start it was with a number of them. Usually they'd start by badgering me. One time I remember at my table in the cafeteria a few physics majors were ridiculing a religious program they'd heard on the radio. "So repetitious," they said. "It didn't advance anything." It turned out to be a broadcast of people saying the rosary.

Some of the early discussions were superficial. But after a while they tightened down. In the end, the big question was what was I doing there at all.

*I'd like to ask that question too, from this setting: the U.S. culture is a technological culture. Critics say it is an impersonal and dehumanizing culture, and there are Jesuits among the critics. Yet here you are, a Jesuit out of Cal Tech and the Ernst-Mach-Institut.*

I agree. It does seem strange, though it shouldn't. Somehow Jesuits don't seem to be very interested in being engineers. The thrust of technology is to liberate man from servitude to matter. Computers and other wonderful new machines give man less work, offer him new leisure, and insulate him from pain. But they give us only slight hints of the true significance of technology. For the common attempt of these machines is to cajole nature into working for man instead of against him. Matter becomes the medium of the spirit's creative self-expression. The rather exciting perspective that emerges is that man's relation to material nature is a dynamically evolving dialogue between himself and matter. As Dr. Vannevar Bush, director of the United States scientific research and development during World War II, said recently, "To pursue science is not to disparage the things of the spirit. In fact, to pursue science rightly is to furnish a framework on which the spirit may rise."

281

*U.S. technologists landed us on the moon on schedule. Now a lot of people are asking why can't they solve some of our local problems, for example, pollution.*

I'm convinced that many of the problems of the world will not be solved without engineers. But, it will not be only engineers that solve these problems. The problems of environmental pollution, racial and social adjustment and deteriorated cities involve human beings and thus involve freedom of choice. Therefore, we don't face the straightforward problem that we faced in going to the moon. There we had machinery. We had environment, not completely known, but nevertheless accountable for. The human astronauts were working in a very highly programmed manner and were able to handle the decisions put to them in their particular situation. All these conditions are part of our earth problems too, but there is also the human freedom to decide whether to go this way or that way, to do this or that. This just makes it a totally different ball game. Take such a thing as environment control. Involved here is the question of municipalities, of states, of large units of people deciding that they have to do something about the problem. Also, they have to be willing to go along with the measures that are necessary to provide the clean environment that they seek. Too many people *want* to throw away beer cans, *want* to litter up property, and so, figuratively, our air and water too. All these problems are of a vastly more complex nature than the getting to the moon.

*What do technologists think of Ralph Nader? Is he making life easier or harder for them?*

I think they feel Nader is making a contribution by drawing attention to shortcomings in products and harmful conditions. His is probably a needed watch-dog activity. But the danger exists that his policy of "mega-overkill" in criticizing industry can create a hopeless and helpless attitude in the public. There is need for action, but there is not cause for panic or despair. Engineers like to look at issues in an objective and professional manner that includes all relevant factors, not an emotional playing-up of one aspect.

I can't speak for the engineers at GM with regard to Nader, nor am I able to comment on any political ambitions he may have. I suppose one would have to say that Nader is making life more difficult for engineers by requiring them to be more thorough in checking designs and products.

*The U.S. and Canada both own half of Lake Erie. There's natural gas and possibly oil under the lake. Canada is short of fuel so is tapping for gas. We complain they're polluting the lake. Canada says our industries on the shore are contributing most of the pollution. Would you comment on this fight?*

It's a complicated issue. If we allow the risk of oil pollution on the Santa Barbara beach, logic would indicate allowing Canadian interests to look for oil beneath Lake Erie if normal safeguards are taken.

*Are the engineers responsible for the budget exaggerations reported in the Government Accounting Office Bluebook and frequently in the press?*

I think it's possible. But, say with the C5A, I suspect that the engineers sitting back at their drawing boards were able to look at that thing and predict, on the basis of rising costs, that the final cost would be much higher than their initial proposal. But the company management is in competition with other companies also making proposals, so they make an optimistic estimate that will get them the contract. Here, again, the technical man is not the sole arbiter of the situation. There is a tendency to underestimate everything as a matter of course.

*Is there such a thing as space morality?*

The morality of man on the moon is basically the same as that of man on earth. The relationships between men in space and between those men and God are not essentially or fundamentally different than they'd be if they were anywhere else.

*We are developing a new medical ethics and morality because of population pressures and the advances of medical science in fields such as genetics. Is a new engineering ethics and morality needed to deal with the advances of technology?*

United States engineers already have a code of ethics that asks me as an engineer to consider the wider and more distant effects of the things I design and make, and to relate them to the common good, the welfare of men around me.

*But we see in the waste of our water, trees and soil, that technological developments can actually work against man's welfare. Hasn't the technologist ignored his code of ethics?*

Not entirely. Not exactly. More than half the blame must be put on our industrialists, our companies that are oriented toward profit without having enough regard for the welfare of mankind. The engineer more or less goes along with this objective. When management says, "Design me this new facility to do this job in an economical way," the engineer does it. Unfortunately, he doesn't pay too much attention to the smoke that's spewed out or the garbage that goes into the river or lake nearby. And unfortunately too, if he does, he might not have the opportunity to design another facility for that manager.

*Since the engineer has access to the equipment and tools that are going to be part of the solution of our environmental problems, isn't he partly responsible for alarming the people of some product's possible side effects?*

284

I definitely see that he must be more socially conscious. If only to do his technical work well, he's also going to have to have these other capabilities. There's a growing interest among engineers in recent court decisions regarding product liability. Such decisions are beginning to reach down to the level of individual engineers. This will certainly push engineers to take possible adverse side effects of their projects or products into account. It's bound to improve overall engineering design.

*How can a priest, whose profession stands for love and peace, conduct research the results of which can be used in war?*

Scientific research is oriented primarily to the development of knowledge of the material universe about us. It participates in the total development of man in his role under God of becoming master of the universe and ultimately restoring it in a more perfect state to the Creator. Although my work is funded by the military to aid in current tasks of providing defense for the country, the fundamental thrust of my current task is one of throwing open more of the secrets of nature. Moreover, regardless of the original support of the work, several immediate benefits to man flow from it. For example, some of the techniques developed for polymer research are currently being applied to a study of the properties of body tissue. New knowledge resulting from this hopefully will contribute to ways of reducing injuries from traffic accidents and improved medical treatment of them.

*Graduate students with research assignments at Massachusetts Institute of Technology are paid tuition and living costs in return for twenty to thirty hours of research a week on projects that may have military connections. One engineering student told a* New York Times *reporter: "What I'm designing may one day be used to kill millions of people. I don't care. That's not my responsibility. I'm given an in-*

*teresting technological problem and I get enjoyment out of solving it.*"

I don't agree with the student; I do care how it's used. But this is where I put together the scientific research and new knowledge aspect with a trust in the good will of government leaders based on the general overall performance and stance taken by the U.S. over a long period of history. The overwhelming evidence is that the U.S. is sincerely interested in the basic freedom and welfare of peoples around the world, despite certain lapses at certain places and times. "We have not a perfect world." Statement courtesy of Linus in *Peanuts*.

*Universities report a drop in the percentage of young men majoring in engineering. Is this serious drop an expression of disgust with technology?*

It's partly that. Fifteen years ago, roughly eighteen to nineteen percent of male students in college were choosing technology as their major in school. Now it's down to ten or eleven percent. We can point to at least three causes.

One is that there's more money to be made in other professions that are also less demanding of time and energy, such as, oh, law or business administration.

The second reason is that we haven't done a good selling job. We haven't been able to get young people to realize the importance of technology as an aid in solving our social and ecological problems. Technologists and engineers are criticized for creating the problems in the first place because they created the dirt makers and noise machines. Yet, obviously, the same technologists are going to have to be called in either to remake their machines or clean up the mess. We need more, not fewer technologists.

A third reason for the drop in young engineers is that people are more interested in the humanistic, the sociological and psychological studies now. That may reflect an urgent need today. This is fine, but technology can be relevant towards our sociological and ecological well-being. All these things fit together. We can't divide ourselves into separate categories.

*How can you make technology attractive to the young people who are now interested in solving social problems?*

Well, we need technologists to solve our inner-city and ghetto problems. A person who has an adequate technical background as well as a real social awareness and commitment towards his community can do a lot to get hold of the problems and to make inroads on their solutions.

*Instead of serving only the industrialist spenders, why can't engineers put their technical skills at the service of the needers and users?*

How do you get a design to a user and have him authorize you to produce the design?

*You don't. The user doesn't authorize you. You're simply his interpreter. If the users have any organization at all, you offer to interpret their needs in design. Let them carry it from there.*

The trouble is that the user is an individual here, an individual there. Consumers are divided. If there is any community organization at the grass-roots level, there is hope for this approach. Take the question of urban renewal. The individual inhabitant in a blighted area knows only that he wants a pleasant place to live. The engineer can build a hermetically sealed house that shuts him off from the rest of the neighborhood. But this isn't the best answer. Suppose the engineer and the planner come in and suggest an ideal place for a park and show how business areas can be better located. These changes release some property to permit home rehabilitation to go forward, and the whole new scene ties together with a new freeway route in the region. Of course, financing must be forthcoming which usually means approaching governmental agencies.

We have a tremendous freeway system here in California. The state and interstate system is designing new routes all the time. This means that new roads are going to have to go through populated areas in some places. A lot of community organizations have been formed to represent those areas through which the roads will go. These organizations go to the freeway people and say, "Look, we want this road to go along the side or through this section rather than right through the middle." So there are community organizations springing up.

The initiative, however, comes from the community. This is not always likely to occur. If it dosn't, maybe a combine of volunteer technical people along with a lawyer, a social worker, a union representative, and a public-spirited businessman could interest several in the community to set the organization in motion. Then these same advisors could see that the plan got a hearing from the appropriate source of funding.

Admittedly this scheme depends greatly on altruistic motivation on the part of the engineer and the others involved, but granted this, it seems feasible in the type of situation described. It's less likely to happen in the design of products or equipment.

Another example of going to the service of the user in a very fundamental sense is with such groups as the Peace Corps and VISTA. Several engineers I've studied with or taught have been engaged in this work.

*The lawyers have Legal Aid for the poor. Can't the engineers offer Technological Aid for the poor? For those who don't even know what they need?*

A community engineering service!

288

*Yeh. The poor never see engineers. They see the surveyors and then they see the constructors putting in the stuff.*

If the community engineering service were a business concern, then the consulting fee required might make for very few customers among the poor. The possibility of support from professional engineering societies is intriguing. Many engineers attend society technical meetings and lectures, take part in carrying out society business, all on a volunteer and non-paid basis, but for the overall purpose of professional self-improvement. After all, engineers have to eat too. But perhaps the orientation of a portion of engineering society activity could be swung around to community improvement with donated professional services by society members. There are incipient signs of this occasionally in editorials of technical society publications.

*Does an engineer approach a problem in a different way than, say, the scientist?*

Oh, yes. Definitely. He has a different point of view. He uses the same mathematics, the same fundamental physics, but his point of view is different. The basic scientist is interested in knowing for the sake of knowing. The engineer is interested in knowing for the sake of creating something, doing with it, making a product or service that benefits mankind in a tangible way, but ideally oriented towards his ultimate development. It may be something very intermediate, like a new candle to replace the fireplace light to read by. So engineers, by the nature of their work, should be highly idealistic people. But, of course, they are human beings with the same interests, selfish or altruistic, good or bad, as anyone else.

*Do the engineer's instruments produce patterns of compartmentalism in society? Are we overspecialized as a result of being overengineered?*

I would say that it's natural for man to make categories. We have to divide out in order to look at in detail. If I'm interested in some subject, I'll maybe take a broad view and then zoom in on a certain area of it. Our comprehension is so finite we take a piece at a time. This seems to be a natural process, to analyze and separate. Yes, the engineering or technological approach subdivides a problem down into its component parts, but I don't think engineers should be blamed for dividing our society. The natural process was prior. Perhaps the need in society now is to synthesize, to see the whole man in order to unify.

We are going in the other direction right now, particularly in the space program. When we get out into space we're not dealing with boxed areas of knowledge, such as chemistry and physics and biology. They all meet there. This has helped develop the systems analysis point of view. Another, more appropriate word, is *interdisciplinary*.

*"Systems analysis" is the same as "interdisciplinary"?*

It involves interdisciplinary activity. You bring in people with all different points of view and abilities and backgrounds and technologies. For example, take weapon systems. You don't simply design the gun that a man carries, you design the gun and the vehicle he rides in, the electronics which relate to other vehicles overhead, the navigation — the whole thing. That's systems analysis.

You could have interdisciplinary activity without systems design, you see. You could just look at the thing without thinking of designing a system for it. The terms are related but not identical. But back to your question: space exploration has forced us to realize that we need people in many different fields to look into the problems that we currently face right here on earth.

*290*

*Technologists are marvelously trained to work out problems on paper and then to construct mechanical or electrical things. But they are too easily frustrated by human beings, who are notoriously unpredictable and, therefore, unmanageable. It requires diplomatic facility as well as technological ability to accomplish the changes we need. Is the engineer or technologist adequately educated to deal with the human "element" in our problems?*

There is a strong movement now in the engineering profession to get its members to be interested in, well, public service, if you will, in helping governmental bodies, advising them and so on. We are aware of the problem, but I admit right now most engineers would be unhappy in public service roles. Engineers who have government contracts have to deal with men in the Pentagon or at NASA. Both may be technically oriented, but there's still the human relationship to be handled. A number of engineers I know say they want to get out of that game. It's too hair-raising and annoying, they say. On the other hand, many are in it right now and are adjusting to it.

The pattern that's developing now in our government setup is that the technical people are acting as advisors and counselors for the lawmakers. The lawyers then combine these technical aspects with the legal and political considerations. We simply don't have a perfect situation. Many things which would be good can't be done merely because of our government's way of doing things. It has to be a compromise. You don't, therefore, achieve what would be best in the abstract because there are other groups that have needs too.

We provide technological solutions for our complex problems, but there's that other item in the feedback loop of society's automatic control system: human response. We've sold our people on the desirability of going to the moon. This was a dynamic goal which appealed to many people, at least it did when it was proposed. It appealed so much it became a national goal. Well, how do we create that same kind of national enthusiasm for righting racial injustices? Or correcting the pollution of our air and water? That's the question.

Most of our citizens and many of our government people still aren't convinced that we're facing crises in our cities. They still don't see the need for money and for massive and immediate action. Technologists who see emergencies and foresee disaster will have to learn how to dramatize their technical visions in order to stir up interest in the people. They'll have to know more about political and governmental decision processes. They'll have to be more active in getting technological facts before legislative bodies.

The engineer will just have to be *more* than merely a technically skilled designer. He'll have to learn politics so that he can work side by side with citizens and government people in solving our social environment problems. These problems will not be solved by any one discipline alone, but by task forces of coordinating disciplines. We are going to have to broaden the humanistic requirements of the engineering student. He will have to study psychology, sociology and political science in order to take his seat on the team.

*My feeling is that the technologist's problems are all tied and wrapped in language. Their problem is one of language communication.*

A contribution of the recent interest in sensitivity sessions and encounter groups has been the growing awareness of how varied may be the way others respond to things you say, and vice versa. That is, a statement from one person means a certain thing to him, but his listener, coming from a different background and with another point of view, may understand it far differently than it occurred in the mind of the speaker. For engineers, who, at least as they advance and become experienced, tend to state things with a certain technical precision and expect that in turn from the people they contact, it proves disconcerting to see questions that lend themselves to precise formulation treated in a literary or perhaps "poetic" type of language. Yet this may be the needed literary genre to get the job done when it involves co-operation with those who do not or cannot communicate in an idiom which logically is more appropriate to the topic.

*Would you comment on a statement by M. D. Morris that appeared in* Engineer *(September 1969). Morris says: "The engineer, by being struck dumb in his lack of professional expression, abandons a principal part of his role as a leader in society when he abandons his communications with the public and with his colleagues. . . . It is only a half truth that specially taught technical writers, hired to produce an understandable report, free a highly educated man to do his specialized task."*

I agree that the technical writer is not the solution. At Loyola University, the engineers must not only demonstrate adequate report-writing ability in senior courses to complete their projects, but they must make oral presentations to typical "review boards" of fellow students, faculty and managers from industry. Even with this, not all display evidence of an adequate high school and college freshman English preparation.

*Bill Cleary uses the term "the hyphenated priest," to describe the man who has a double dedication, one to the priesthood and one to another profession. It's the title of his book in which I first saw your name . . .*

Yes, I'm the priest-engineer in Bill's book.

*That hyphen disturbs some people. To a student it means another three or four years of study. To the conservative it suggests restlessness or disillusionment or even a kind of part-time purity.*

I've experienced that last attitude. People ask how can you really be committed to engineering and research when your first commitment is to your religious organization?

It seems to me that I have to look at my vocation as a technically oriented Jesuit in a rather long-range way. Many of the things I do, both as a priest and an engineer, will not see any visible effect until perhaps after my lifetime. The physicists at Cal Tech used to wonder: how can you possibly say you're interested in our material welfare when you're supposed to be committed to the spiritual? For me the two are not divorced. Religion, particularly the Catholic religion, is oriented towards the total welfare of man, which includes his material welfare as well as his spiritual. The welfare of mankind in the hereafter is definitely connected with our welfare here in this world. We are creating right here and now our eternal destiny.

My long-term goals, I think, are even more important than my direct and immediate activities for others, such as counseling or teaching, say, one hundred students a year. Through activities with people, through correspondence and research, I should — at least this is the faith that I work on — I should have some ultimate effect in them who know me both as a priest dedicated to the spiritual and an engineer and researcher committed wholeheartedly to science and technology. They will eventually see these two commitments coming together in one individual. This is my own long-range picture. Over a period of time the hundreds and perhaps thousands of technically involved people around the world who come to know me may be prompted to search for the material-spiritual unity within themselves.

*You believe it will be your full presence as a person that will educate others?*

Yes, that's a very big part of it indeed.

*The presence and dialogue, this is what Martin Buber would say: you being who you are both as scientist and priest.*

Right. If I were simply to use technology as a means to get in touch with people, I would be false to my technological goals and therefore fail in my total goal. This is the implicaiton of Teilhard de Chardin's *omega* point — that the physical universe is an important component in the evolvement of all creation toward ultimate fulfillment.

Max Planck recently proposed that advanced technical circles are developing a spirit of complementarity. Reality will be open to the interacting insights of scientists, philosophers, poets, theologians, and mystics. Many scholars think that when this openness filters down to the campuses and laboratories, religion will be in an advantageous position to show its relevance. Undoubtedly, the priest-scientist should be on the scene when this occurs.

*How many Provincials*
*have their phones bugged?*

# Ken Feit, S.J.

*Paul Weber wanted me to meet Ken Feit because he didn't want all of my impressions of the Society to come from middle-aged men: — "I don't think Jesuits ought to get all hung up on Ken Feit. He makes mistakes and he knows he makes mistakes, but at the same time he is biting at the heels of the established people and he makes them move, and he makes them think and talk. Which is good. Because we can get so dead-center nothing moves . . . I disagree with him sometimes. We argue about things, but as intelligent men. If it's something that's going to make him happy and it's of no relevance to me one way or other, I'll give in. If it's something I think is important, I'll fight until we come to some agreement."*

*I was up in what used to be the Coronado Hotel (now Lewis Memorial) in St. Louis talking with Weber when Feit walked in. Hello to Margaret Flanagan at the tape recorder, hello to me and Weber, apologies for interrupting, then Feit sat down on the floor. Miss Flanagan offered him booze, Coke, milk or coffee. No to everything. Would he like a pillow? No, he had his blanket roll. He wore green work suspenders strapped over a green shirt, big shoes that had once been black, red-brown hair, mustache, glasses. He was about six feet four, not fat. His shoes looked lived in, like "There Once Was an Old Woman" — that kind of shoe. I remember his shoes, I suppose, because for a while they were busier than*

299

*he was: supporting his haunches, ending his legs stretched out in front of him, like brackets; thumping heads, laboring over each other when he crossed his ankles.*

*Feit didn't talk, just sat listening to Weber. When he did start to talk, he talked for four hours, pausing only briefly to let Weber leave. His was a marvelous verbal spectacular, baroque in delivery and configuration, frank, strong. You'll read some of what he said in his interview following. He said it fast, unspooling his words in long breakless lines, using few gestures: he faults Jesuits for living and working in physical and psychological cloisters that insulate them from the tensions and conflicts of our times. Young Jesuits are exempt from the agonizing decisions that harass their non-Jesuit peers. Later as priests, how will these Jesuits be able to understand their people? Feit believes Jesuits should live among the poor in order to sensitize themselves to the problems of the poor. He would like laws changed so that young Jesuit scholastics could renounce their draft exemptions. He would like Jesuit scholastics to be draft counselors.*

*Feit, like John Padberg and Ted Cunningham, has a trained respect for history. He tries to support radical action with radical documentation. Together with Richard Zipfel, S.J., he has produced a study "The American Resistance and the American Church." Examining documents of Jesuit-owned slaves in Missouri, he wrote, "St. Louis Area Jesuits and the Inter-racial Apostolate, 1823–1969." In April of 1970 the Council on Urban Life in Milwaukee, Wis., published his latest report: "The Milwaukee Police Department: An In-Depth Study."*

*Ken Feit, thirty years old, is a "young Jesuit." He's an action poet in love with the sounds and sights of language. He loves words, not as a reader, but as a minstrel. He is not a typical young Jesuit, but novice masters all over the country are inviting him to speak to their new men. Some older Jesuits are hopeful, some disgusted at the thought that Ken Feit may be the Jesuit of tomorrow.*

Just ten years ago a friend of mine stood up in a class at Loyola University in Chicago, a bad class. He wasn't a bright fellow, but he had a knack of asking very root questions. He knew what he wanted to do with his life. That was his gift. He looked at the professor and said, "I'm paying tuition, right?"

The professor said, "Yeh, I assume so."

"And you're on salary, right?"

"Right," the professor said.

"You're my employee then. You're teaching a poor class. If you continue to do so, I'm going to fire you." Then he sat down.

No one knew how to handle that. He had asserted a relationship that was really genuine. Ever since then I've never regarded the Church the same way. Or any official, or myself. We're all servants. We've got to be, or else we're slaves to ourselves.

I think that our spirituality has to be grounded in the art of asking questions — full-bodied questions, not amputated ones. Like in the past whenever we planned something new we asked: "Is there enough money?" "Are there enough men?" "Is there enough time?" "What will people think?" "Can we get permission?" All these qualifiers that choked the question in the throat of the asker. Wow! How many unborn ideas — real abortions and you know what the pope says about that. Instead, I think, we should ask whole questions like: "What kind of world do we want to create?" "What kind of persons do we want to be?" "What kind of values do we want to see alive?" And then see where the questions take us — what language develops, what institutions form.

*Did you stay at Loyola?*

No. I also went to Berkeley, St. Louis University and Xavier. My mind was really blown in grad school. But at Berkeley I started reasking elemental questions. Then I spent some time in Mexico as director of a student project in a little pueblo. Hard work — teaching, construction, staffing an infirmary, farming — hard, but good.

I entered the Society when I was twenty-four. I had all but finished my master's in history and had completed most of my philosophy requirements. I was six years older than most of my fellow novices. I felt I was forced to forget a lot of things I had experienced in order to survive the two years of novitiate.

When I entered the juniorate things began to revive. I attended classes at the nearby Jesuit university and helped organize a discussion group. We wanted to have a Mass for an Early Peace, but the president of the university said: "This is a political use of the Mass." I said, "No. It's just a Mass for an early peace, and if 'early' is the word that's political, then we'll have a Mass for a late peace. How's that?" He didn't like that idea, but we got the Mass — mostly because I went on a fifty-hour hunger strike to mobilize the faculty and students.

When I first came into the philosophate in St. Louis I went to each of my superiors — the rector, the minister, and the director of scholastics — and I said, "Look, I lived in fear for two and a half years and I didn't like it. Now I see that I wanted to stay in the Society because for some reason then I was afraid to step out of it. But I'm not afraid any more. I'm not afraid of you and I don't want you to be afraid of me. If I ever have occasion to be afraid of you, I'm going to walk right out. I'm going to be doing a lot of strange things, but I trust you and I want you to trust me."

I explained as much as I could what my vows and my spirituality meant to me, and at the end I thought we had the beginnings of an understanding. I've never had a problem since then with any superiors. It really has been beautiful.

. . . A group of us stopped St. Louis University from participating with other universities in a hundred-million-dollar government defense contract. I got a copy of the contract, made 350 copies of it. We spread the copies throughout the campus, conducted a forum to discuss this. Then started a letter-writing campaign. And the army withdrew its contract . . . The university workers, the janitors and people, went on strike. The university didn't recognize their right to unionize and threatened to fire them if they didn't go back to work by a certain date. A group of us, students and faculty, got hold of the issue. We had a benefit for the striking workers so that they would have groceries during their strike . . . We had a benefit for Biafra at our coffeehouse, Act II, raised $150. We were the first academic group in this whole city to respond.

The board of trustees who make the decisions see this university [St. Louis] as a corporation. They determine its success in terms of profit or loss each year. I can sympathize to a certain extent with their vision. It's not mine. I think of the university as a forum for dissent, for growth and innovation, creativity, irrespective of profit or loss . . .

I used to feel that my vows were made to God through my superiors and fellow Jesuits. Now, more and more, I feel they're made to God through the poor, especially when I think of the vow of obedience. I really conceive of myself as a servant of the poor, subject to immediate dismissal at their pleasure or displeasure.

*And paying you?*

I'm self-supporting now.

*Then who can fire you?*

When I go into a poverty neighborhood where I'm living now in Milwaukee, or among the Dakota Sioux, *chicanos,*

303

Appalachian whites and blacks, the firing is in the glances, in the hearts, in the exchange.

*You're talking about a relationship that isn't a money thing, it's a heart and love thing.*

That's what I mean by service, yes. That's really the root Christian notion of service as a priest.

To get back to the vows, the vow of chastity is a delicate thing to talk about. I'm a very passionate person, a very physical, sensual person, an intuitive person. When I meet a friend, I don't just shake hands, I embrace him. I say all this to give background. I see no problem at all with physical and personal contact with women. I think it's a very good thing.

Now, I know that because of my temperament and my calling I will always lead a life of celibacy. I have very little choice, really on a psychological plane, just as I am psychologically unable to live in an affluent neighborhood. Yet, at the same time, I want and feel the need and presence of a woman, of a woman's companionship. The kind of questions I ask, the loneliness with which I must live is often assuaged by any personal presence, very often by a woman's presence. I don't want to underplay the tremendous affection that a community of dedicated men can display either. I have no hesitancy at all about seeking this presence and enjoying it but always honestly.

My interpretation of poverty, again, is determined by my commitment to the poor. I find myself called to live out my vow in a very Spartan fashion, partly because that's the way I read it, and partly because that's the only genuine way I could function among the poor. I realize that some men can use tape recorders and seismographic instruments as poor men, as servants. I'm not a technician. I don't need those tools. A typewriter might be a handy thing, but the way I move, I carry everything on my back and if I can't carry it I leave it. I feel a gift is meant to be held for the moment and passed on to someone else so that it can grow richer.

*Where are you at in the Society, Ken?*

I'm somewhere between philosophy and theology. There is no term for it. It used to be called regency.

*There isn't a regency any more?*

Not for me. Unless you want to define it differently. I'd rather invent a new word for it or better yet leave it unnamed.

*Whatever you call it, is it still three years long?*

Not necessarily, maybe two, maybe five years, depending on when I'm ready to approach formal priesthood.

*Most scholastics spend regency teaching in one of the schools. Is that what you're doing, Ken?*

No. I'm unassigned. When I finished philosophy, my provincial said, "We need a man to teach in the school." I said, "Why don't you hire a man?" Then I went before the board of consultors and told them: "I trust that your decision to have me teach in the high school was made on your knees and wasn't merely a planning-board decision. If you feel after prayerfully considering this matter, that I really belong in one of the high schools, I'll go there and do as you say because I have faith in this thing they call *grace of office.* But I don't want to go there merely because there's a need for just another man for just another job. I believe the work I'm doing for the poor has tremendous spiritual implications for me and for the Society." The consultors thought about it and gave me a free hand at working out my own regency program.

*Can't you work for the poor from a high school base?*

The question I have to ask is not, "Given the existence of this high school, how do I adapt it more to the needs of the poor?" but rather, "What are the needs of the poor? How can I respond?" The first question is, "Do we even need a high school?" If, working from the needs of these people a high school turns out to be relevant, then what kind of a high school? Must it be a Jesuit high school? If the Jesuit high school is useful, then how can we revise it to meet the needs? The principle of questioning should apply to all of our ministries with all classes of men — rich and poor. Personally, I would like to see us work in preschool and early grades. That's where real values are born.

We style our high schools as being college-preparatory. Now, my vision is limited by the voices I hear, those of the poor, the economically and socially oppressed. Loan companies and corporations, supermarkets, selective service systems, and universities, have a way, unconsciously maybe, of exploiting the poor. This is my working assumption. This is a given part of our social and economic and political structure today. Now I see our universities and colleges providing personnel to feed this system and provide its leaders and directors. Then the question for us as Jesuits who are preparing men to enter college is this: "What is our moral responsibility in promoting a system which in part at least, exploits the poor?"

We talk about involving the poor in our college-preparatory systems. This is ironic, for we're then preparing them to enter a system which is going to perpetuate this system.

There are many students who want certain courses that don't fit in our high schools because we define our curriculum and methods in terms of college expectations. Our success is measured by the percentage of men that enter college. And how does a college measure its success? By the number of men who enter careers — academic, business, military, social service. The whole stream of our education is geared to stabilizing our society *on its terms* and *in its language;* no wonder we're so sensitive to benefactors.

Personally I think we need a new language, and I say that as a man who truly loves his country and his order, and wants

306

to help save both from possible suicide. Now that's a value judgment but I think there's enough evidence to warrant it — I mean militarism, racism, colonialism.

But where does that put the Jesuit high school teacher? If he's sensitive to the conveyor belt he and his students are on, he should be in a crisis of decision. Maybe the best thing to do is to raise questions and practice innovative methods that would make college less attractive, but enable the student to create alternatives. We desperately need creative alternatives, like *free schools* for students who wish to shape their own curriculum. I'd like to help coordinate a series of courses in the history of the peace, civil rights and resistance movements, or maybe labs in civil disobedience.

Jesuits enjoy a certain autonomy in terms of the archdiocese and the federal government. Should we not radically innovate, as we once did when we were the schoolmasters of Europe, emphasizing self-determination, goal orientation, value formation on an individual basis that would create individuals who would ask the questions we are talking about?

Our schools could help orient people towards the fine arts, social planning, social psychology, and that sort of thing. We wouldn't be interested so much in the continuity that comes from studying medieval history or modern European history. Our students wouldn't be the technicians or the engineers or the physicists that our society cries out for today, and maybe will continue to need tomorrow. Our students would see future society is leisure-oriented. They would create a wider range of options in the fine arts and self-expression.

I'd like to see Jesuit regents doing some draft counseling in the high schools. The close personal contact that a scholastic enjoys with his students places him in a position to serve in this way. Besides, this same close contact may help the regent's own development by keeping him close to the problems facing the young men he's working with. By draft counseling I don't mean making a predecision for the guy.

Maybe the best thing for him is to enlist. But it's something he'll have to determine for himself. I guess I prefer a republic of freedom to one of coerced virtue. The regent could let him know what his alternatives are, could help him form his own questions about the morality of modern warfare, and other moral issues in a sort of counseling fashion. This is important for the seventeen-year-old guy who's immature and approaching an important decision-making period. I wasn't prepared to approach this period. I had no help and could have used some.

Two historical experiences — the civil rights movement and the peace movement — are confronting all young American men constantly. We as Jesuits have insulated ourselves from these experiences by our draft exemptions, tax exemptions and by academic involvement. Wow! I mean it's so easy to philosophize and theologize about revolution and violence and racism and war. But none of us are in jail (with a few notable exceptions) or have our phones tapped (probably the same exceptions). I was vulnerable to draft until I was twenty-four and entered the order. It was in '64. Things were getting hot then, issues were sharpening, but it wasn't the same as now. My friends now face alternatives of imprisonment or flight to Canada, or getting strung out on drugs or developing some sort of homosexual relationship or freaking out so that they get their I-Y. Or maybe joining a seminary. Right? Marrying early and having a lot of children or else prolonging a meaningless education.

These alternatives are very limiting. What I'm trying to say is that we Jesuits tend to pursue our education without any awareness of the pressure that our brothers are under. Right now, day by day we're creating the language gaps of tomorrow. How will we be able to speak to our peers a generation from now through this sort of insulation? Part of the style of being male and young and asking yourself questions about your manliness means facing the draft. It's sort of a puberty rite. It's something the young Jesuit may never do. We can't internalize what the students are going through. It's an unreal question to us. The tensions of soldiers and draft resisters are as abstract to us as those of blacks. Now, I'm trying to find a way in which we as Jesuits can personally experience the choice of going to jail or serving. We could do this by renouncing our draft status but the government won't let us do it, although in France and Korea and elsewhere Jesuits routinely serve in the army or show good reason for not.

I'd like to set up a resistance probation for novices. That may sound like I'd like them to throw their bodies into the wheels of the Czar's carriage. I don't mean that. I mean have them live and work in a poverty community for a time. Suppose Jesuit novices were not draft exempt and preferred jail to serving an immoral cause. Maybe jail could be novitiate or at least one of the tests. It could be a maturizing experience, morally and emotionally. I'd be glad to be a novice master in a prison situation like that. I see a lot of points of comparison between the novitiate and prisons. Maybe I could learn a little more about revising the novitiate by studying efforts at prison reform. I'm open.

My work is opening me more each day to the pressures my brothers face outside the order. Last year I testified at a judiciary committee hearing of the Milwaukee Common Council on three police-reform resolutions. The chief eyed me suspiciously — Roman collar and all — then wrote my name on a yellow sheet of paper. Next day I was tipped off by an alderman friend (who got a leak from the police department) that the chief was having my phone tapped, had ordered a complete investigation of my background, and had a detective trailing me. Wow! I went to bed at eight that night — first time since novitiate — like I was scared knowing the arbitrary power of the police. They could plant marijuana on me, beat me up, and throw a switchblade on the sidewalk claiming aggravated assault, et cetera. I've seen that happen.

The next morning I called the provincial to fill him in. I wanted him to know what I was going through. I was being watched and he wasn't. I knew if he didn't understand the difference that made in our communication, a growing language rift would separate us. How many provincials have their phones bugged? Maybe if they did, we'd sense a new urgency in our efforts to renew the Society and Christianity.

*I know you're a nonviolent person. Do you endorse at least the language of violence as a tactic?*

You mean like calling a policeman a pig? No. I don't endorse that. It's stupid. Maybe that's just a counter-category but I think it only dehumanizes the ones who use it and it sterilizes language. I guess I see violence as being like private property — something which closes off communication. It's self-fulfilling and self-contained even when used in the service of others since it closes off openness and usually reduces itself to rhetoric. Rhetoric is bastard language, narcissistic and narrow. The problem is there's so much violence around us, between us, within us that I can understand *why* we use it, especially when it's being used against us. The alternative is a kind of self-crucifixion. Let's just not pretend that we're communicating or loving.

I was in Chicago at Lincoln Park during the Democratic Convention. It reached a point there when the police were coming on and it looked pretty hopeless. Everybody was shouting these slogans that were provocative and anti-intellectual like the Hitler youth in the Berlin Sportzpalast, like gabbling geese. Then rocks started flying and tear gas and clubs and screams. No one was talking. No one was listening. There was no language, only irrationality. It was absurd. I knew those policemen were afraid of being hurt and that those people really didn't want to get tear-gassed or clubbed. No one really wanted what was happening, but circumstances forced them into it. I stood on the pavement and

310

wept bitterly wanting to do something but knowing that I couldn't. I couldn't do the one thing my priesthood called me to do — to humanize chaos. It was only a question of whether I too wanted to be brutalized and hateful, so I slowly walked away despising myself.

The same thing happened in Charleston in the hospital strike last summer. I was prepared to get arrested and take my thirty days. There was a principle at stake there that I valued and I was willing to accept the consequences. Hosea Williams and Ralph Abernathy had already been arrested that night. I was sitting there on my blue blanket, just waiting for the moment. Then some kids started throwing stones and bottles at the police and the police started moving forward to clear the area. Then people panicked and started to stampede. I jumped up and got to the side. Again, it was the irrationality that destroyed the humanism of the moment (or maybe that itself was the humanism?). At any rate, I saw a guy get hurt and said, "Come on. Let's go to the hospital." We went and I got out.

Underneath it all I guess I act on the basis of whether or not I will grow more human in a situation. Sometimes that means the suffering of action, other times the suffering of silence which is another form of action. Maybe that's selfish, but I don't see how we will co-redeem the world on an inhuman base.

*Do you belong to the Missouri Province?*

No. Legally in the Chicago, bodily in the Wisconsin Province. But I'm in and out of St. Louis a lot. This past summer I traveled thirteen thousand miles, mostly hitchhiking. I was out in California with the grape pickers. That used up many miles. Then I was east, too.

PAUL WEBER: Isn't it possible that we're being so damn mobile that we never stay in one place long enough to do a job? Like the novice probation: six weeks in the ghetto. Big hairy deal. Isn't this another kind of exploitation of the poor? All right, so a guy doesn't stay as intellectually alive and doesn't have all the best questions and that, but he's there day after day after day. Isn't that better for the poor?

KF: Okay. The sociology major who comes down to Pedro House or Sophia House to write a term paper is exploiting the situation. Okay. Now where does that put me? I have a base. I have a five-year commitment to Milwaukee where I live as a neighbor in a poor community. The other work I feel called to do requires me to be mobile enough to move to other poverty areas, to East Harlem, or south El Paso, or east Los Angeles, to ask questions and understand what's going on.

PW: But, Ken, you were very successful at Pedro House working with delinquents. When you pulled out of there you left a vacuum behind you. There's work there to be done which you haven't stayed around to do. Now, I think perhaps you have to follow your own charisma and I agree you do more valuable work by moving around. But don't you think there is also a necessity for other Jesuits to stay there and not move around so much?

KF: Okay. Yes. I do.

PW: I just want to make a comparison. Canisius was great. He went around Europe and set up all the universities. The real saints were the Jesuits who came behind him and had to staff them, and solve the day-to-day problems and make them work. He didn't make them work. They did. The nameless ones.

KF: Okay. I would like to set the record straight. I saw the implications of the work I was doing and I wanted to continue it. St. Louis is a natural crossroads. I asked the provincial if I could stay in St. Louis and use Pedro House as my base of operations. I could have been doing in St. Louis what I'm doing out of Milwaukee. Instead of working in police-community relations I could be working to change the conditions of St. Louis detention center. He was afraid of this. "Manpower and continuity." That's all he could say.

*Why are you and Paul laughing? What does "manpower and continuity" mean?*

KF: Those are the stock objections to new ideas.

PW: "We need the men in our high schools."

KF: "Can you guarantee someone will follow this work up?" — continuity.

*It means a Jesuit to take up another Jesuit's work?*

KF: Yes, but I think that's an obsolete notion of continuity. The community should undertake the work that you've maybe just begun to raise questions about, open possibilities in. If Jesuits are going to take over Jesuit work in poverty areas, we're just enforcing the outdated image of the patriarch. The leadership has to come from a place within. *They*'ve got to do it really, otherwise, wherever we do something we create dependencies. That's just not good.

I see the need for a temporary presence, for strengthening people, then moving on. If I stayed, I could . . . oh, wow! I could create a world full of vegetables around me waiting to be vibrated. I've got to be a guy who moves through.

*All right, Ken. You're a free-lance regent. Do you spend most of your time traveling? What do you do?*

I'm very conscious that the time I spend is earned for me by a lot of poor people who really believe in what I'm doing and what I stand for. That doesn't mean I don't relax, but it means that I know inside when I'm wasting time. I'd consider that sinful.

My work in regency is pretty involved. I team-teach a course in minority group history at Marquette High School in Milwaukee. I also research the field of police-community relations for the Council of Urban Life. My goals are to find, if possible, ways in which the control of the police department as a unit of society can return more to the community. I think historically it began there and should return.

Our community is experimental. There are three of us Jesuits living there but the house is open to all who need hospitality — vagrants, students, displaced persons, political prisoners, et cetera. Right now we have three non-Jesuit members in our family. The numbers vary with the season.

PW: Let me just interrupt here to say that in Milwaukee, Ken and some other Jesuit scholastics wanted to set up a house to work with the war resisters, the Milwaukee 14, and that type of thing.

It came up at the province consultors meeting that I attended as scholastic consultor. The consultors asked a lot of peripheral questions like, "How can you have a house of Jesuits working with resistance people attacking a Jesuit university and high school?" There was a lot of interesting discussion about that, but the key question they finally asked was: "Are these men good Jesuits?" That was the issue, and it was an excellent issue. People who knew the three guys involved said, yes. They're good Jesuits. They're loyal Jesuits. They're obedient Jesuits. They're very interested in the Church and the spiritual life.

Once that question was settled, we came to the unanimous opinion that they ought to be allowed to set up this house, and to start asking the type of questions that Ken is asking.

*Do you have a leader in that house — a superior?*

KF: Our authority is something that has evolved in a consensual way. We have a priest in our community now. The vice-provincial described his role as a "catalyst for decision making." We said, "Forget it, man. He's the newest member of our community. He isn't going to be a catalyst for anything. He's going to listen. He doesn't know what we're about." And he agrees. We decide house policy as a community. That's just another version of the old notion that the Jesuit leader coming into the community with ideas and vision is going to lead these people to a solution. We've got to listen to the people we serve. For me it's the poor.

*Who pays the rent?*

We're pretty much self-supporting, but times get rough like last week we only had fifty-seven cents in the bankbook.

*The Society of Jesus is not a mendicant order. Are you trying to make it one?*

No, not in the sense of a life-style of begging. That's a full-time job and we have other important work to do: teaching, researching, organizing, writing, preaching. I do think that we ought to return to the sense of material dependence that the mendicants experienced. If we live with or near the poor, our understanding of poverty won't be so abstract. We must renounce our autonomy, our buildings, our self-contained communities. We have to do more mixing of Jesuits and non-Jesuits to break down our sense of exclusiveness and separation.

My image of the priesthood began to form two years ago when I got a letter from a couple of lawyer friends who knew I was working in poverty communities. The letter said, "Here's some money: feed the hungry, clothe the naked, shelter the homeless, but don't send this over to the Church because we're tired of them making statues with it." I went to my superior and showed him the letter. I asked him: "What shall I do with this?" He said, "Well, do what they say." So I did.

A Jesuit house in a poor neighborhood can lock the poor out at the doorstep. We can pray and eat and recreate together, then go to the door and find the poor still waiting. That's been the tradition in the past. It's got to be changed by opening doors, abolishing cloister — especially psychological and emotional cloister — so that we can break bread together in real brotherhood.

The neighborhood I live in is itself poor and interethnic, centering around Casa Maria, a Catholic Worker house of hospitality located two blocks away. There are six or seven other houses nearby and together they coordinate a total program which feeds over one hundred people daily, and operates a free clothing center, a Montessori school for the poor, a halfway house for alcoholics, a bookstore and a coffeehouse. *The Catholic Radical* is our neighborhood publication.

PW: There is another problem which worries the older Jesuits. We get our vocations largely from our own high schools, and the middle class. If we start emphasizing work among the very poor, we'll be killing ourselves. We won't be getting the vocations we need to perpetuate the Society. So the Society will die out.

KF: Okay. Of course that assumes that dying out is a bad thing. I'm not sure it is. I mean we were suppressed as an order in the 1780's once. And what happened? We rose from the dead a little transfigured. Maybe we should be suppressed again. Let's face it — we won't get the poor blacks, Indians or whites to join the Society. Poor Mexican-Americans, I don't know. But there is so much unconscious exclusivism that's in our training, and that really bugs the shit out of me. I mean, look, why is it that practically every canonized Jesuit saint was an aristocrat of some sort? Berchmans was about the only exception and he was processing his papers to leave the order I understand. Is there some kind of positive correlation between sanctity and affluence? That's not the way I read Scripture: the rich young man, the eye of the needle and that jive. But that's the way we seem to act. Today everybody's dropping out of school, not just because it's tough but because it's a hassle. People are getting real education elsewhere — a generation on sabbatical, communes, rock, acid, yoga, macrobiotics — environmental education. We keep using old standards to define vocation. We've got to listen to the voices of the new age and discern Christ's call there. I mean we've identified the spiritual and cultural factors for too long.

We have about thirty *chicano* Jesuits — Mexican-American — in Texas, California, Colorado, Arizona, New Mexico and Nevada. I don't know how many come in but most leave in the early years of training. The *chicano* who stays loses contact with his culture, his traditions, language and food. He enters an Anglo world of competition and formalism where he sees himself as almost white. Unconsciously, he tries to forget his past, his *barrio* and friends. Later, when he sees how divided he is, he may try to straighten himself out by leaving the order. He may stay and live as a marginal man, a "castrated" Jesuit.

I'd like to see a Jesuit *chicano* caucus develop across the country. It could set up a novitiate for Mexicans, Cubans and Puerto Ricans and help them appreciate the roots of their cultures, while they establish their own style of study, their own ministry and their personal prayer.

It kills me to think that we gringos have culturally defined the Jesuit ideal in such a way as would exclude Ignatius or his modern-day counterparts from his own order.

*What will you teach the poor? To be happy with poverty and dependence on welfare? Or to strive for middle-class life?*

I'm not interested in idealizing poverty as a permanent condition of life in itself. Voluntary poverty is a means to experience faith and brotherhood and for building community. It avoids the pitfalls of competition, formalism and private ownership.

Involuntary poverty is not the same. Frequently, it creates as much divisiveness as affluence. It may drive people to incredible delusions that are both violent and dehumanizing. I'm interested in eradicating that kind of poverty and creating a base for sharing, not merely material but aesthetic and spiritual resources. The lesson I hope to bring to the poor is the realization of their dignity and beauty as brothers and of their ability to create alternatives to their condition.

*Do you really feel poverty?*

I experience it, but I feel thrift too, and that's different. I don't like to waste money. My parents did a good job of communicating the Depression to me. They told me to save for a rainy day. Then one day I realized that for some people it was raining right now. Every day was a rainy day for them.

In 1969 I went to Atlanta to join the poor people's march. In Atlanta I learned that the march got stuck in Jackson, Mississippi. I didn't have the money to join it. My first instinct was a beautiful middle-class instinct: I've got to get a job. So I went to Traveler's Aid, and said, "Look, I need a job. I don't have any money and I've got to get down to Jackson, Mississippi." I didn't want to hitchhike at the time because I didn't savor hitchhiking across Alabama you know, *Easy Rider* and all that. They said, "Okay. We'll get you a job." They sent me to Manpower. The guy at Manpower asked what could I do. I said I could handle French, Spanish, German, Russian and Greek. The guy said, "Well, that's good. Here. Unload these swimming pool fixtures."

Four tons of swimming pool fixtures from a warehouse. Five-and-a-half hours' work, seven dollars pay! Five dollars at the end of the day and two dollars in the mail.

*Did you steal anything?*

No. Well, what can you do with swimming pool fixtures? So I said, "Feit, you really are a stupid shit. You wasted a valuable day. You didn't learn anything" — maybe *that's* learning something.

On the way to the warehouse the guy said, "Yeh, you guys like to work a day, get enough to get some wine, find a fleabag hotel and get drunk for a couple of days." I walked out of the warehouse with just enough money to get me to Jackson plus seventy cents and feeling very sweaty. I felt I had to get a shower and be clean. I went to the YMCA and said, "Look, I need a shower, man." And he said, "It'll cost you fifty cents." I said, "All I've got is seventy cents and I haven't eaten for thirty-six hours." "It'll still cost you fifty cents." So I said, "Look" — and then I played the card I didn't want to play — "I'm a seminarian and I'm studying to be a priest, and you call yourself a Christian association. I'm a poor man and I'm Christian. Can you give me a free shower?" "Sorry, it'll cost you fifty cents." And stupid jerk that I am, I paid fifty cents and I took a shower.

As soon as I did it, I said, "Wow, you really are middle class, Feit!! Your stomach really demands priority but you want to feel and smell clean." So I said, "Screw it all. I'm not going to work tomorrow. If I'm the pilgrim I claim to be, if I'm dependent on people around me and want to give them a chance to feel my need and respond to it, I better start begging." So I went to the first church and said, "Look, I'm a pilgrim and haven't eaten in thirty-six hours. What can you do for me?" "Come on in and have something to eat."

They gave me a place to sleep and I stayed on for two weeks — teaching and reciting poetry in a summer school

*319*

and coffeehouse, studying the Southern Christian Leadership Conference, attending classes at Atlanta University and helping out at two local resistance and parish communities. After that I got a ride to Charleston where SCLC was directing the hospital strike.

*Was that a Catholic Church you went to?*

Yes, but I would have tried any. I chose the Church of the Sacred Heart. It just seemed like a good name.

*You call getting clean a middle-class instinct?*

I think under the circumstances a poor person with seventy cents and thirty-six hours of hunger would have spent seventy cents for a meal. He wouldn't spend it to feel clean.

*You said earlier that your first instinct to find a job was "middle class." Are you saying that very, very poor people don't want to work?*

No. I meant to emphasize that when I ran out of money, it didn't occur to me that I should try to trust somebody to help. Like if I did have money I wouldn't have to trust. As long as the difference between trust and nontrust is money or property or a job and not people then I'm lost and alone. I've cut myself off from other people and from God, who really is behind all the trust anyway.

*Is hitchhiking the only way you travel?*

No. I drive too. Car. Motorbike. Once last summer I got a ticket for speeding and had to appear in court at Mundelein, Illinois, a small, white, middle-class suburb. The judge fined me twenty-five dollars but I just stood there and said, "I'm a poor man." So he looked me over and finally said,

"Okay, hardship case — twenty dollars. Pay the clerk." I didn't move. "You didn't hear me, Your Honor," I said. "I'm a poor man. I don't have *any* money. And even if I did I couldn't pay it to this court." Silence. Then I explained about my work in Milwaukee among the poor and how we shared what we had.

I told him I was a Jesuit and had taken a vow of voluntary poverty. I read it from my rule book. I explained how I just didn't believe in a money ethic since I was more concerned with people. I admitted that the law was just and that I had broken it, but instead of paying a fine I offered to attend driver's education classes or do some socially serviceable work for the county or report on my work in Milwaukee. I concluded that a fine wouldn't rehabilitate me. If I paid the fine I'd be giving to the court what belonged to my poor brothers and sisters who couldn't pay rent or grocery or hospital bills.

More silence. Then the district attorney objected. "What if everyone felt this way?" I said, "I think we'd have a better world." The judge informed me that I must choose between a fine or jail. I didn't think jail would rehabilitate me either but figured that at least it wouldn't be robbing the poor, so I said, "Let's go to jail." Again the district attorney objected that sending me to jail would stop my good work and I really had to agree, but reminded him that it wasn't my decision. The judge by now was edgy and said, "You're putting me in an embarrassing position." I answered that the law was embarrassing both of us and that we had to find more humane alternatives. Then he got extremely agitated and stammered, "Go . . . go to Milwaukee and don't come back."

As I got ready to leave I asked the clerk for my license but she refused because I didn't pay the fine. She had been totally unmoved by the courtroom scene and kept saying, "I've got to send your license to Springfield unless you pay your fine." Finally I just said, "This looks like the court of Pontius Pilate. No decision was made. You're just sending me on to Herod." She shrugged her shoulders, saying, "You've got your principles and I've got mine."

Later in Milwaukee I received a notice from the court that my case had been suspended, so I wrote Springfield for my license. Instead of the license I got a nice letter telling me that my case number was 69–T–30169. Since then I've been driving without a license. I carry the letter.

*When you wear a Roman collar out on the sidewalk and a guy comes up to you for money, how do you respond?*

It depends. If he wants a drink, sometimes I'll say: "Let's have a drink together." Sometimes I'll pull out my harmonica and say, "I don't have any money, but I've got some music." And I'll play a song for them. That's happened lots of times. One guy started dancing on the sidewalk and he pulled a bottle out of his pocket and we shared a swig as we walked along together. No one has ever been angry about that because songs are beautiful and there's something about sharing that's good. Most often I'll just sit and talk and listen to a guy talk about the old days. Once I gave a guy my shoes and had to walk home barefoot. If he needs clothing I'll get something for him. Same for food. Once I took a guy up and gave him my room to sleep in that night; he was gone before daybreak. Another time I took a guy in and let him shave and shower while I washed his clothes and got him some food and — it really depends on the rhythm of the moment. But I try in general to respond to the guy. I can smell a con man usually. But a con man is just conning himself in the end. He's being screwed by the system as much as by the loan shark.

I've developed what I call a Good Samaritan Guide. It's a list of all the flophouses where you can get medical treatment, de-lousing, de-alcoholization, clothing, housing, food, employment, traveler's aid — you know, stuff like that. I like to pass these out to people looking for help, then I give them a dime so they can make a call. If they're serious about wanting help they can get it. The list is only good for St. Louis. Each time I pass one out I get a different response.

I used to feel bad talking to derelicts, making them realize how manful they are, once were, and then walking away knowing that they're left alone with themselves again. But then who knows what's really going on inside a man? I mean maybe his life has begun to change. Probably not, but maybe. Who knows? Like one time I was talking with an alcoholic guy who wanted me to put him up for a week or so, so he could straighten himself out. He had a good vocabulary — educated. I listened a few hours, then I pointed to his half-filled wine bottle and said, "Look man, if you want me to believe you, pour that shit out." He couldn't do it. He wanted a bed, food, money, but he wanted his slavery too. So I did a hard thing. I walked away. Like he was the rich young man all over again. If I'd given him a flop, I'd have been saying, "You're just a vegetable; not free." Jeez, if only he had poured out that wine, I would have stayed with him through the DTs, helped him find a job . . . If *only*.

I'm convinced that all men can be in charge of their own future. Yet when I walk away from a man like that and all he sees around him is broken bottles and someone calls, "Hey, bum, come over here," the whole vision of his manful past and the possibilities of a future must collapse. It seems cruel. Yet there were a few moments there where he was a man, and maybe that's important. Maybe that's the only gift I can share then.

That's why sometimes I feel that my real work is to help set up a hospitality house in St. Louis where we could share soup and bread. It would be good for all of us: for the derelicts, for the student searching for livable values, for the Church that's right now confused by change and self-compromise. Wow! It would be like living the first years of Christianity again: works of mercy in a community of prayer and service. Think of the new political and social and economic consciousness that would grow out of this way of living. I can almost taste it! . . .

There's a part of Ken Feit that's an activist, that's trying to remake things. There's a part that's fatalist, that sees that the poor are always with us, sees war as something that's eternal (especially the war within the person), that sees life in terms of rhythm and seasons, cycles and orbits, and that delights in nature and leaving things as they are.

There's a constant dialogue between the two voices, the fatalist and the activist. At one point, I say, "No one really cares. Why don't you realize that these beautiful things around you are to be enjoyed?" — the sound of two clouds bumping against one another, or a car clearing its throat. Sometimes I like to do nutty things like liberate ice cubes, you know, jailed water. The students will buy a bag for fifty cents at a filling station and we'll go down to the pond and set them free, let them go back to raindrops again. That's good.

I could do a lot of things like that, have fun, leave the agonies to others. But then my activist voice says, "Yeah, but man *can* change, *can* control his destiny. People *can* evolve and live together and love if they make the effort." So the dialogue reaches equilibrium.


*Scholastics used to sneak smoking. Do they now smoke pot? Have you ever taken drugs or smoked pot?*


I don't think scholastics do. I've never taken LSD. I've taken marijuana. No problems. I have a powerful imagination. I don't feel the need for that kind of stimulation. In fact I'm a little apprehensive about what a drug would do to me, since I'm bothered by such wild questions without them.

I see something good in heightening perception, in being aware of what's going on around us. But it's like masturbation in a sense. If it's just to delight the self and not to involve others then I'm suspicious of it. To use political language, it's counterrevolutionary. It's sort of egocentric diversion from trying to, let's say, redeem the world, bring new meaningfulness to it, and redeem yourself.

I see a problem with law, but I don't see a problem for civil society. I can't say I myself know much about drugs, except that some of my non-Jesuit friends go on acid and I've talked them down and spent time with them.

What I'm more concerned with is, "What does a drug do to help somebody ask questions?" Insofar as drugs are an escape from asking questions and they frequently are, I'm against them just as I'm against booze or religion or snowmobiles or television when they are used that way . . .

I was just smiling and thinking of the last time I was in Jersey City. (There just seems to be something about Jersey City that I find makes it real missionary territory.) It has a Jesuit military school and I went there to see a friend of mine who had been in philosophy with me. He started introducing me to fellow Jesuits as "the Apostle to the hippies." Then he said, very seriously: "I'm going to take a stand, Ken." I thought, "That's good" — like maybe he was going to announce some dramatic confrontation, you know, draft counseling for his ROTC kids. Instead he said, "I'm going to make sure you can eat dinner with us." That was a revolutionary thing. A Jesuit could eat in a Jesuit house!

*He was serious?*

He was putting me on. In my travels I've received hospitality without exception everywhere in the United States and Mexico and Canada. I was put in the provincial's room at Loyola University, Los Angeles. It was embarrassing, but then that just shows the hang-ups I still have. Whether it's out of love or sheer puzzlement, I don't know, but they've all been good to me.

*Do you have the feeling they change the sheets right after you leave?*

I can't say. Maybe there's a lot of grumbling behind my back.

*Aren't you imposing what you consider to be your style onto the whole Society of Jesus and, if so, don't you go beyond your own limit of merely raising questions?*

I feel I'm speaking for many other Jesuits. Most of the guys doing the yeoman's work by maintaining the schools are fundamentally open to what I represent, and the searching I'm doing. In general, I've got far more support than dissonance in the Society. A lot of puzzlement, but a lot of trust. I mean, I really love those guys and they know it, even when I make mistakes.

*The jobs you've chosen encourage trust because they're not glamour jobs. You work for the poor and you're interested in novice Jesuits. If you said your mission was to bring Christ to film starlets we might suspect your motives.*

I get a little nervous when you say you don't suspect my motives. *I* sure do. Hell man, if I keep hearing people say, "Good work, Feit, you're our prophet," I'm liable to start believing that shit and that's when real prophecy (whatever that means) dies. If I begin to think I've got some monopoly on vision, I'm going to stop listening, I'll start worshiping myself. I need to listen, especially to good, loving criticism. I feel I may have become insensitive and intolerant because other people don't want to suffer and serve exactly the way I do. I have to remember their suffering and service is often more genuine, though less spectacular. Besides Ken Feit isn't doing anything. It's Christ and my brothers in me or it's nothing.

*Ken Feit at times sounds egoistic, vain and self-promoting. Isn't it possible some resistance to your ideas may come from people who are resisting you personally and your ego?*

When my brother Jesuits know that prayer means something important to me, it confronts their whole spiritual posture, as their prayer confronts mine. My life-style is asking a lot of questions, questions not only about the future of the Society, but about the role that our men today are living. They're in danger of becoming organization men who are just putting in time. At that point, the order becomes a gentlemen's club. That danger was true of me at least and it's something I have to keep fighting in myself. I once conceived of my Jesuit role as trying to earn enough money to bring back a profit on that twenty thousand dollars, or whatever that mythical sum is that they invested in my schooling. My role was to be that of a good investment. But I abandoned that notion very early . . .

*As being middle class?*

No, as just being inhuman. As being stupid. I don't want to equate middle class with *that*. I think there are some real values in the middle class. But the notion of being a marketable commodity is typical of our technological society. We say we want to produce the best student "products." I was a Jesuit product at one time. I'm not any more. They can't say, "Well, look what the system spat out. Isn't *he* a fine functioning piece of machinery!" I'm rejecting what I think was a self-imposed dehumanizing notion of my role as a Jesuit: to be a fine cog in a questionably fine machine.

*If you don't want to see yourself as a "good investment," what value in your estimation are you to the Society?*

My gift lies in asking some of the root questions — that's what "radical" means, *root*. My life is an attempt to answer those questions. My motives, I hope are Christian — I'm not sure. I think I generate more resistance, or uncertainty, or fear, or apprehension on the part of the young men than on the part of the old men, because it's harder to ignore someone your own age. That really disturbs me. Because I need peer support. I experience a lot more excitement from them too. They give my work both the strongest support and the strongest resistance. Partly because they feel, perhaps not, I'm not sure, that my work and my style is a commentary on them. That's really important to me. When a brother confesses to me that my life-style makes him feel guilty about his own, I want to cry and embrace him and say, "Brother, there's no 'my' life-style. It's ours. You're me and I'm you, and if you feel guilty, let's share it. Let's live it together."

*I wonder if age has anything to do with it. The older fathers accept you but not Dan Berrigan. The young men accept Berrigan but have their doubts about you. Is that too tidy?*

I don't know. Did you hear St. Louis University wouldn't allow Dan to say Mass here on campus? There were complications on both sides, but Berrigan suffered. I circulated a petition among fellow Jesuits letting Berrigan know that he wasn't standing alone. Lots of Jesuits signed. I sense Dan's more skeptical about the future of the Society than I am. I'm really optimistic.

*He's skeptical about the future of the Society in its present structure. You've already broken free from many of the conventional structures.*

Many people feel that I'm telling them that's what *they*'ve got to do. I'm not. I'm saying that there are questions you ought to ask yourself. I was living three lives last year. I'm

surprised I didn't physically break down. I was putting forty
hours in on apostolic work, while carrying a full course load
each week. I was running a coffeehouse, tutoring at Sophia
House, directing a sort of drama course there, living at Pedro House, and teaching in the free university. I was active
in the student radical movement on campus, and was teaching
catechism out in Webster Groves. Time just made itself. But
I think guys might have felt that was a reproach and I didn't
mean it to be. I didn't have time even to tell them that I didn't
mean it to be.

*Is the Society of Jesus going to last?*

I fear that two Societies are developing. In one Society are
Jesuits who are dedicated to social and political activism
which calls them away from an institutional expression. In
the other, *older* Society are Jesuits who are committed as educators to teaching and to research. I don't mean to judge
one over the other, but I do sense a different life-style, a different notion of community and sometimes of poverty, a different area of effectiveness, and I sense very little communication between these two Societies.

What we need is a common lived spiritual language so that
we'll trust one another enough to live in different cultural
worlds. Paul Weber and I, from different perspectives, feel
that we can bridge the language gaps. I'd like to think that
men who've gone through the same novitiate training, and
share a common vision, can transcend their differences. At
the same time, I'd like to really broaden the language toler-
ance that we get in training by greater experimentation in
studies and community and prayer.

*Do you think these two "Societies" could split like the order
of St. Francis separated?*

I see signs that the number of activist Jesuits is growing.
But also I see many men leaving because they find themselves

standing alone. And I've also seen men who have been castrated by their ministries. I think this is tragic. This is why we are all called to reform the Society of Jesus. That means a lot of things, but basically it means listening to one another and creating a new language. It also means helping the prophets return from their deserts to their communities, and even, maybe, interpreting their language, their vision, and asking questions of the community that will force it to see itself in a more complete context. It also means testing prophecy against self-deception by criticism, prayer, mortification and community.

It is important to me that I grow more human, that I become a more sensitive and compassionate servant, more Christ-like. The questions I ask myself are: "What kind of a Society of Jesus do we want to create? What kind of persons do we want to be? How do I see institutional expressions, like the family, like the Church, the school, the corporation, conducting or resisting the future direction?"

PW: Would you agree with me that we can make the kind of Society of Jesus we feel is necessary for our times because we're not hung up on a lot of tradition in the Society?

KF: Basically, yes. Jesuits can change their future. Many of us are afraid because we've been hurt by a system we're trying to change, or maybe we just don't have enough self-confidence and faith. Ever since Claude Aquaviva began to structuralize studies with the *Ratio Studiorum*, ever since Canisius set up a vast educational system throughout Europe, we've been living with the consequences of commitments that were made in history. The same is true of us here in the United States after we accepted the task of educating an immigrant population in the nineteenth century. The style Ignatius established was possible perhaps because he had only a few men to work with. His men were moving at great speed and speaking from great distances so there had to be a lot of implicit trust. The personal visions were part of a larger corporate vision. I feel this early style ceased to be possible a hundred years later.

St. Ignatius was a real risker. His only concern was God's service no matter what it cost him. Like one time he had a dream that the order would be shut down. That was a possibility then because many cardinals objected to his experimentation and didn't like his religious life-style. The dream scared him for about five minutes ; then he shrugged his shoulders and said if that's the way God wanted it, it had to be okay. That was the kind of detachment he expected from his followers, especially from his many chosen superiors. Early superiors had it. They sent novices on long pilgrimages without provisions, to hostile lands, to open schools without money. It was only after the order started acquiring property and expanding in numbers that superiors started becoming defensive about their jobs and playing it safe. Then Aquaviva began to consolidate and impose order on the diversity of the Society. The days of open-ended experimentation were over and a more rigidly defined program of studies was substituted.

It doesn't surprise me that Aquaviva hesitated sending Jesuits to certain martyrdom in England on the grounds that they would be more useful elsewhere. It's also not surprising that the same Aquaviva kept Jesuits from intervening in the Galileo affair. A concern for continuity and security now replaced earlier concerns for mobility and experimentation.

Somewhere in the seventeenth century Ignatian obedience lost its guts and in acquisition developed into a kind of hard-shelled conformity that merited the Suppression. Fortunately, today, we face the same pivotal times of crisis that Ignatius faced. Our own history tells us we must return to the same open-ended trusting, imaginative styles of authority and obedience that once made our order strong. Maybe it's good that our numbers seem to be shrinking. It'll force us to be more resourceful.

*331*

*Why do you say "seem to be shrinking?" It's a fact, isn't it?*

Maybe they're just shifting, since many of the men who have left continue to share the Jesuit vision.

I see the American Jesuits at a point of change. There is real value-questioning going on in the larger human society. There is a move toward replacing job and prestige and property with personal values.

It's exciting to feel that we today can shape our own destinies, that we need not work wearing institutional harnesses that we've inherited or make a virtue of continuity. Maybe we'll be forced now to act as Xavier and deSmet did when they faced the wilderness and had to depend on their own human resources and, of course, on divine resources.

I regard the Society as a corporation, as an academic multiversity, as a unit of tremendous political activism, as a family and a spiritual force, as many things. As many, many things. The Society today is in conflict with itself, sensing change and unable to contend with it, experiencing commitments made by others in the past, yet hearing prophetic voices urging it to seize the future. Not knowing quite what to do.

We are creating a new Society now, with new questions to be asked. A new Jesuit style is emerging, of which I feel I'm a part, a style that is mobile, communal, personal, deinstitutionalized and poor.

I find many men on the verge of ordination saying, "Man, I can't predict the future. All I can do is react." I don't feel that way. I'm part of this wave shaping things. I don't feel that I'm watching a parade.

# Acknowledgments

I'm grateful to Margaret Flanagan, my project assistant, whose keen Yorkshire ear picked more than four hundred thousand Jesuit words out of the tape recorder and moved them over to paper where we could see them. She guided each of the eleven manuscripts through its various stages toward the publisher and managed to keep each Jesuit and his words together. Her faithful i.t.a. spellings of unfamiliar terms and names provided me with an excellent sample of regional pronunciations of Latin and French.

My thanks to John Teeling for his periodic reminders that *"the best* is the enemy of *the good."* And thanks, finally, to James Nolan, Michael Gallagher, Pat Cotter and Bill Cleary for arguments, information, feedback and leads.

George Riemer